Classical
MYTHOLOGY

Classical
MYTHOLOGY

Myths and Legends of Ancient Greece and Rome

CHIEF CONSULTANT
Dr. Alice Mills

GLOBAL BOOK PUBLISHING

Managing director	Chryl Campbell
Publishing director	Sarah Anderson
Project manager	Dannielle Doggett
Art directors	Stan Lamond
	Kylie Mulquin
New title development manager	David Kidd
Chief consultant	Dr. Alice Mills
Commissioning editor	Helen Bateman
Picture research	Helen Bateman
Cover design	Kylie Mulquin
Designer	Lena Lowe
Cartographer	John Frith
Typesetting	Dee Rogers
Index	Glenda Browne
	Jon Jermey
Production	Ian Coles
Foreign rights	Belinda Vance
Publishing assistant	Jessica Luca

First published in 2003 by
Global Book Publishing
Level 8, 15 Orion Road, Lane Cove,
NSW 2066, Australia
Ph: (612) 9425 5800   Fax: (612) 9425 5804
Email: rightsmanager@globalpub.com.au

ISBN 9781740480109

This publication and arrangement
© Global Book Publishing Pty Ltd 2007
Photographs from the Global Book Publishing Photo Library (except where credited otherwise on pages 214–215)
Text © Global Book Publishing Pty Ltd 2007
Maps © Global Book Publishing Pty Ltd 2007
First printed in English in 2009

Printed in China by SNP Leefung Printers Limited
Film separation Pica Digital Pte Ltd, Singapore

Photographers
Global Book Publishing would be pleased to hear from photographers interested in supplying photographs.

CONTRIBUTOR

Dr. Alice Mills is an associate professor of literature and children's literature at the University of Ballarat located in the Australian state of Victoria. One of the many interesting subjects that she teaches is Myth and Mythmaking. She began learning Latin when she was just 11 years old, then classical Greek when she was 12, and has had a lifelong interest in the mythical stories and characters that underlie contemporary Western culture. Dr. Mills has published many scholarly articles on the topics of children's literature and fantasy, and has edited several anthologies of children's literature including the Random House *Treasury of Children's Literature*. She is also a Jungian psychotherapist, and she brings Jung's ideas about the human psyche to bear on her understanding of the ancient myths of Greece and Rome.

Captions for preliminary pages and section opener
Page 1: Marble sculpture of Centaur ridden by Eros, first–second century CE
Page 2: Gilded bronze head of Medusa, detail from the Temple of Asclepius in Ulpia Traiana, Romania, second–third century CE
Page 5: *Psyche Receiving Her First Kiss From Cupid* by François Pascal Simon Gérard (1770–1837)
Pages 6–7: Stone sculpture of Pan, detail from the Baroque Zwinger Palace in Dresden, Germany
Pages 8–9: Theseus slays the Minotaur, from Reliefs of Painted Vases of the Count of Bamberg, 1813
Pages 10–11: *Les Sabines* by Jacques-Louis David (1748–1825)

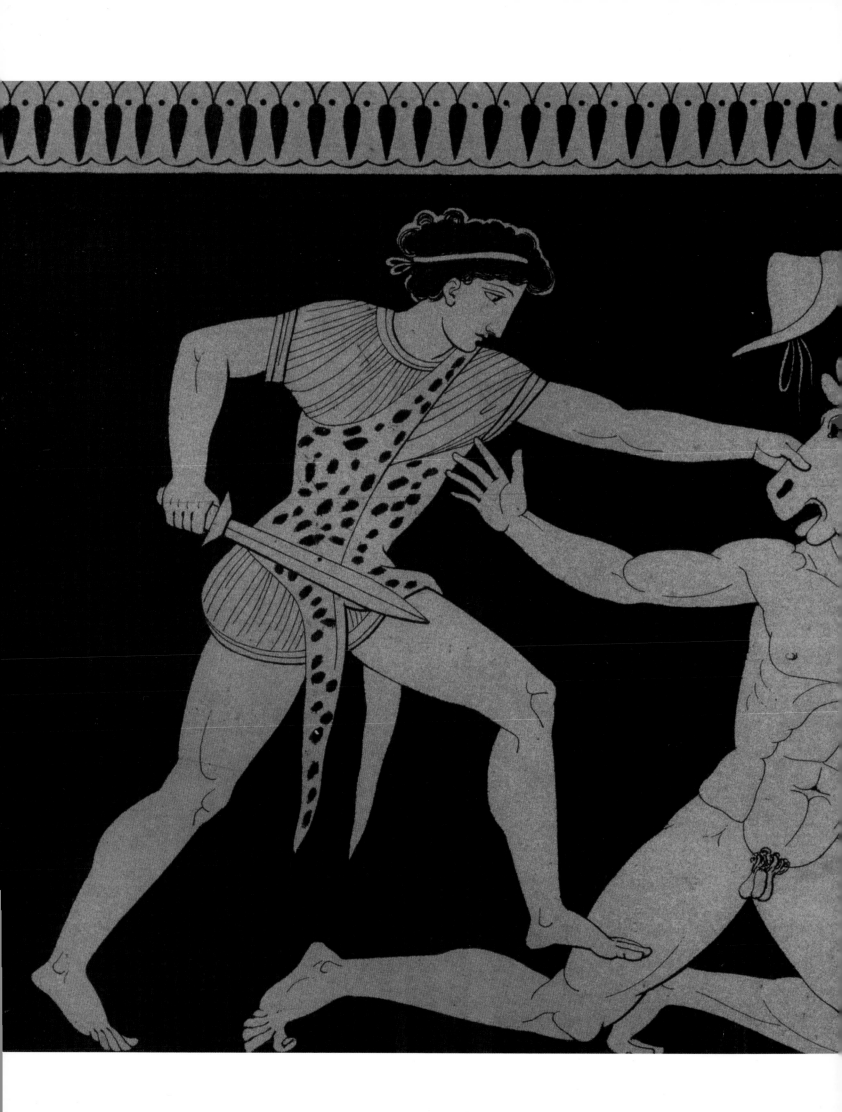

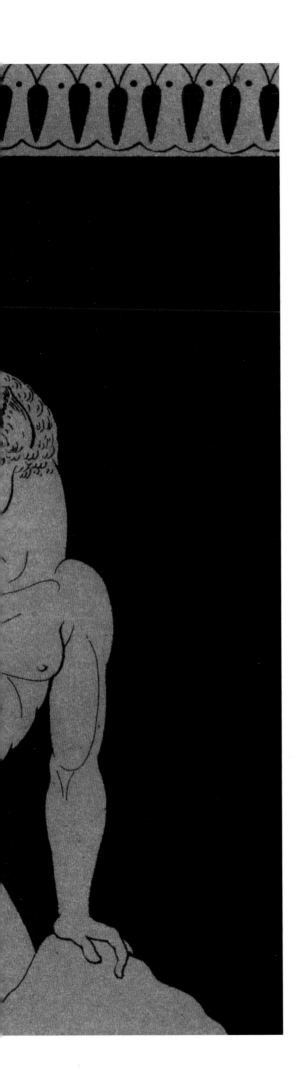

CONTENTS

THE CLASSICAL ERA

GREEK AND ROMAN MYTHOLOGY

Below *Zeus and Hera* by Ambrogio Figino (c. 1550–c. 1595). The goddess Hera was honored by the Greeks as the goddess of women, marriage, and childbirth. However, Zeus's wandering eye meant Hera spent much of her time plotting revenge against his lovers.

W hen Westerners think of myth, they think in terms of Greek and Roman myths. For Western culture, Greek and Roman myths are the foundation of myth, with their well-worked-out stories of gods and heroes, wars to fight and monsters to defeat, and families suffering their way through the workings of a curse. No other myth system is so familiar, or permeates Western culture so thoroughly. The Greeks produced the most culturally resilient myths that the world has known, partly because their myths concern the middle of things rather than their beginnings or endings. Their myths do not focus primarily on how things came into being. Hephaestus (Vulcan) invents individual items for the first time, but most Greek and Roman myth takes place well after the world has come into being, and the gods and their antagonists are already in place. Greek and Roman myth is equally unconcerned with endings, with questions of how the world ends or what happens after death. There are stories of heroes descending into the underworld for brief visits, but only the philosophers spent much time speaking about the fate of the soul. Greek and Roman myth focuses on the here and now of life for the gods feasting and quarreling on Olympus, for heroes seeking immortal fame, for both gods and mortals wanting revenge. Its themes are divine and human hopes and pains, disappointments, and tricks and transformations. These myths are not often set in sacred space, but take place among fallible characters—the gods being as fallible, temperamental, irascible, and prone to tantrums as any human being. Such stories transcend cultural boundaries.

The Gods

The gods of Greek myth, and of Roman retellings of Greek myths, are much closer to human beings than the gods of most other mythologies. They endlessly interact with human beings. In Greek and Roman daily life, any girl out on her own fetching water or visiting a temple, any ship on a voyage over the wine-dark sea, any trader wanting to make a profit, anyone wanting to gain revenge or to win love, was aware of the gods' powers to change a human life. Anyone wanting to know about the future relied on the gods' priests and priestesses to transmit their words of truth. In the myths, the gods regularly took on the disguise of human bodies to tease and test human beings. This meant that one of the gods might at any time substitute for a member of your family, your neighbor, the person you worked for. A prime directive of Greek myth was to honor and be generous to strangers, for no one could be

ANCIENT GREECE

certain just who was human and who might be a god in disguise. The gods took many other nonhuman forms, especially when they came to Earth in search of desirable human beings to rape or take as lovers, and they also took the form of ideas, inspirations, moments of particular clarity, or confusion. When Ares (Mars) walked on the battlefield, battle frenzy, terror, and fear accompanied him. When Athene (Minerva) accompanied her favorite hero, Odysseus (Ulysses), she whispered bright ideas to him, so that the hero's ingenious mind became indistinguishable from the cleverness of the goddess. When Eros (Cupid) struck someone with his arrow, the overwhelming desire and love that he inflicted was felt both as falling in love and as an affliction sent by the god. Aphrodite (Venus) made her favorites gleam and glow with beauty. Hera (Juno) clothed her favorites with stately majesty. Human beings' glory was the glory of the gods, for who could tell the inspiration of the gods from that of the humans that they befriended, harassed, and molested?

These gods were not moral beings. The gods of Greece and Rome were neither good nor bad. They are best described as being more like energies, whose use could be judged right or wrong, fair or unfair by humans, but they used their powers without being bound by any system of morality. The only thing that they insisted upon was proper respect from mortals. Many of the myths of Greece concern people who claimed to be equal to the gods or had the insolence to set themselves up as

greater than the gods. Such claims attracted instant retribution. The gods did not always punish murderers, but they always punished those who dared to act insolently toward them.

The gods of the Greeks are the most human of the gods of myth, but with powers that often destroyed the humans with whom they mixed. To take a god as one's lover often led to suffering and death. To resist a god's attentions, however, guaranteed an unpleasant fate. These gods also had favorites. Aphrodite favored Paris, the Trojan prince who gave her the apple destined for the fairest of the goddesses. Artemis (Diana) favored those who loved the hunt and vowed themselves to chastity. Zeus (Jupiter) took an interest in the rulers of the world, and wars that involved the whole of the known world. Ares loved battle, and Athene loved subtlety of mind. Hermes (Mercury) could not resist a clever liar and thief.

Greek myth is as alive and changeable as fairy tales. Retellings of fairy tales frequently put forward very different details to the story, especially its ending. In Greek and Roman times, different

Top left **Zeus flanked by soldiers while being nursed.** While the nymphs nursed Zeus, it is said that the Curetes danced about, clashing their spears and shields to hide the child's cries from Cronus. The Curetes were believed to be semidivine counterparts of Cretan youths who performed ritual dances to honor Zeus.

Left *Eros* by Praxiteles (c. 400 B.C.–c. 330 B.C.). Over time, there came to be many different traditions and perceptions of the god of love. The Greeks named him Eros, referring to love of a sexual kind, while the Romans called him Amor, meaning love, or Cupid, meaning desire.

NAMING THE GODS

NAME IN GREEK MYTHOLOGY	NAME IN ROMAN MYTHOLOGY
AIAS	AJAX
APHRODITE	VENUS
ARTEMIS	DIANA
ASCLEPIUS	AESCULAPIUS
ATHENE	MINERVA
CRONUS	SATURNUS
DEMETER	CERES
DIONYSUS	BACCHUS
EOS	AURORA
EROS	CUPID
HADES	PLUTO
HECABE	HECUBA
HELIUS	SOL
HEPHAESTUS	VULCAN
HERA	JUNO
HERACLES	HERCULES
HERMES	MERCURY
HESTIA	VESTA
HYPNUS	SOMNUS
NYX	NOX
ODYSSEUS	ULYSSES
OURANUS	URANUS
PERSEPHONE	PROSERPINA
POLYDEUCES	POLLUX
POSEIDON	NEPTUNE
RHEA	CYBELE
ZEUS	JUPITER

versions of the myths kept arising. Greek drama transfigured the heroes and gods from noble to villainous, from scandalous to blameless. Genealogers reconfigured family trees to suit the local nobility for whom they worked. As a result of this, there is very rarely one, and only one, right version of a Greek or Roman myth.

The Myths of Heroes

The myths of the Greek and Roman heroes merge into history. Many myth systems set their myths in sacred time, a dream time, or a time outside human chronology. For the ancient Greeks, the myths of the fathers of the gods were longer ago, but still in time that could be measured in years. The hero myths were believed to be history of just a few generations ago, when the Trojans and Greeks fought over Helen of Troy, or a couple of generations before that, when Heracles (Hercules) walked the earth and the Argonauts went in quest of the Golden Fleece. For modern scholars, these myths merge into history in a different way, by reflecting such events as the collapse of the Minoan empire or the development of trading routes north of the Black Sea. The myths were also a source of local prestige and every town and city wanted to claim that one of the heroes was born or buried there. There are discrepancies between different lists of the Argonauts, fostering the claims of different city-states to have sent a hero

on the quest for the Golden Fleece. There were only 50 places available on the Argo, but in the story of the Trojan War, the number of ships sent by the Greeks was easily expanded to fit in new claimants. In this way, modifying the myths remade local history.

Greek myths also merge into everyday geography. Many of the details of the myths are quite specific about the mountain path where a monster used to lurk, or the temple where a god raped a girl, or the route taken by a ship keeping close to land. These locatable details merge into mythic space, which cannot be reconciled with the details of the atlas. In the story of Odysseus's return, for instance, the journey of his son Telemachus can be mapped accurately to show where Mycenae and Pylos are located, but it is a fruitless endeavor to try to locate the island of the Sirens or the land of the Lotus-Eaters from Odysseus's travels. Even Odysseus's Ithaca, described in loving detail by the Greek poet Homer, cannot be mapped with confidence on the island now called Ithaca. Mount Olympus stands in Greece, but in our everyday reality it does not house the gods of Greek and Roman myth. They live on in the mythic geography of the imagination.

Perhaps the stories of Greek gods and heroes live on also in everyday psychology. Carl Jung argues that the Greek myths (like all others) tell truths about the human psyche, especially those overpowering impulses and uncontrollable behaviors that affect groups rather than individuals. Jungians would see

the god Ares in action as nations go to war, Hermes playing the trickster in every business that tries to lie and deceive its way through financial difficulties, Dionysian energies at work at rave parties, Aphrodite's glamor evident in each new film starlet's box office appeal, and the hero's descent to the underworld in every bout of depression. To this way of thinking, the Greek gods do not live on Mount Olympus, but their stories can be read afresh in every news broadcast or newspaper headline. Greek myths are more often than not remarkably specific in their location, but for the Jungians, their psychological truths transcend the millennia and are still being acted out today by people all over the world.

Thus have the gods spun the thread for wretched mortals: that they live in grief while they themselves are without cares

HOMER (800 B.C.–700 B.C.),
THE ILIAD

The Romans were not great inventors of myths like the Greeks. They were great empire builders, and in the course of exploring, conquering, and administering nations, they assimilated each nation's myths. Where a similarity could be found between gods, for instance, this was interpreted as signifying the same god under different titles. Thus the Greek goddess Athene was assimilated into the Etruscan and Roman goddess Minerva. In the following collection of myths, the Greek names of gods and humans are given first and then the Roman equivalent, except for the two sections on Myths of the Romans and the Roman tale of Aeneas, which put forward the Roman names first.

Above *The Rape of Helen by Gavin Hamilton (1723–1798)*. Although some authors refer to the "rape" or "abduction" of Helen, other scholars are not so convinced. Many believe that Helen chose to go with Paris of her own accord because she fell in love with him.

IDENTIFYING THE GODS

When they are not in disguise, each of the Greek and Roman gods can be recognized by their body features or their special emblems. These emblems may be weapons or they may be animals and birds that are always associated with them. Zeus (Jupiter), for example, wields the thunderbolt as his weapon, and his bird is the eagle. Athene (Minerva) is associated with the owl, while Aphrodite (Venus) is associated with the dove and Hera (Juno) with the peacock. As messenger for the gods, Hermes (Mercury) has small wings at each ankle and a winged cap. He carries the caduceus, a staff whose handle is made up of intertwined snakes.

The emblem of Cronus (Saturnus) is the sickle with which he mutilated his father, but since he is often confused with Chronos, the god of time, he is sometimes represented as an old man with an hourglass. If that is the case, the artist has introduced emblems of time that should in fact belong to Chronos.

Right *Zeus and the Eagle* by the Naukratis Painter *c.* 575 B.C. In some tales, Zeus is simply accompanied by an eagle, his special emblem, whereas in other tales, he is actually transformed into the bird itself.

hatched Eros (Cupid), the god of love? Did everything start off as a giant chaos of water and mud, fire and air, from which Earth slowly came into being? Was Chaos a god, whose wife was Nyx (Nox), the goddess of night? And did their son Erebus overthrow Chaos before he was overthrown in turn by his children Aether and Hemera, Light and Day? Or perhaps was the goddess of Earth, Gaia (or Ge) there from the very beginning, giving birth to the seas, the mountains, and the sky?

THE FATHERS OF THE GODS

There is no all-powerful, all-wise, and totally good father god in Greek myth. Instead, the story of the gods of Olympus is a complicated tale of crime, conspiracy, mutilation, and murder. One god after another claimed sovereign power, but their hold on kingship was shaky. Pictures and sculptures often show the gods sitting in confident majesty, but the myths tell a different tale.

How it all began was really never quite clear. Was there a gigantic egg, perhaps, from which

Gaia and Ouranus

The ancient Greeks thought of the earth-mother goddess Gaia as a gentle giver of life and nourisher of all her children. And she had a multitude of children. From the union of Gaia and her son, the sky god Ouranus (Uranus), were born a family of gods who were called the Titans. Oceanus was the Titan god of the great oceanic river that forever circles the world, and Tethys was his sister and wife. The Titan Hyperion was the first sun god, and his sister-wife was Theia. Coeus and Phoebe the moon goddess, Cronus (identified by the Romans with

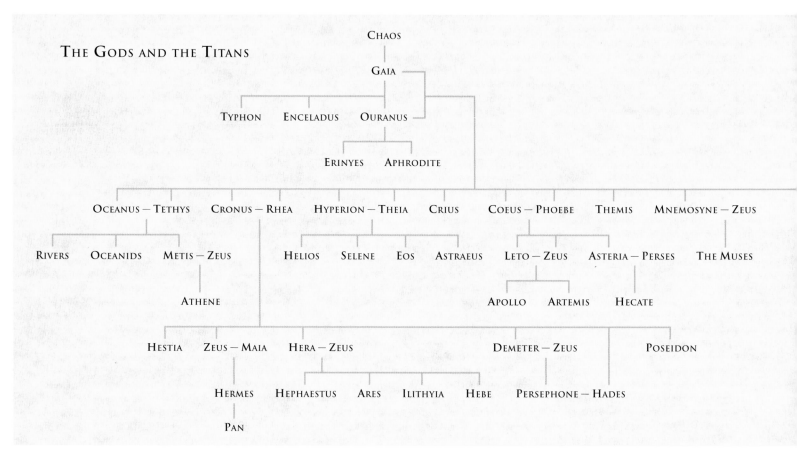

THE GODS AND THE TITANS

CHAOS

GAIA

TYPHON ENCELADUS OURANUS

ERINYES APHRODITE

OCEANUS — TETHYS   CRONUS — RHEA   HYPERION — THEIA   CRIUS   COEUS — PHOEBE   THEMIS   MNEMOSYNE — ZEUS

RIVERS OCEANIDS METIS — ZEUS   HELIOS SELENE EOS ASTRAEUS   LETO — ZEUS   ASTERIA — PERSES   THE MUSES

ATHENE   APOLLO ARTEMIS   HECATE

HESTIA ZEUS — MAIA   HERA — ZEUS   DEMETER — ZEUS   POSEIDON

HERMES   HEPHAESTUS ARES ILITHYIA HEBE   PERSEPHONE — HADES

PAN

their god Saturnus) and Rhea (identified with the goddess Cybele), Crius, Japetus, Themis (the goddess of justice), and Mnemosyne (the goddess of memory), made up the rest of the 12 Titans. Gaia also gave birth to the Hundred-Handed Giants and to the Cyclopes, giants who each had a single eye in the middle of his forehead. Gaia had many grandchildren, including the three Fates, and the nine Muses, and the two young Titans Prometheus and Epimetheus.

Ouranus did not allow his children to see the light of day, because he was afraid of their power. Perhaps he was mindful of his family history, the overthrow of Chaos by his son Erebus, and then of Erebus by his children. Even though Ouranus ruled all the wide heavens, his sons and daughters were forced to stay underground, chained in the black cavern of Tartarus. Gaia became angry with her husband, and encouraged her children to conspire against him. Her youngest child, Cronus (Saturnus), made himself ruler of the world when he attacked and castrated Ouranus with a sickle. He threw Ouranus's severed genitals into the ocean, and where they fell the sea foamed up and gave birth to Aphrodite (Venus), the beautiful goddess of sexual

desire and love. Drops of Ouranus's blood fell to the ground and from them were born the Erinyes, Furies who torment the minds of criminals.

How Zeus Overthrew His Father

Cronus was as fearful a king as his father, Ouranus, and for better reason. Cronus's mother Gaia had once prophesied that one of his children would grow up to overthrow him, or perhaps the words were uttered as a curse from his mutilated father's mouth. Cronus and Rhea had three male children, Poseidon (Neptune), Hades (Pluto), and Zeus (Jupiter), and three female children, Hestia (Vesta), Hera (Juno), and Demeter (Ceres).

As soon as each baby was born, Cronus swallowed it whole, and there it stayed in his stomach helplessly. Rhea was determined to stop her husband from eating his children, but she was afraid of his great strength. She needed to overthrow him not by force but by trickery.

When she was about to give birth to her youngest child, Zeus, she hid a large stone in her bed, and when Cronus demanded the child, she offered him the stone instead. Cronus must have gulped the stone down, because he did not notice the trick, and Rhea hid her newborn son in a cave. The goat Amaltheia supplied him with milk to drink, and he was fed honey by the bees. Rhea asked some minor deities, the Curetes, to keep her child safe, and when he cried, they made a loud noise with their spears and shields so that Cronus would not hear the baby.

As soon as the child Zeus was strong enough, he forced his father to vomit up all the babies that he had swallowed, then threw him underground to Tartarus again. Some myths say that Cronus was not imprisoned in the depths of Tartarus but lives on in Elysium. The fields of Elysium are the place where the fortunate dead, those who have pleased the gods,

Left **The birth of Aphrodite.** The goddess of love, beauty, and sexual ecstasy, Aphrodite was born from the *aphros* (Greek for "sea foam") that was churned up where Cronus cast the severed genitals of his father, Ouranus, into the ocean. Some myths say Aphrodite was carried by the sea to Cyprus, others say to Cythera.

Above *Cronus Devouring His Son* by Peter Paul Rubens (1577–1640). Cronus was always shown carrying the sickle with which he castrated his father. He swallowed his children whole as soon as each was born.

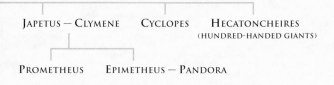

JAPETUS — CLYMENE   CYCLOPES   HECATONCHEIRES
(HUNDRED-HANDED GIANTS)

PROMETHEUS   EPIMETHEUS — PANDORA

Above *Enceladus Buried Underneath Mount Etna* by Bernard Picart (1673–1733). Giants differed from mortals mostly in their size rather than in their appearance, but some giants were much larger than the rest. The hundred-headed, fire-breathing giant Enceladus was so enormous that he had to be buried underneath Mount Etna in order to be subdued.

War With the Titans and Other Troubles

But before the troubles of the human race began, Zeus had to deal with his brothers and sisters. He married his sister Hera, gave dominion over the hearth to Hestia, and put Demeter in charge of the crops and the world's fertility. Zeus and his brothers divided up the kingship of the world, with Poseidon taking charge of the oceans and Zeus, as oldest brother, becoming king of the gods. It is because Rhea's other children were all born again from their father's belly that Zeus is considered to be both the youngest and the oldest of her sons. Hades was given the underworld to rule, and he was not satisfied with his share. That is why Hades so rarely appears in Greek myth, for he usually keeps his distance from the other gods who, in turn, do not care to visit Hades' realm. Instead, most of the greater gods of Greek myth have their palaces on Mount Olympus (an actual mountain in Thessaly).

Only four of Gaia's other children accepted Zeus as ruler of the gods. The rest went to war with the gods of Olympus, and they seemed likely to win by sheer numbers. Zeus remembered the Hundred-Handed Giants and the Cyclopes, who were still chained down in Tartarus. He offered them freedom on the condition that the Hundred-Handed Giants would fight alongside the gods of Olympus, and the Cyclopes would forge a weapon that no god, no Titan, and no monster could withstand. Zeus soon gained his weapon, the jagged thunderbolt, but even with its help he took 10 years to bring the war to an end and cast the rebels into Tartarus.

The war against the Titans was over, but Gaia was angry with Zeus for seizing power from the rest of her children. She gave birth to the hundred-headed giants Typhon (Typhoeus) and Enceladus, who could breathe fire and pile mountain upon mountain. The gods of Olympus were terrified at the sight of these giants and started to run away to Egypt, disguising themselves as animals. To escape Typhon's attention, Hades put on a helmet of invisibility, made for him by the Cyclopes. The giant Typhon took Dionysus (Bacchus) by surprise on the banks of the Nile, and the god jumped into the river, transforming himself immediately into a creature that was part-goat and part-fish; the constellation of Capricorn commemorates this event. Aphrodite and Eros disguised themselves as fish, a transformation which

enjoy a most happy existence. Nothing about his treatment of his children would have pleased the next generation of gods, but although Cronus was the worst of fathers to his own children, he was a generous ruler over humankind. The age of Cronus is called the Age of Gold, when the earth provided food without the need for labor, and murder was unknown to humans who lived peacefully together. As soon as Cronus was cast down from his throne by his son, the Age of Silver began, and the seasons came into being. Then came the Age of Bronze, an age of war, and finally the Age of Iron, an age of toil and injustice, crime and punishment. This is the age which all of humankind is still suffering through.

> *It is not possible either to trick or escape the mind of Zeus.*
> HESIOD (C. EIGHTH CENTURY B.C.), *THEOGONY*

Opposite page *Four Ages of Life* by Pietro da Cortona (1596–1664). The Age of Gold was a tranquil era devoted to peaceful existence.

THE GAIA HYPOTHESIS

The idea that Earth is a living goddess has long been rejected by science, and played no part in the development of the earth sciences, biology, or meteorology. In 1979, however, James Lovelock published *Gaia: A New Look at Life on Earth*, a book in which he argues for something like the idea of a nurturing earth goddess. He puts forward the Gaia hypothesis that all that is alive on Earth can be understood as one organism. Just as human beings regulate their own body temperature, for example, the planet

Earth seems to regulate its temperature to exactly the range needed for life to survive. The Gaia hypothesis talks of a planet that is friendly to the life on its surface, just like the Greek goddess Gaia, the mother and nurturer of all life.

Right **Goddess of Earth.** Gaia, once thought of as the source of all the gods in Greece, later fell from favor. She is often depicted suckling her children, and is shown here with the mother goddess Thalassa.

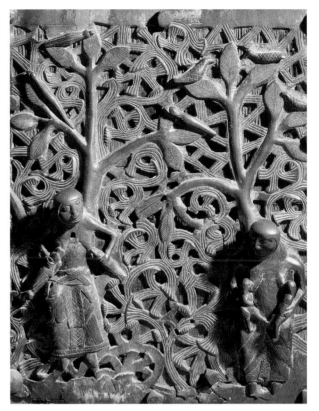

is commemorated in the constellation of Pisces. Even Zeus, king of the gods, disguised himself as a ram. Zeus alone found the courage to return and fight each of the giants with his new weapon, the thunderbolt. The struggle was fierce and, even when the giants were defeated, Enceladus kept on breathing fire, writhing in his prison under Mount Etna. That is why Etna is such an active volcano; each time the giant tries to break free, the earth shakes, and each time he breathes fire, lava spouts into the air.

The Children of Zeus

Zeus was married to Hera, goddess of marriage, and their sons were the god of war, Ares (Mars) and the blacksmith god Hephaestus (Vulcan); but he fathered many other children, who, if their mother was a goddess, were born gods and goddesses. Apollo, the sun god, and Artemis (Diana), the moon goddess and huntress, were the children of Zeus and Leto. Hera was so jealous that she did not allow Leto to stay anywhere on solid earth when it was time for her to give birth. Only the floating island of Ortygia gave her sanctuary, and as a reward, it became fixed with pillars of adamant. Hermes (Mercury) was the son of Zeus and the minor goddess Maia, and the maiden Persephone (Proserpina) was the daughter of Zeus and Demeter.

Zeus's first wife was the goddess of wise prudence, the Titan Metis, daughter of Oceanus and Tethys. Gaia prophesied that, like his father and grandfather, Zeus would be overthrown by a son. She said that Metis was destined to give birth first to a strong-minded daughter and then to a son who would be the next ruler of gods and men. Zeus

found a way to avoid this prophecy: he promptly swallowed the pregnant Metis, as his father Cronus had swallowed his children, so that she would have only the one child, a daughter. Metis's daughter grew within the body of her father until one day his head started to ache unbearably, so badly that he ordered Hephaestus to take an ax and split his brains open. Out sprang his daughter, the goddess Athene (Minerva), already dressed in full armor and ready for battle.

Even though Athene was born as a fully grown warrior goddess, she was not about to challenge her father or try to rescue her mother in the same way that Cronus had challenged Ouranus and Zeus had rescued his brothers and sisters from the stomach of his father. When Zeus had swallowed Metis, he was incorporating prudence and wisdom into his life, and this put an end to the cycle of resentment and anger that had brought about the overthrow of his father and grandfather and generations before them. Athene was Zeus's favorite daughter and was always loyal to her father. She was the goddess of craft and craftiness, cleverness and ingenuity, and she enjoyed the trick that her father had played on the Fates. With the birth of Athene, a pattern of murderous hate and fear between parent and child in the family of the Olympian gods comes to an end.

Opposite page **Detail from *Zeus Launching His Thunderbolts* by Giulio Romano (c. 1499–1546).** As well as being the ruler of the gods, Zeus was believed to be the weather god. He controlled thunder, rain, and lightning. He used thunderbolts as his main weapons of war.

Left **Warrior goddess.** The goddess Athene, daughter of Zeus, was renowned for her clever strategies and practical wisdom. She was the goddess of war, industry, craft, and justice.

Above **The gift of fire.**
In some myths Prometheus
is blamed for the origin of
death. His act of stealing
fire from the gods to give
to humans brought about
the creation of Pandora,
who in turn let loose
disasters on the world.

PROMETHEUS, PANDORA, AND LYCAON

Prometheus and Epimetheus were two
of the sons of the Titan Japetus. Their
mother was Clymene, a nymph of the
sea. In Greek, the name Prometheus
means "looking forward" and Prometheus
was indeed someone who planned for the
future. The name Epimetheus means
"looking back," but although Epimetheus
may have been good at looking back at
what had already happened, that did not
help him in his time of trouble. In the end,
neither of these Titans managed to live a
happy life, whichever way they looked.

After Zeus (Jupiter) and his brothers
and sisters had overthrown the rebel
Titans, the gods of Olympus wanted
humans to worship them with animal
sacrifices. The people making the sacrifices
looked forward to the sacred festivals as oppor-
tunities to eat plenty of meat. Humans and gods
alike wanted to have the best parts of any
animal sacrifice, the meat and not the
bones. Prometheus was chosen to
cut up an animal for sacrifice so
that Zeus could choose which
half he preferred, to decide
once and for all just which
portions went to the god and
which to the hungry people.

Prometheus always wanted to help
humankind, and perhaps he thought it
unfair that the gods should get all the meat when
they had done none of the work. He cut up the
carcass very carefully, and piled all the edible meat

When every spark was
quenched on every hearth
Throughout the earth,
I brought to man the fire
And all its ministrations. My reward
Hath been the rock and vulture.

HENRY WADSWORTH LONGFELLOW
(1807–1882), "BIRDS OF PASSAGE"

underneath the animal skin, putting the stomach on
top so that the whole pile looked unappetizing. In the
other pile he put the inedible bones,
covered with a thick layer of
animal fat so it looked ready
to be cooked for a feast.

No one knows if Zeus
was fooled by Prometheus's
trick or whether he only
pretended to think that the
pile of bones and fat was the
choicest part of the sacrifice.

Prometheus was clever, but perhaps
it was Zeus who looked farther ahead this time,
foreseeing an opportunity to get his revenge on the
Titan and all humankind. Whatever the truth, from

that moment on, whenever an animal is sacrificed
in honor of a god, only the bones and fat are burned
on the altar. The gods must content themselves with
the sweet smell of hot fat while the humans are
feasting on the meat.

The Theft of Fire

Zeus had to keep his word. He could do nothing to
change his own decision that Prometheus's division
of the carcass would set the rules for every sacrifice
to come. The king of the gods could, however, take
his revenge on both human beings and the Titan
who was so fond of them by making a new ruling.
No human being was now allowed to use fire. They
could not warm themselves with fire, they could not
work metals in the forge, and, most importantly, they

could not cook their food. If the gods were to be
denied cooked meat on their altars, mortals would
be denied cooked food at their tables.

Prometheus climbed Mount Olympus in secret
and stole fire from the gods. Some say that Athene
(Minerva) helped him, for she was always fond of
cleverness and craftiness. He
held the fire in a hollow reed
or perhaps a fennel stalk as he
climbed back to the world of
mortals. He traveled to every place
where humans lived, to farmhouses,
to palaces, to fields where shepherds
were shivering, to kitchens where cooks
were complaining. Everywhere he gave the
gift of fire. Soon there were so many fires in

so many fireplaces that the gods could never put them all out. Prometheus had given humankind one of the greatest gifts of civilization.

Pandora

Zeus was furious, but he decided not to use the thunderbolt to gain his revenge. Instead, he played a trick of his own on the Titans and humankind. He was wary of trying to trick the clever Prometheus, but he was quite confident that his brother, at least, could be easily fooled, for Epimetheus, the one who looked backward, was not the cleverest of Titans. Zeus asked Hephaestus (Vulcan), the blacksmith god, to make a beautiful woman out of clay, and he named her Pandora (a name that means "full of all gifts"). Zeus put in Pandora's arms a large box that was closed and sealed, and told his son Hermes (Mercury) to take her to Epimetheus as a bride, a present from the gods.

Prometheus warned his brother to be very wary of any gifts coming from Zeus, who had no reason to be friendly, but Epimetheus saw how beautiful Pandora was and decided to marry her. Hermes had told her never to open the box, and for days and weeks she tried not to think about it, but every day she felt more curious about its contents. Surely there must be something very precious in there, she thought, and it was unfair of the gods to give her something and then forbid her to enjoy it. In the end she broke the seals and opened the box. Out flew all the diseases, sorrows, and disasters that afflict humankind. Pandora tried to close the box, but more and more troubles surged out, covering the whole Earth. The only thing that she was able to keep hold of was Hope.

One version of the story of Pandora tries to excuse the behavior of the gods. If, in fact, Hope was in the bottom of the box, surely the rest of its contents must have been equally delightful. In this version, the box was really brimful of good things, the gods' gifts from Olympus, and all of them except Hope are lost to us through the curiosity of a foolish woman.

This story of how evil came into the world (or goodness was lost) through a woman's folly is reminiscent of the biblical story of how Eve was tempted to eat the apple, which brought death into the world along with other woes. Some theologians have argued that the myth of Pandora is a faint reflection of biblical truth. Secular critics of myth often classify all stories that blame women for the introduction of evil into the world as a product of a patriarchal society. Where men are in power, who better to blame for evil than women?

Left *Eva Prima Pandora (Eve, the First Pandora)* by Jean Cousin, the Father, (c. 1490–c. 1560). Hephaestus created Pandora, and the gods endowed her with many gifts. Among them were the gift of beauty from Aphrodite and the gift of music from Apollo.

Above *Pandora Opens the Box* by Walter Crane (1845–1915). In one version of this myth, Pandora released all types of disasters on humankind. In another, the box was full of her wedding presents— gifts and blessings given to her by the gods.

VIRGO AND LIBRA

The Age of Gold was the first age of the world, without hardship or toil for those who dwelt on Earth, and was without crime. The most recent age of the world, full of troubles and evils, is called the Age of Iron, but perhaps it would be better to call it the Second Age of Gold, for many of its troubles began when gold first tempted humankind to wickedness and war. Through the Ages of Gold, Silver, and Bronze, Astraea, the goddess of justice, still remained on Earth, but when the Age of Iron began, she found she could stay here no longer. Now she shines down from the sky as the constellation Virgo, the virgin. Astraea once carried a pair of scales with which she weighed up the rights and wrongs of any dispute. Now Astraea's scales shine close by Virgo, as the constellation Libra.

Opposite page **The chariot of Mercury and Virgo.** Astraea, which means "the star maiden," was the last deity to leave Earth. She and her scales became constellations.

The Punishment of Prometheus

Humankind was now punished with the contents of Pandora's box, and the next target for Zeus's revenge was Prometheus. Not only had the Titan disobeyed Zeus, stealing fire for humankind, but he was also keeping a dangerous secret. He had heard a prophecy that the goddess Thetis would give birth to a son destined to overthrow his father. Zeus knew part of the prophecy, but not the name of the goddess.

Above **Eternal torment.** Prometheus knew that he could end his torment if he simply gave in to Zeus and told him the goddess's name. It is his resistance that has made Prometheus a symbol of endurance and strength of will. Here he is shown being tortured daily by the eagle.

Right *Prometheus in Chains* by Nicolas Sebastien Adam (1705–1778). Prometheus is often represented in Greek myths as being the friend of humankind who interceded on their behalf with Zeus. This drew the wrath of Zeus down on him and led to him being chained to the mountain as punishment.

He was tormented with doubts. So many of the goddesses and nymphs had been his lovers, and one of them was perhaps already pregnant with the son who would overthrow him. Or did the prophecy name a new goddess? Or did it point to his wife, Hera (Juno), so that he would have to keep his distance from her as well? Prometheus refused to name the goddess, and Zeus decided that he would have to torture the secret out of him. Prometheus was seized and hurled into Tartarus, where so many of Zeus's family had suffered in the past. He still would not speak, and so Zeus brought him out and chained him to the side of Mount Caucasus. Every day a huge bird flew to the rock and pecked out his liver, and every night the flesh healed again. Some say that the bird was a vulture, others that Zeus sent his own royal bird, the eagle, to torment the Titan.

Prometheus could not die, nor could he break free from his chains. He knew that he would be free only if another of the immortals went down to the underworld, to Hades' realm of death, of his own free will. Human lifetimes came and went, and still he hung, burning and bleeding in the sun by day and freezing by night, until Heracles (Hercules) found his way to Mount Caucasus and shot the eagle. Heracles was in the middle of accomplishing the tasks that made up his 12 labors, and he had just accidentally shot his friend, the wise Centaur Cheiron with a poisoned arrow, leaving a wound that could not be healed. Cheiron was eager to die and go to the underworld instead of Prometheus. The Titan might have refused his offer and stayed silent even then, to make Zeus suffer still more, but he felt pity for the Centaur's unending pain. "Thetis," he groaned, "that is the name of the goddess whose son will surpass his father."

At once Prometheus's chains fell from him and he was free. He was even welcomed back to Olympus, on condition that all his cleverness was to be put to use for the gods, not against them. Zeus promptly arranged a marriage between Thetis and a mortal man, making sure that any son she gave birth to would surpass only his mortal father and not endanger the throne of the king of the gods.

The Banquet of Lycaon

As soon as the gods had won their war with the Titans, trouble began among the people of Earth. Some say that the first human beings were created by Prometheus, and that is why they proved to be so disrespectful to the gods. In the northern part of Greece, in Arcadia, the tyrant Lycaon refused to worship the gods and mocked his people for believing in them. Zeus disguised himself as a mortal man and traveled to Arcadia to find out for himself just how badly Lycaon could behave. When the king of the gods told peasants and townsfolk that he was no mortal man but a god, they believed him and started to worship him as he deserved. But Lycaon would not listen to the traveler and began to mock his people for their credulity. He even went so far as to promise the people that he would put this charlatan to the test, a test that he felt could not fail. "Everyone knows that the gods are immortal," Lycaon said. "All I have to do is to kill this fellow and you will all see how foolish you have been." He did not say this within Zeus's earshot, of course, because he planned to sneak into his guest's room at night and take him by surprise, stabbing him to death.

This was not the worst part of his plan. He wanted his guest to pollute his mouth and stomach by eating forbidden food, and Lycaon himself wanted to feast on the same food, to wallow in evil, to perform the most abhorrent of acts in defiance of the gods. He had a captive in his prison cells, a hostage whose life should have been sacred to him, but Lycaon cared nothing for proper treatment of hostages. Instead, he slit the prisoner's throat and carved up his body, using some parts for the roasting spit, and cutting other parts into meat for the stew. Lycaon cooked this meal with his own hands, and put the dishes onto the table with freshly baked bread and wine. Some say that it was a baby that Lycaon killed and served to his guest, and most horrible of all, in some accounts, it was his own baby son.

LYCAON AS WEREWOLF

Lycaon's name is related to the classical Greek word for wolf, *lykos*, and his metamorphosis is an example of lycanthropy (from the Greek words *lykos* and *ánthrōpos* meaning "human being"). Lycanthropes, which are more commonly called werewolves, display a preference for human flesh, especially that of babies. The myth of Lycaon's banquet provides a prime example of the lycanthrope as a cannibal, although here the serving up of human flesh occurs before his transformation into wolf. Werewolves in literature and film tend to change repeatedly between human and animal form, often at the occurrence of the full moon. Lycaon is an unusual lycanthrope in that he changes only once and does so irreversibly.

Above **Metamorphosis of men into wolves.** Stories of werewolves are told all over the world. In some countries, if wolves are not common, other wild animals are cited instead.

Zeus immediately struck the meat from the table in anger and sent his thunderbolt flying against the walls of the palace. Down crashed ceilings, walls collapsed, and the palace was devoured by flames. Lycaon was quick enough to escape the fire, but the vengeance of Zeus followed him as he fled into the countryside. As he ran, he tried to cry out for help, but instead of human words he began to snarl and howl. His clothes ripped and fell off as his body

changed shape. He could no longer run like a man, but found himself on all fours, with his arms changing to thin legs, his skin growing coarse hairs, his ears lengthening, and his mouth stretching forward into a snout. Zeus had transformed Lycaon into a wolf. However, even as a wolf, he was still the same bloodthirsty Lycaon. He continued to prey on the sheep and goats of Arcadia, his mouth still slavering and his eyes still gleaming with the lust to kill.

Left *Lycaon Becomes a Wolf* by Bernard Picart (1673–1733). Some versions of this myth say that Lycaon's disrespect for Zeus's status prompted Zeus's plan to destroy the world with the flood in the age of Deucalion.

Above **Deucalion and Flood by J. Briot (c. 1610).** Some believe that Zeus's main reason for wanting to destroy humankind was because he was alarmed that so many gods continued to have children with the mortals, making humans more powerful.

Below **Zeus throwing a thunderbolt.** Zeus's name is from an Indo-European word meaning "to shine." He was the god of the sky and all its phenomena.

TALES OF ZEUS

After the horrors of Lycaon's banquet, Zeus (Jupiter) decided that the whole of humankind deserved to die. The other gods thought anxiously about their temples and their festivals. Who would make sure that the sweet smells of sacrifice would continue to rise up to Mount Olympus if there were no more human beings? Who would be left to worship the gods? Zeus promised that the human race would not die out completely. He would find a way for a new breed of humans to come into being, people who would be properly respectful of the gods and careful to observe every festival with its proper rituals.

Zeus stood on Mount Olympus with the thunderbolt in his hand, choosing his first target. He was just about to hurl the thunderbolt into the marketplace of the closest city when he remembered a prophecy that the world was doomed to end in fire. Carefully, he laid aside his weapon, for he wished to cleanse the world, not to destroy it utterly. "Let the waters carry my revenge and then subside," he decreed, "so that life can return once more."

As he spoke, the winds began to blow up a tempest. The South Wind gathered black storm clouds that poured their rain down onto the land. The crops were washed away; this year, all of humankind would go hungry. But Zeus was not satisfied with this revenge. He wanted not just to hurt the troublesome human race, but to drown almost all of them.

He called to his brother Poseidon (Neptune), lord of the sea. Poseidon commanded all the rivers and streams of the world to flood, and then he struck the surface of the earth with his trident. Poseidon is sometimes known as the Earth Shaker, and on this day he shook the earth until it cracked open, letting the sea flood in. Gigantic waves smashed across the land. Cities were washed away. No temple, no palace, could stand against the roaring tide. There was no more boundary between earth and water, nowhere to take refuge on solid land, and when people tried to outride the storm by taking refuge in ships, they ended up starving to death on the ocean.

Deucalion and Pyrrha

Almost every human being was now dead. Only two people, Deucalion and Pyrrha, were still alive, afloat on the ocean in a small boat, and Zeus knew that if the human race were to survive, he would have to let these two live. Deucalion was the son of Prometheus and Pyrrha the daughter of Epimetheus, but they were neither disobedient nor stupid. In fact they were the best of humans, and always quick to honor the gods. They would make the best possible parents for the new race of human beings.

Little by little, the ocean grew calm and the highest peaks of mountains began to appear. As the flood receded, the two summits of Mount Parnassus, which before and since the flood reared high enough into the heavens to pierce the clouds, now pierced the surface of the ocean, and the little boat stuck between them. The first thing that Deucalion and Pyrrha did was to give thanks to the gods of Mount Parnassus and pray for their help, as they watched the waters diminish and the mountain grow tall again.

From their vantage point high on the mountain, Deucalion and Pyrrha could see far across the countryside. They watched as the rivers began to flow once more within their banks and the trees shook mud off their leaves. They could now see the ruined temple of Themis, but no other signs that humans had

ever lived on Earth. Quickly, they walked down to the River Cephisus and sprinkled drops of its water onto their wet clothes and wet hair, as a mark of respect for the goddess. Then they knelt down close to the temple, praying that Themis would help them rescue the entire human race from extinction.

Themis is a gentle goddess who is remarkably skilled at foretelling the future. She announced to Deucalion and Pyrrha, "You must walk away from the temple, veiling your heads and loosening your garments, throwing behind you the bones of your mother." Pyrrha was totally

Zeus is the air, Zeus the earth, Zeus all things and what transcends them all.

AESCHYLUS (525 B.C.–456 B.C.), *FRAGMENTS*

appalled at the thought of digging up the grave of her mother and throwing away her bones, but then she remembered that oracles usually spoke in riddles. Together with Deucalion, she puzzled over the goddess's command. "The oracle would never tell us to do anything that would offend the gods," said Deucalion. "The mother that she speaks of, must mean the great mother of all, Gaia the earth goddess, and the mother's bones must be the stones in the ground."

Neither Deucalion nor Pyrrha was confident that this was what the oracle meant, but they could think

Below **Poseidon on his chariot.** Poseidon, the god of the sea, lived in the ocean and drove a chariot pulled by horses. One of his emblems was a trident, with which he would strike the ground to cause tidal waves and earthquakes.

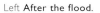

of no better interpretation of her words. With their heads veiled and their garments loosened, they picked up stones from the muddy ground and began to walk away from the temple. At every step they threw a stone or two behind them. Each stone, as it fell back into the mud, started to change shape and grow larger. They began to look like roughly carved marble statues, then like statues as big as life, and finally they grew warm and started to breathe. Each stone that Pyrrha threw behind her turned into a woman, and each stone that Deucalion threw behind him turned into a man. This is why the peoples of Earth are strong and tough, because their origin was the strong, tough stones of Parnassus.

Zeus and Io

Io was the daughter of the river god Inachus, and she became a priestess of Hera (Juno). Hera is the goddess of marriage, and she had much to complain about in the behavior of her royal husband Zeus. It was beyond forgiveness when Zeus fell in love with Io and tried to persuade her to lie down with him in the secret woodlands of Lerna. Io was horrified by the idea, and ran away as quickly as she could, but Zeus spread rain clouds over the countryside so that it became as dark as night, and she could not see where she was going. When she stopped running, he took her virginity by force.

Hera looked out from the Olympian palace and noticed a patch of darkness in Argus while the rest of the world was in bright sunshine. This had to be one of Zeus's tricks, she thought, and she hurried down to Earth and ordered the sun to disperse the clouds.

Opposite page *The God Hermes Plays Flute to Argus While Io Disguised as a Cow Watches* by Jacopo Amiconi (Amigoni) (1682–1752).

In the sunshine, she could see no sign of any woman or nymph. There in the fields was a beautiful white heifer, with her husband standing beside it. The cow's eyes looked almost human to her, and the goddess began to wonder if this might be her rival, metamorphosed into animal disguise to fool her. "Give me this beautiful creature as a present," she asked Zeus, and as he could think of no good excuse to refuse her, he gave her the heifer.

Hera became convinced that the heifer was her missing priestess, Io, and she thought that Zeus might try to steal her back again, and so she gave the creature to Argus to guard by night and day. Argus had a hundred eyes, and he was never completely awake and never wholly asleep. His eyes took it in turns to sleep, so that some of them were constantly on guard, and the eyes in the back of his head meant that no one could possibly creep up on him from behind to surprise him.

Io hated her new body. She hated eating grass and lying in the open on the hard ground. She stood by the banks of the River Inachus and tried to explain to the river god who she was, but she could not speak human words. Then she wrote her name in the mud using her hoof, and the river god wept for the fate of his dear daughter.

Zeus watched from a distance, longing to rescue Io from the troubles that he himself had brought upon her. He sent his son Hermes (Mercury), the trickster, to kill Argus of the hundred eyes. Hermes

Left **After the flood.** Some say that Zeus had no intention of allowing Deucalion and Pyrrha to live to repopulate the earth. Instead, they say Prometheus warned his son and daughter-in-law to build a boat so as to thwart Zeus's intentions.

HEPHAESTUS'S LIMP

Once Zeus (Jupiter) had become king of the gods, there were no more killings of gods by gods, but they were still capable of injuring one another. The blacksmith god, Hephaestus (Vulcan), walked with a limp, which was caused by either his father, Zeus, or his mother, Hera (Juno), depending on which version of the story is accepted. In one version, when Hephaestus was born, his mother thought he was the ugliest of babies and threw him out of the palace and down the side of Mount Olympus. His legs were permanently broken and twisted in the fall. In the other version, Hephaestus was an ugly baby but his mother did not reject him. He grew up without ever being injured until he was foolish enough to become involved in an argument between Hera and Zeus. When he agreed with his mother, his father threw him down the mountain.

Left *Hephaestus at Forge* by Peter Paul Rubens (1577–1640). Hephaestus, the god of the forge, was the patron of craftsmen.

31

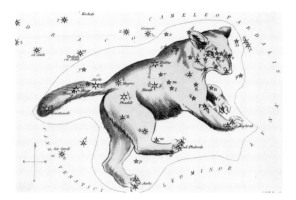

Above **Constellation of Ursa Major.** Callisto, from "Kalliste," meaning "most beautiful," was eventually joined by her son, whose constellation is said to guard her. Hera saw to it that Callisto could never rest—she is doomed to revolve ceaselessly around the North Star.

Below *The Goddess Hera Receives Head of Argus from Hermes and Places Eyes in Tail of Peacock* by Jacopo Amiconi (Amigoni) (1682–1752). Argus has been described as a man, a giant, and a monster. He had many eyes that were placed in the tail of Hera's sacred bird, the peacock.

did not try to outfight Argus, but walked up playing the flute, and sat close by him playing sweet tunes until the hundred eyes all closed. As soon as Argus was asleep, Hermes cut off his head. Hera took those hundred eyes of her faithful servant and placed them on the tail feathers of her bird, the peacock. This is how the male peacock was given its splendid and uniquely patterned plumage.

Hera was already angry with Zeus for betraying his marriage bed, and angry with Io for abandoning her vows as priestess (no matter that she had been raped by the god). Now she was even angrier, after the killing of Argus, and she made up her mind to torment Io. She sent a gadfly, the kind that bites at cattle in the hot weather, and it drove Io across country after country without rest. She visited the shores of a sea that was named in her honor, the Ionian Sea. She swam across the straits that join the Black Sea and the Mediterranean, and that is why they are called the Bosphorus, a word which in Greek means "the straits of the cow." She struggled up the slopes of Mount Caucasus, where she met Prometheus, chained to his rock. She traveled as far as the Nile, where the poor heifer fell to her knees and prayed to Zeus for help.

Zeus promised Hera by the waters of the Styx that he would be a better husband to her, if only she would let Io take human form again. An oath that invokes the River Styx is binding on anyone, god or mortal. Hera decided to let go of her anger and jealousy, and Io became human once more. Now she is a goddess in her own right, worshipped in Egypt, and her son by Zeus is called Epaphus.

Callisto

Callisto was a companion of Artemis (Diana) the huntress, and along with all the other virgins who attended upon Artemis, she had vowed never to take a sexual interest in any male, whether man or faun, satyr or god. Zeus saw her and desired her passionately, and because he knew that she would never accept a male lover, he disguised himself as Artemis. Callisto was deceived by this disguise until he forced himself upon her, and she was unable to defend herself from him. She tried to keep her rape secret, but it soon became very difficult to hide the fact that she was pregnant. On a hot day, Artemis called all her companions to bathe with her in a cool stream. Callisto undressed with everyone else, and at once the goddess noticed her swelling body and ordered her to go away, never again to be her companion in the hunt.

This banishment was punishment enough for trying to conceal what had happened from the virgin goddess, but Callisto had to face the angry Hera as well. Hera found out that Callisto had given birth to Zeus's son, Arcas, and came down from Olympus to destroy her rival. She grasped Callisto's hair and pulled it hard. Then the jealous goddess transformed Callisto from human form into the frightening shape of a bear, with a huge snout and dangerous teeth, with powerful legs and claws that could rip a man to shreds. Callisto was appalled at the loss of all her past happiness, and her sufferings increased even more when she found that she was now terrified of hunters and dogs.

For 15 years Callisto suffered life as a great bear, until one day her son Arcas was hunting in the forest. He did not know what had happened to his mother, and so, when he spotted the bear, he was terrified for his life. Callisto recognized her son at once and tried to speak to him, but all that came out

of her mouth was a frightening growl. Arcas then took his hunting spear and readied his arm to kill the bear as she stood close by, neither attacking him nor defending herself. His aim could not miss.

At the very moment when Arcas thrust the spear toward the bear's heart, Zeus grasped his hand and held him back from the crime of killing his own mother. Then the god carried them both into the sky where he transformed her into the Great Bear constellation, known as Ursa Major, and her son into the Little Bear constellation, Ursa Minor.

*Who would not love,
if loving she might be
Changed like Callisto to
a star in heaven?*

HENRY WADSWORTH LONGFELLOW
(1807–1882), "BIRDS OF PASSAGE"

Hera became even more furious than before. Not only could her rival boast of a son fathered by Zeus, but Callisto was now also shining gloriously in the night sky. In her anger and frustration, Hera turned for assistance to the Titans Oceanus and Tethys, asking them to find a way to prevent the Great Bear from ever dipping below the horizon into the ocean that rings the world. The Titans agreed to Hera's request, which is why, in the night sky of the Northern Hemisphere, the distinctive constellation of Ursa Major never entirely dips below the horizon.

Above *Arcas and Callisto* by Jean-Francois Millet (1814–1875). There are differing accounts as to when Arcas was transformed into the Little Bear constellation. At some stage during his life he succeeded his uncle, Nyctimus, to the throne and became king of Arcadia. He taught his people the arts of bread-making, weaving, and the cultivation of crops.

TALES OF APOLLO

Apollo was the son of Zeus (Jupiter) and Leto, and one of the 12 gods who lived on Mount Olympus. In many myths, he is the god of the sun, but there is also another Greek sun god, Helius, as well as the Titan sun god Hyperion (who lost his powers when Zeus became king of the gods). Apollo first showed his powers when he was only four days old. One of the children of Mother Earth was the great serpent Pytho, as big as a hillside. Pytho was the serpent who harassed Leto when she was trying to find somewhere to give birth to Apollo and his sister Artemis (Diana). The baby Apollo asked for weapons to avenge the treatment of his mother, and Hephaestus (Vulcan) gave him a bow and arrows.

Apollo overcame the serpent on Mount Parnassus, letting fly a thousand of his new arrows until the poison bled from the snake through a thousand wounds. Then he set up a festival of athletic games, called the Pythian games after the serpent Pytho, so that his victory would never be forgotten. Every athlete who triumphed at these games was rewarded with a wreath of oak or beech leaves. Later in Greek and Roman history, victors were rewarded with laurel wreaths, and the story of Apollo and Daphne explains how the laurel tree (*daphnē* in Greek) came into being.

Apollo and Daphne

Like most love stories, the tale of Apollo and Daphne begins with the god of love, Eros (Cupid). Eros had his own bow and arrows, but he wanted to try out the much bigger bow of Apollo. He had just managed to bend the bow, ready to loose an arrow, when Apollo caught him and said, "What use is a warrior's bow to you? Your task is to use your dainty bow and arrows to wound the heart, while the great bow belongs to me when I hunt my enemies, like the huge serpent Pytho that I killed even though it stretched over a whole hill. Stay within your own province, Eros, and do not intrude into mine." It was a rash comment. Eros was determined to show Apollo who was master, and he flew high into the air and shot two arrows. One wounded Daphne, a nymph of the woodlands, daughter of the river god Peneus, and the other found its mark in Apollo's heart. But they were not both arrows of love. Apollo burned with desire for the nymph Daphne, but Eros had wounded her with a blunt-tipped arrow, the kind that deters the heart from love.

Daphne immediately decided that she wanted nothing to do with men or male gods, sexual desire, or marriage. Apollo used all his arts to woo her, but she ran away whenever she saw him. At first he pretended to be a mortal man, and then he revealed himself as Apollo, god of oracular wisdom, god of music, god of the sun, god of medicine. Nothing that he said made any difference. Daphne ran away again, and Apollo could think of no better tactic than to run after her. She was spurred on by fear and he by desire. On they ran, until the nymph could feel Apollo's breath as he gasped for air just behind her, and she could hardly keep on her feet for weariness.

Now she was running downhill toward the River Peneus, and she called out, "Help me, father! If you have any powers as a river god, use them now to save me from Apollo. He loves my beauty, he says. Father, destroy my body and keep me safe for ever!" Then she stopped, unable to run another step, and as she stood on the riverbank, her feet were held fast in the wet soil. Her body became thinner and her skin grew a layer of bark. Her arms became branches, her fingers became leaves; she had changed into the first laurel tree.

Apollo could not forget the nymph, and promised that he would always wear a wreath of her laurel leaves. Every athlete who won at the games would wear a laurel wreath in memory of Daphne, and the prize for the best poet would always be a laurel wreath.

> *Till Daphne,*
> *desperate with pursuit*
> *Of his imperious love,*
> *At her own prayer transformed,*
> *took root,*
> *A laurel in the grove.*
>
> WILLIAM WORDSWORTH (1770–1850),
> "THE RUSSIAN FUGITIVE"

Apollo and Phaethon

Phaethon was the son of Apollo and Clymene, but he was born months after she had been left by the sun god. Phaethon boasted that he was the child of a god, but no one believed him. "No one knows who your father is," he was told, "but if he is really a god, surely he will give you some proof of it, and you can take your rightful place on Olympus with the rest of the gods." Everyone laughed at the idea, until Phaethon could no longer bear their mockery.

Left **Apollo crowned with laurels.** The emblems of Apollo were the lyre, the bow, and the tripod. There were many animals sacred to Apollo including the wolf, the swan, the hawk, the raven, the snake, and the mouse.

Opposite page *Apollo and Daphne* by Antonio Pollaiuolo (1432–1498) and Piero Pollaiuolo (1443–1496). When his beloved Daphne was transformed into a laurel tree, Apollo resolved that a garland of laurel leaves should decorate his lyre, his quiver, his own head, and the heads of his minstrels in Daphne's honor.

Below **Daphne.** Daphne was not the only maiden in distress rescued by the River Peneus. Known also by its Arcadian name, the River Ladon, the Peneus also rescued the nymph Syrinx when she was transformed into a reed while fleeing from Pan.

Above **Detail from a carriage showing Apollo dismounting from the sun chariot.** Apollo rose every morning from the ocean in the east and rode in his sun chariot across the sky. Every evening he descended from his chariot in the west, leaving his helpers to tend the horses.

He ran home and entreated his mother to give him some proof that he really was the sun god's child, and she faithfully swore that she had told him the truth. "If you do not believe me," she said, "you can easily walk to the edge of the world where the chariot of the sun rises every morning. That is where his palace is built, and you can ask Apollo himself if he is your father."

Phaethon set off at once, and within a few days he had reached the palace of the sun, bright and glistening with gold and ivory. There sat Apollo in glory among the Seasons and Hours, the Days and Months and Years. Apollo noticed the young man standing on the threshold and recognized him. "You are welcome, my dear son," the god said, but this alone was not enough to satisfy Phaethon. He asked for clear evidence that he was in truth the son of Apollo, evidence that would convince all the mockers and doubters back home.

PHAETHON'S REQUEST

Apollo promised to grant any request that would help Phaethon prove his parentage. He promised by the waters of Styx, and that is an oath that neither gods nor men can break. As soon as he heard the sacred oath, Phaethon asked to be allowed to drive the chariot of the sun for one course across the heavens, from morning to evening of a single day. Apollo was appalled at Phaethon's request, for the horses of the sun would endure no hands on the reins but his own, not even the mighty hands of father Zeus. Only the sun god himself could drive this chariot, and sometimes even he was terrified at the heights of noon, and how now and then the horses nearly dragged the chariot astray in their hurry to get home at dusk. The father begged his son repeatedly to ask for something else, from all the treasures of the world; anything that Phaethon cared to ask for would be his.

Tartarus, where Hades (Pluto) and Persephone (Proserpina) blinked their unaccustomed eyes in the glare of noon. The seas began to boil wildly, and Poseidon (Neptune) and Gaia appealed to Zeus to save them. Life on Earth was in danger of absolute destruction, and a cry went up to Olympus from every nymph and satyr, every river god and every human being, begging the king of the gods to save them from the sun.

Zeus threw a thunderbolt across the sky toward the hurtling chariot and struck the charioteer, setting him on fire and hurling him down to the ground. The chariot was wrecked

Above *Apollo and Phaethon* **by Giovanni Mannozzi (1592–1636).** There is speculation as to the origins of the god Apollo. In earlier times Apollo and Helius had been regarded as two separate deities, but in later tales Apollo seems to have taken over the functions of the ancient sun god, including the parentage of Phaethon.

But Phaethon would not listen. He was afire with longing to drive the chariot of the sun, and could hardly wait until morning. The dawn began to brighten the sky with her rosy fingers, and the night stars faded. Up sprang the horses, but Phaethon could not hold them on their proper course. How far away it looked now, the path that the horses should be treading toward noon and on to evening. As his fingers dropped the reins, the sun raced a zigzag path across the sky, sometimes little and pale and far away, and then scorchingly close to the earth. The boy looked down from the sky in panic, longing to be back on firm ground, but as he looked, he could see the forests bursting into flames, then the cities burning, until the whole world seemed to be on fire.

That was the time when the Ethiopians' skin darkened, to save them from being burned alive by the sun, and deserts spread across all of North Africa. The earth cracked open as far as the chasms of

and the horses ran home to their stable in terror. Leaving a trail of fire, Phaethon fell like a shooting star into the waters of the River Eridanus, and the nymphs of Italy found his scorched body. There in Italy he is buried, far away from his native Argos.

His mother and his sisters, the Heliades, daughters of the sun, found his grave and wept for him without pause, for four days and four nights. Eventually the girls' bodies began to change to trembling poplars. Clymene tried to stop the metamorphosis, pulling down their branches and tearing the bark from their trunks. The trees wept sap which dried in the sun to become

Left **Apollo and his bow.** Apollo was also called "the lord of the silver bow." Apollo had the god Hephaestus fashion him his own bow and arrows. It is said that once forged, Apollo declared these weapons sacred to him.

CYGNUS THE SWAN

The river god Eridanus, into whose waters Phaethon fell, became a constellation in the

heavens, now called simply the River. Cygnus was a friend of Phaethon who was also later transformed into a constellation. He mourned for his dead friend until his skin grew feathers and his feet became webbed, his face grew a beak, his neck lengthened and curved elegantly, and his arms turned to white wings. This is how the first swan came into being, and because he hated the flames that had killed his friend Phaethon, he chooses to live in rivers and keeps dipping his head below the water where the sun's heat cannot reach him.

Left *Cygnus Transformed into a Swan and Phaethon's Sisters into Poplars* by Bernard Picart (1673–1733). The tears of Phaethon's sisters continue to fall as drops of amber.

amber. This is where amber is said to originate: it is the tears shed by the sun god's children.

Niobe and Tityus

Niobe was the daughter of Tantalus and Dione, and she married Amphion, king of Thebes. Queen Niobe gave birth to six sons and six daughters, though some say that she had seven sons and seven daughters. Niobe was foolish enough to mock Leto, who had once been the lover of Zeus and had given birth to only two children, the gods Apollo and Artemis (Diana). Leto complained to her children about the intolerable remarks that the insolent mortal woman had dared to make against her. At once Apollo and Artemis took their bows and arrows, with which they bring a gentle death to

those mortals who die from diseases. They shot down all of Niobe's children in the royal palace, and her husband subsequently killed himself with grief.

As a result, there was no one left alive to help Niobe bury the dead, and she was too distressed to do anything but sit and weep. As she sat still, for day after day, her body turned to stone, but even the stone wept with grief. It can still be seen somewhere in the mountains of Greece, with a stream of tears endlessly coursing down its face.

Leto asked for the help of her children again when she was attacked by the giant Tityus—son of the earth goddess Gaia—who had tried to rape her. Once more they took up their bows, killing the giant and sending him down to the underworld where he is even to this day tormented for his crime. His enormous body is secured down on the ground, covering as much area as that of a small town, and his punishment is the same suffering that Prometheus once endured, only twice as bad. While Prometheus was mutilated night after night by a vulture pecking at his liver, he was at least left alone during the day for his body to regenerate. Tityus is savaged by two vultures, pecking at his liver night after night and day after day, without any respite.

Coronis and Asclepius

The raven is a bird with black feathers, but there was a time when all ravens were as white as swans. This story explains how the raven's once fair plumage turned from white to black.

GOD PRAYER CHART

WHICH GOD	COULD BE PRAYED TO FOR:
APOLLO	MODERATION IN ALL THINGS; ORDERLINESS; ORACULAR ADVICE ABOUT THE FUTURE
ARES (MARS)	THE ONSET OF WAR; SATISFACTION OF AGGRESSIVE IMPULSES
DIONYSUS (BACCHUS)	FREEDOM FROM SOCIAL EXPECTATIONS; ECSTATIC UNION WITH THE GOD
EROS (CUPID)	WINNING THE LOVE OF THE BELOVED
HADES (PLUTO)	DEATH TO ONE'S ENEMIES
HEPHAESTUS (VULCAN)	SKILL AT MAKING MACHINERY AND WORKING AT THE FORGE
HERMES (MERCURY)	PROSPERITY AS A TRADER OR MERCHANT
PAN	SUCCESS FOR HUNTERS IN FINDING THEIR QUARRY
POSEIDON (NEPTUNE)	SAFE JOURNEY BY SEA
ZEUS (JUPITER)	SUCCESS IN BUILDING AN EMPIRE; FIRM RULE AND CONTROL

Coronis was Apollo's beloved, but she also secretly shared her bed with a young man from Thessaly. She was careful to hide what she was doing from gods and mortals alike, but she did not think of hiding from the birds of the air. A white raven saw her and her Thessalian lover together and flew as fast as it could to take the news to Apollo. He was beside himself with anger, and taking up his bow and arrows, he shot his beloved Coronis in the heart. Before she died, she said to him, "Apollo, I was foolish but you were far too hasty in punishing me. I am carrying your child, and in killing me you have killed him too."

Apollo was angry with himself for acting so impetuously, and angry with the bird that had brought him the bad news. He turned the raven's beautiful white feathers to black as a punishment. Apollo is a great healer as well as an expert killer, but he could do nothing to bring Coronis back to life. All that he could achieve was to remove the unborn child from the dead mother's womb and take him to the cave of the Centaur, Cheiron, who was also a great healer, asking him to take great care of the child until he was a fully grown man. The Centaur did as he was asked.

The Centaur's daughter, Ocyrhoe, was able to prophesy the future, and when she saw the baby, she said, "This child will become the greatest healer among humankind. He will even surpass his father, the god Apollo, for he will be able to bring the dead back to life, but he will use his healing powers too often and displease the ruler of the underworld. Then he will die and be reborn." This was all that the gods allowed her to say.

Apollo's son was called Asclepius (Aesculapius) and, just as Ocyrhoe had prophesied, he became the greatest of healers. Hades started to fear that no more of the dead would come to his realm, and asked Zeus to put an end to Asclepius's miracles. Zeus struck Asclepius dead with his thunderbolt, but he was made a god and worshipped in temples where the sick came to find the answer to their diseases in a dream.

Admetus and Alcestis

When Zeus killed Asclepius with a thunderbolt, his father Apollo took revenge by killing the Cyclopes who had long ago made the thunderbolt as a weapon for Zeus. Now it was Zeus's turn to take revenge on his son, Apollo. He ordered the sun god to serve a mortal king for a year. Apollo chose to serve Admetus, king of Thessaly, as a shepherd.

Apollo grew fond of his master and helped him to win Alcestis, daughter of Pelias, as his wife. Pelias had decreed that she would marry only the man who could drive a chariot drawn by lions and wild boars;

Left **Asclepius the healer.** Asclepius, the god of medicine and healing, was schooled in the use of drugs, love potions, and incantations. It is said that Athene gave him two vials of Gorgon's blood, one drawn from the veins on the right side and the other from the left. One vial could be used to destroy life, while the other could restore it.

Below **Admetus and his carriage drawn by a boar and a lion.** Admetus showed Apollo such kind hospitality that the god was only too happy to return the favor. As well as taming the wild beasts to help Admetus win Alcestis, Apollo caused all his cows to have twins so that his wealth would increase.

THE NINE MUSES

Apollo's companions were the nine muses who inspire all artists and scientists. They were the children of Zeus and Mnemosyne, the goddess of memory. Calliope is the muse of epic poetry, Clio the muse of history, Erato the muse of love song, Euterpe the muse of lyric poetry, Melpomene the muse of tragedy, Polymnia (sometimes called Polyhymnia) the muse of sacred song, Thalia the muse of comedy, Terpsichore the muse of the dance, and Urania the muse of astronomy. They could be found on the slopes of Mount Parnassus where the Castalian spring rises near Apollo's oracle of Delphi, or alternatively on Mount Helicon.

Above **Muses** attributed to Francesco Primaticcio (1504–1570). The name "Muses" denotes "memory" or "a reminder," since, with no books, poets had to rely on their memories.

it was easy for Apollo to help Admetus tame the wild beasts. Admetus and Alcestis lived happily together until the king became so unwell that he was on the point of dying. Apollo once again served his master to the best of his divine ability, going to the Fates to ask them to spare his life. But the Fates had already ordained his death, and the most that they were willing to do for Apollo was to allow Admetus to live as long as he could manage to persuade some other mortal to die in his place.

Admetus was sure that someone in his kingdom would die for him, but his people all refused. He turned to his old parents, but they said that the few years left to them were too precious to throw away. The only person willing to die for him was his adored wife, Alcestis. Admetus was torn between joy that he would be allowed to live and shame and grief that his life was saved at the expense of his wife's death.

She grew sick as fast as he grew well, until she was lying on her bed very close to death. As Alcestis lay dying, Heracles (Hercules) arrived to visit his friend Admetus. The king tried to hide the truth, but Heracles soon found out why everyone was in tears and promised to help. That night, he waited at the doorway of Alcestis's bedroom until he spotted Death coming to take her to the underworld. Heracles seized Death and forced him to leave empty-handed, and Alcestis came back to health again.

ORACLES

The word "oracle" refers to both what the gods say and where it is said. An oracle in Greek myth can be a prophecy, or it can be the sacred spot where visitors come to ask the gods for advice. Such prophecies shaped many of the stories in Greek myth, for both gods and humans wanted to know the future. When an oracle foretold disaster, both gods and humans took action to prevent this unwelcome future. Oracles were almost infallible, and those who tried to avert their prophetic words most often brought upon themselves the very doom that they were trying to avoid. Oedipus and his parents, for example, acted in ways that seemingly guaranteed that the oracle could not be fulfilled, but those actions led directly to the very fate predicted by the oracle. Zeus (Jupiter) was more successful at averting those oracles prophesying that a son would surpass his father, but at a cost. In the case of Metis, he ate his sexual partner to prevent her from bearing him a son, and in the case of Thetis, he did not act upon his desire for her and he married her to someone else. Zeus's success in averting the prophecy of Thetis was clever, however, the oracle was still fulfilled when Thetis's son surpassed his mortal father; the god's success in thwarting the prophecy of Metis was much more unusual. This is a rare example of an oracle not being fulfilled at all. In general, though oracles were spoken in the name of many of the Greek gods, what they really stated were the decrees of the Fates, and the Fates were ancient powers that ruled even the gods.

Oracles were not only common in the myths but a fact of life in ancient Greece and Rome. People went to the oracles and consulted the gods there, for over 1,000 years. There are archaeological records of many votive offerings by grateful clients of the oracles, and a Roman visitor speaks of 3,000 statues at Delphi, all given in thanks to the oracle over the centuries. The oracles' prophecies must have been helpful and accurate on enough occasions for people to keep coming back to ask for more advice. Rulers of Greek city-states consulted an oracle when making decisions as important as whether to wage war, whom to make an alliance with, or where to found a new colony. At least one Roman emperor is also believed to have consulted a Greek oracle.

Both in myth and in everyday life, oracles were notorious for their ambiguity. The oracle given to Deucalion and Pyrrha, for example, told them to throw the bones of their mother behind them, a command which turned out to refer to rocks, the bones of Mother Earth, rather than to the literal bones of a dead human mother. Heracles was told that he could be killed only by a dead man, a condition that seemed impossible until he was

Left **Detail from a mosaic floor of a figure carrying an offering**. Gifts, often of fruit, from suppliants were common as offerings accompanying requests for advice from oracles.

Below **Ministers of the Fates**. The oracles were the ministers of the Fates who handed down the decrees of these ancient powers. In this painting, Admetus and Alcestis consult an oracle seeking advice on how to prevent Alcestis's death.

Above **The Oracle at Dodona**. Zeus's oracle at Dodona was the oldest oracle in Greece. The prophecies from the Fates were delivered from the rustlings of the sacred oak, which is shown here as having human form.

Right **Detail from a vase fragment showing Apollo at Delphi.** Apollo, the ruler of Delphi, is said by some to have set up the oracle there. Suppliants would make a regular pilgrimage to Delphi to consult him. This was once said to be the site of a shrine first of all to Gaia, and then later shared by Poseidon.

Opposite page *The Sibyl* by Domenico Zampieri Domenichino (1581– 1641). Sibyls, prophets who were said to be under the influence of Apollo, possessed the power of prophecy or divination without it being requested of them. They simply foretold the future.

poisoned by the blood of a long-dead enemy. Cynics argue that the oracles were deliberately couched in ambiguous language so that the words could be twisted to correspond to one of several futures. If someone asked, "Who will win the war?" the oracle might reply symbolically, or phrase the answer in such a way that both sides could argue that it favored them in battle. Then, whichever side actually won, the oracle could claim prior knowledge of its success. The first Greek historian, Herodotus, tells of King Croesus's visit to the oracle at Delphi, where he asked whether he should make war against the Persians. The oracle replied that if he crossed the River Halys, a mighty empire would be lost, and Croesus took the answer to predict his success. When he was vanquished, the oracle was reinterpreted to predict the loss of his own mighty empire. Most of the other historical evidence (as distinct from the evidence from myth), however, is much less slippery, as the oracle gives advice on how to honor gods or whether it would be good to institute a new law.

How the Gods Spoke
The most famous of Greek oracles were those of Zeus at Dodona and Apollo at Delphi. In Dodona, in the north of Greece, the words of Zeus were heard in the rustling of the leaves of a sacred oak tree. The priests and priestesses of the shrine interpreted the rustling noises to the petitioner. Originally there were three priestesses, who always slept on the ground and went barefoot, and never washed their feet, to keep as close contact to the sacred oak's way of life as they could. Later in this oracle's history there were priests as well as priestesses, and they, too, went barefoot and slept on the ground. Prophecies were also

derived at this oracle from the casting of lots, from birdsong, and in an elaborate ceremony involving a cauldron and a statue. The statue of a boy held a whip with three chains that could move if the wind blew it. When it moved, the buttons on the chains hit the cauldron and made a ringing sound. It was this sound that was believed to convey the words of the king of the gods.

The Oracle at Dodona
The oracle at Dodona was established, so the myth goes, when two black pigeons flew from the Egyptian city of Thebes, where a temple of Zeus already existed. One pigeon went to Ammon in Libya and the other to Dodona. Both started speaking in human words when they arrived, commanding the people to establish an oracle of Zeus at that spot. The Greek historian Herodotus interprets this story as reflecting a historical truth, that an Egyptian woman was captured and sold as a slave in Ammon and another in Dodona, and that these women were priestesses of the temple of Zeus in Thebes who eventually set up similar oracles in Ammon and Dodona. They were represented in the myth as pigeons because the Greeks could not understand their language and thought they sounded like birds.

The Oracle of Apollo at Delphi
The oracle of Apollo at Delphi was the greatest of Greek oracles, and its buildings can still be visited on Mount Parnassus. These buildings are the latest in a series of temples, each replacing the last as it was destroyed in an earthquake. A huge stone still stands in the temple, known as the Omphalos stone, the

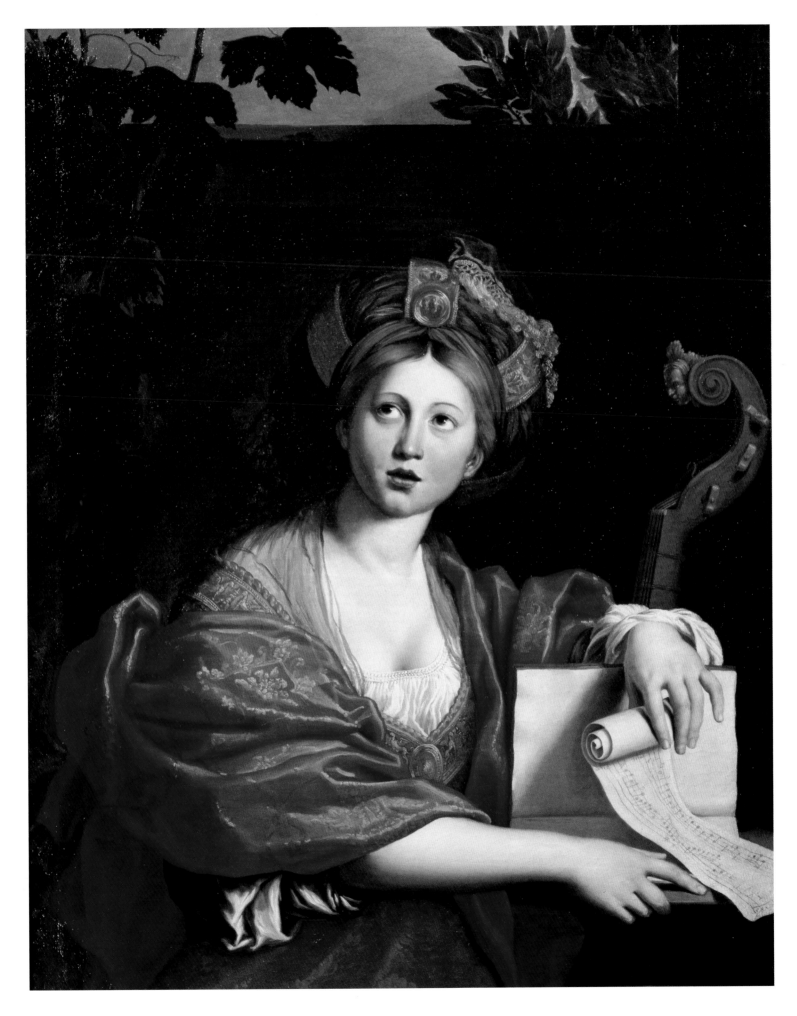

navel of the world. In some accounts, Apollo set up the oracle at Delphi, but his fight with the giant serpent Pytho on Mount Parnassus has also been interpreted as an allegorical account of the invading race of Dorian Greeks conquering the older Pythian oracle, replacing its female deity with an Olympian male. Those who heard the voice of the god were always female and were each called Pythia. Some (more or less) historical accounts of the oracle are unexciting, with the Pythia of the moment behaving like a professional, calmly transmitting the god's message. More thrilling are those accounts that describe the Pythia as sitting on a tripod above a fissure or cave, an opening in the ground inside the temple, where she chewed laurel leaves and inhaled volcanic gases from Mount Parnassus. In these versions, it was in a prophetic trance that she spoke the words given to her by the god. The words came out sounding like incoherent babble, and it was the priests' business to interpret and transmit the message to the petitioner. Nowadays there is no sign of a cave emitting volcanic gases on the slopes of Mount Parnassus, but this is a geologically active part of Greece and it is not impossible that such a cave did exist but has been destroyed in one of the region's earthquakes.

While the Pythia was unique to Delphi, the Sibyls were female prophets who spoke Apollo's words in many regions of the world, including Babylon, Egypt, and Libya. The Sibyl of Cumae was given the

*The word
by seers or sibyls told,
In groves of oak, or fanes of gold,
Still floats upon the morning wind,
Still whispers to the willing mind.*

RALPH WALDO EMERSON (1803–1882),
"THE PROBLEM"

gift of very long life by Apollo, when she allowed him to become her lover. She scooped up a handful of sand and asked the god for as many years' life as there were grains of sand in her handful, but just like Eos's lover, Tithonus, she forgot to ask for long-lasting youth as well. She shriveled with age until she became so tiny that she was kept in a bottle. There she kept whispering, over and over again, how much she longed for the death that the god had denied her.

It was common for prophets to be disbelieved, mocked, or reviled for the messages they brought from the gods. The blind seer, Teiresias, offered the gods' unwelcome truth to Oedipus and Creon, and his fate was to be ignored or accused of conspiracy, rather than respected and believed. The seer Cassandra of Troy heard directly from Apollo what was to happen to her city and herself in the future, but her fate was always to be disbelieved. Seers tell the truth in Greek myth, but their words rarely bring a story to a happy ending.

On many occasions, a god appeared directly to a favored human being and spoke clear words of advice or command, but more usually, the god came in disguise as a stranger, acquaintance, relative, or friend. No one could be altogether sure, then, that the passing stranger was really just a human being and not a god come to set a test with a fearful penalty for failure. The strong reverence for guests in Greek myth derives from this sense that a god might be wronged whenever a human stranger was maltreated. Some gods sent messages in dreams, and it took great skill to determine which dreams were false and which spoke a divine truth. Some gods sent portents in the form of birds in flight. Sometimes the entrails of sacrificed animals were read to provide a prophecy, or seers practiced foretelling the future in bowls of water, a skill known as scrying. In Pharae, the oracular advice of Hermes (Mercury) was transmitted in the first words that the petitioner heard while walking out of the marketplace (an appropriate place to seek help from Hermes, god of merchants). Zeus's anger was manifested in bad weather. When a thunderstorm raged, his displeasure was very clear.

THOSE WHOM THE GODS LOVE, DIE YOUNG

The twin brothers Agamedes and Trophonius built a stone threshold for the temple at Delphi. Apollo was pleased with their work, and his oracle told the brothers that they should live life to the fullest for the next week. Then, on the seventh day, they would be given their heart's desire. On the sixth night they could hardly sleep for excitement, but eventually they fell asleep, and in the morning they were found dead in their beds.

The same gift was given to Cleobis and Biton, sons of Hera's (Juno's) priestess at Argos. One of the rites of Hera involved a chariot drawn by white oxen. The day of the festival dawned, but the oxen were missing. Cleobis and Biton pulled the chariot a long and sweaty distance to the temple. The priestess prayed that Hera would give these dutiful young men the best gift that the gods could give to mortals. In the morning, they were found dead.

Left and Right **Cleobis and Biton.** The Greek gods believed that death was the best thing that could happen to mortals because it released them from their human life that was so full of suffering.

EROS AND PSYCHE

The Greeks usually imagined their god of love, Eros, in the shape of a boy with wings, his weapons a bow and arrows. Renamed Cupid by the Romans, he steadily grew smaller over the centuries until by the time of Renaissance art, he became a chubby-cheeked infant who hardly seemed strong enough to bend his bow and loose his arrows. In the story of Eros and Psyche told by the Roman writer Apuleius, however, the god takes the shape of a young man, though not yet old enough to be quite independent of his mother Aphrodite (Venus).

The gods of Olympus were always quick to punish the arrogance of any mortal who dared to claim equality with a god. Tales of human folly and arrogance almost always ended badly for the human being concerned, but the myth of Eros and Psyche is an exception to this norm, though the foolish princess

Psyche had to endure struggles and suffering before she finally reached her happy ending.

Perhaps her story ends well because it was not Psyche herself who dared to compare her beauty with that of a goddess, but her proud parents, who

Above **Eros.** Eros used to be seen as one of the creative powers of nature who was born at the beginning of time with Chaos.

BEAUTY AND THE BEAST

The fairy tale of *Beauty and the Beast* was strongly influenced by the myth of Eros and Psyche. Both are stories of love being tested by outward show. Beauty and Psyche both fail the test at first, as Beauty does not learn to love the Beast until he lies dying, while Psyche believes her sisters' story that her husband is a murderous monster. Where Beauty is literally confronted with a Beast, however, it is only in Psyche's imagination that Eros is anything but a most desirable god in the shape of a man. In the fairy tale both Beauty and the Beast have something to learn before they can fully love one another. In the myth, there are numerous ordeals for Psyche but not for Eros, who manages to stay hidden at his mother's house while his beloved is suffering. Perhaps this helps to explain why Eros is so often depicted as a little boy who never grows up.

Left **The god Eros.** Eros is often portrayed as a wild and mischievous god who did what he wanted without regard for former commitments or any consideration for the future welfare of those he targeted.

Below *Psyche Showing Her Sisters Her Gifts from Eros* by Jean-Honore Fragonard (1732–1806). After Psyche's sisters learned of her husband's true identity and that he had abandoned Psyche, they climbed the mountain in their wedding gowns and leaped off, hoping to be swept away by the west wind. Instead, they plummeted to their deaths.

claimed that their youngest daughter was more beautiful than the goddess of love, Aphrodite. Worse still, all the people of Greece and the lands around began to visit Psyche's palace to worship her, while the temples of Aphrodite stayed empty. The goddess begged her son, Eros, to punish the girl by wounding her heart with his arrow, so that she would fall in love with some miserable wretch of a man and make an unhappy marriage. In the meantime, Psyche became sad because people were treating her like a goddess and no one was bold enough to love her as a woman and try to marry her. Both of her older sisters married, but Psyche stayed at home, unhappy and lonely.

The king became worried as time passed and no one came courting his youngest daughter. In the end, he asked the oracle of Apollo where a husband might be found for his lonely child. The oracle's reply was terrifying. Psyche must be dressed as a bride and taken to the top of a steep mountain. Her husband would be no mortal man but a poisonous monster, a creature powerful enough to frighten even the greatest of the gods, Zeus (Jupiter) himself.

Psyche and her parents walked to the top of the mountain in tears, as though they were going to her funeral instead of her marriage. Everyone knew that she was being punished by Aphrodite, but there was

nothing that they could do to calm the offended goddess. They had to walk away from Psyche while she waited fearfully at the mountain top for the monster to arrive.

She tensed her body, expecting an attack, but instead, a soft wind blew at her garments until she was swept off her feet and carried gently down to the foot of the mountain. There she saw a marvelous palace, so magnificent that she guessed at once that it belonged to one of the gods. The whole palace seemed to be empty, but she could hear kind voices, and invisible hands fetched food and drink and played sweet music for her. There was no sign of any monster, and she went to bed wondering who her husband would be. In the middle of the night she was woken by someone—a person, not a monster—climbing into the bed. It was her new husband, but she could not see him in the darkness. He left while it was still dark, and every night he came back to her bed in the darkness and left again before daybreak. Psyche was falling in love with someone that she had never seen.

Psyche Loses Her Husband

One night, he warned Psyche that her sisters were about to climb the mountain in search of her, dead or alive. He begged her not to pay any attention to them, but when Psyche heard her sisters calling and weeping, she could not help asking the wind to blow them gently down to her palace. The two sisters grew jealous when they saw all of Psyche's jewels and rich clothes and all the treasures of her palace, and the next day they came back to find out if there was any way that they could hurt Psyche and spoil her marriage. "What is your husband like?" they kept asking, and eventually Psyche had to admit that she had never seen him. "He is a monster," they told her, "and that is why he has never had the courage to show you his face. Now you are

Celestial Cupid her fam'd son advanc't, Holds his dear Psyche sweet intranc't After her wandring labours long

JOHN MILTON
(1608–1674), "COMUS"

pregnant, and everyone knows that a monster's favorite food is a pregnant woman. He is just waiting for your baby to grow big inside you, and then he will feast on both of you together. You must kill him before he kills you; use a lamp to see by, and cut off his head with a knife!"

Psyche believed everything that her sisters told her. She found a lamp and a knife and hid them both beside the bed. That night, after her husband had fallen asleep, she lit the lamp and saw his body for the first time. There beside her lay the god of love in the shape of a man, but more handsome than any mortal could be. Close to his hand were his bow and arrows, and Psyche scratched herself on an arrow as she bent closer to kiss him. The wound from the arrow ensured that she would love Eros for the rest of her life.

Psyche was just about to kiss the god when the lamp in her hand tipped forward and a drop of burning oil fell onto his shoulder and woke him. Eros sprang up from the bed and started to fly away, but Psyche clung onto him for a few moments, so that he carried her out of the palace and onto the mountainside. She could hold him no longer, and fell to the ground. Eros told her that he must return to his mother so that his shoulder would heal from its burn. Aphrodite would be furious when she found out that instead of tormenting Psyche, he had fallen in love with her and married her. If only the foolish girl had kept silent about him, her baby would have been born a god, but now she would be lucky to stay alive long enough for her baby to be born, for he could not protect her against Aphrodite's anger. Then he flew away into the night.

Psyche's Tasks

Psyche felt so miserable and so frightened of Aphrodite that she tried to drown herself in a river, but the river god recognized her as the bride of Eros and would not let her die. Then she asked Hera (Juno), the goddess of married love, for help and Demeter (Ceres), who knew the pain of losing her daughter Persephone, but neither of these goddesses was willing to offend Aphrodite by helping Psyche.

Left *Psyche Carried off by Zephyrus* by Egisto Ferroni (1835–1912). The divine personification of the west wind, Zephyrus was known by the Romans as Favonius. Represented as a young man with wings, he glided through the air bringing freshness and bountiful rain.

Below *Psyche Abandoned* by Augustin Pajou (1730–1809). The jealous and spiteful nature of her sisters weighed heavily on Psyche. She lost faith in her lover and had to pay a heavy price for her doubt.

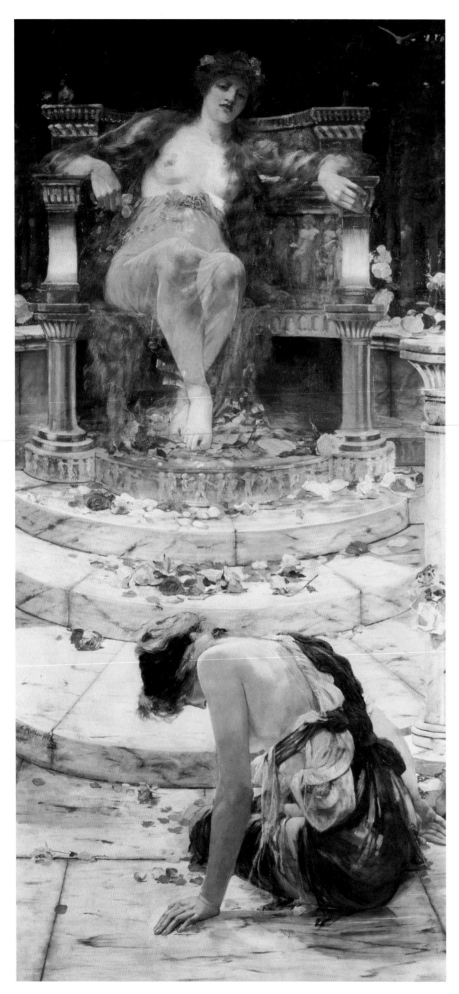

THE MISSING HALF

The philosopher Plato explained the nature of love by telling a myth about the first human beings, who were circular creatures each with two faces on a single neck, four legs, and four arms. They traveled by rolling their bodies along the ground. Zeus (Jupiter) grew angry with these early humans when they challenged the rule of the gods, and sliced each of them in half, leaving humankind with only one face, two arms, and two legs. Zeus threatened that, if ever there were any more serious trouble from humankind, he would cut everyone in half again. Then, with one leg and one arm each, reduced to hopping everywhere, people would finally learn how to treat the gods with respect. According to this myth, we are all halves of lost wholes, each longing and searching for its missing half. Love, according to this myth, is the desire and pursuit of the whole.

In the end, Aphrodite found Psyche and began to punish her at once with a flogging. Then she decided to torment the poor girl with tasks that could not be accomplished, so that she would have endless excuses to beat her again. First, Aphrodite took handfuls of all the grains and beans and poppy seed and mixed them together. Then she threw them on the hearth and demanded that Psyche separate them again before nightfall. If she failed, she would be whipped. Psyche started to sort out a little pile of millet seeds but after a few minutes she realized that she would never sort all the seeds by evening. She began to cry, but then noticed an ant running as fast as it could across the hearth, calling out to all the other ants in the palace, "The bride of Eros is here, and needs our help." Immediately all the ants in the goddess's palace raced to the seeds and began to carry them into separate piles. By evening, the task was done.

"You must have had some help, you sly creature," the goddess complained, "but do not think you can escape my anger so easily. Tomorrow I want you to go to the field where the golden sheep are grazing, and fetch me a handful of their shining wool." This task sounded easy, but in the morning, as Psyche walked toward the field, she could see that all the sheep had long, sharp horns. She had to cross a little stream to reach the sheep, and as she stood there hesitating, a reed from the stream said to her, "Psyche, if you cross over the water now, you are going to your death. The sheep will use their horns on you, and if that does not kill you, their teeth are also poisonous. But these sheep are only dangerous in the daytime, when their golden fleeces grow burning hot in the sun and enrage them. Wait until the evening, when they will be calm and peaceful. Then you will be able to walk among them safely and gather all the wool that has been caught on thorns and briars."

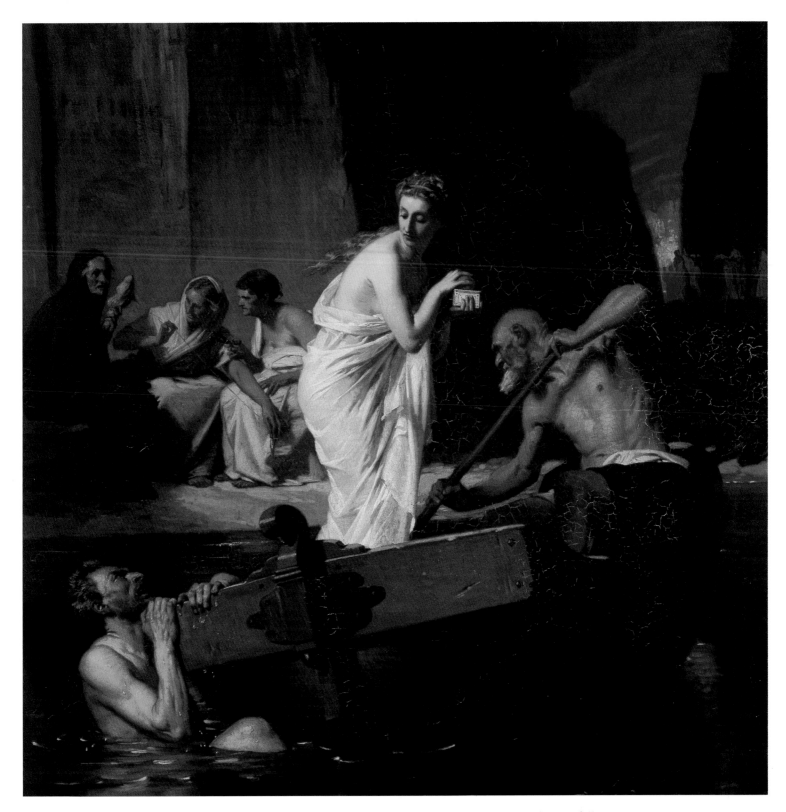

That night, Aphrodite was even more angry with Psyche. "Surely some mischievous god has been helping you," she scolded, and Psyche remembered how Pan's beloved Syrinx had been transformed into a reed. Perhaps it had been the great god Pan who had helped her, in the guise of a reed. Aphrodite was quick to devise a new ordeal for Psyche. "Your next task will be harder to find help for, because even the gods are in awe of the river of death. You must go to the River Styx and bring me back some water from its source, high in the mountains, where it falls down a cliff before pouring down into the underworld. I want water from the middle of the river, not just from its edge."

Psyche understood all too well that the goddess intended to kill her, when she came to the cliff and the waterfall and saw that dragons guarded both banks of the dark river. She started to think again about killing herself, but the eagle of Zeus noticed her just as she was about to run toward the dragons

Above *Psyche in the Underworld* by Ernest Hillemacher (1818–1887). Psyche collected water from the River Styx.

Opposite page *Psyche at the Throne of Aphrodite* by Edward Hale (1852–1924). Psyche pleaded for clemency from Aphrodite.

Above *Psyche Receiving the Casket Back from Persephone* by Sir Edward Burne-Jones (1833–1898). Eros swooped down to rescue his beloved Psyche. He carried her to Olympus where she was made immortal. In due course, she bore Eros a daughter called Volupta (Pleasure).

in despair, and flew down to help her. He recalled the time that Eros had helped him, when Zeus had ordered him to abduct the beautiful boy Ganymede and carry him to Olympus to be the gods' cupbearer. The huge eagle snatched the jug from Psyche's hand and carried it to the middle of the river, then brought it back full of dark water.

Descent to the Underworld

Aphrodite was angrier still. Surely all the gods were conspiring to thwart her, but she could think of one task that would bring Psyche to her death, no matter who tried to help her. The rule of the underworld, for the Greeks as for the peoples of Mesopotamia, was that anyone living could go there but none

could return. She ordered Psyche to go down to the underworld to visit its queen, Persephone (Proserpina) and ask her to give Aphrodite some of her beauty.

Once again Psyche thought of killing herself, for that would be her speediest way to the underworld; she could see no prospect of going there and coming back alive. She began to climb the steps of a high tower, getting ready to jump to her death, when the tower started to speak to her. "Psyche, do not be so quick to despair. You can go down to the under-world alive and come back alive, if you do what I say. You must take two barley cakes and two coins, because Charon, the ferryman over the River Styx, takes no one across without payment, and the three-headed dog, Cerberus, will tear to pieces anyone

---

who tries to pass without feeding him. You must ignore anyone who asks you for help, you must eat nothing but bread and drink nothing but water, and even if you are offered a throne to sit on, you must sit on the ground. If you do all of these things, Persephone will give you a box of beauty and you will be able to come back to the world of the living, feeding Cerberus the second barley cake and giving Charon the second coin. Remember that you must not open the box; it is not wise to uncover the secrets of the underworld."

Psyche ran down the road that led to the underworld, and soon found Charon with his ferry. On the way a man was struggling to load a donkey with wood, and asked Psyche to help him tie the load on securely, but she remembered the tower's advice and ran past him. While Charon was rowing her across the Styx, she saw an old man drowning and heard him call out to her, but she sat still in the boat and did nothing to help. On and on she went, and Aphrodite sent more and more poor victims to tempt her into helping them, but even when Psyche saw dying children, she remembered to ignore them. They were only phantoms, sent by the goddess to entice Psyche into letting go of the barley cakes that she held in her hand. At last she saw Cerberus standing in the roadway, snarling at her from each of his three mouths, and she threw him one of the cakes. Now she was close to the palace of Persephone and Hades, and the goddess was waiting to give her the box of beauty.

But there was one more test. The tower had warned Psyche not to open the box, but as she walked back to the upper world, feeding the second barley cake

to Cerberus and giving Charon the second coin, she kept imagining being with Eros once again, and longed to take just a little of Persephone's beauty for herself. She opened the box and found that it was empty, except for the air of the underworld. As she breathed it in deeply, she fell to the ground, dying.

Just in time, Eros flew down and blew the lethal air away. His wounded shoulder had healed and he was ready to defy his mother and make sure that Psyche became a goddess and his unborn child a god. He carried Psyche to Olympus where Zeus gave her ambrosia, the luscious food of the gods that makes the person eating it immortal. Like her husband, Psyche now had wings, but hers were like the wings of a butterfly rather than the feathered wings of Eros. As a caterpillar leaves its familiar earthbound life and later emerges as an air-traveling butterfly, so Psyche left her life as a princess among human beings and she became one of the goddesses of Olympus.

Left **Winged Eros and his lyre.** Far from being the monster Psyche had expected, Eros was kind and patient, fetching food and drink for Psyche, and playing music for her on his lyre.

Below *Eros and Psyche* by **Antonio Canova (1757–1822).** The tale of Eros and Psyche is seen by many as a statement about life and love. It embodies the idea that the soul (*psychē* in Greek) must endure suffering before eventually finding love.

Above *Aphrodite and Hermes* by Filipepi Botticelli (1445–1510). Some have said that Aphrodite was originally a Middle Eastern goddess, similar to the Mesopotamian Ishtar, the goddess of love and fertility, and the Syro-Palestinian goddess Ashtart.

TALES OF APHRODITE

Aphrodite (Venus), the goddess of sexual desire, was born from the foam of the sea. She stepped out of a seashell and first set foot on land in Cyprus or else in the island of Cythera. She was sometimes celebrated as a goddess of orderly affection and community, like Hestia (Vesta), goddess of the hearth, or Hera (Juno), goddess of marriage, but the love that she inspired was most often urgent and unrestrained, beyond reason and common sense. She was the goddess of infatuation and sexual obsession, of desire that leads its sufferer to sacrifice everything in order to obtain the beloved, but when she was thought of as a sea-born goddess, sailors prayed to her for calm waters and safe passage. Like most of the other Olympians, Aphrodite was a combination of opposites, but the best-known stories about Aphrodite all focus on passion beyond control.

Aphrodite and Ares

The god of war, Ares (Mars) was the son of Zeus (Jupiter) and Hera, and he was usually to be found on the battlefield. Not many of the other gods of Olympus enjoyed his company, for he had a fierce temper and thought that violence was a good answer to most problems. One of the Olympians, however, not only liked him but enjoyed a passionate love affair with him. Aphrodite was as capable as Ares of being carried away by her passions, regardless of her husband Hephaestus (Vulcan). She even managed to persuade Hephaestus that he was the father of her four children, Phobos (meaning "fear" in Greek), Deimos (meaning "terror"), Eros (Cupid), the god of love, and Harmonia, the harmonious one; but they were really her children by her lover, Ares.

One morning Aphrodite visited Ares' palace overnight and stayed too long in his bed in the morning. The sun god caught sight of them together. He was quick to tell tales to Hephaestus, who usually said very little but felt so angry at the news that he let all the gods of Olympus know that he was planning revenge. All that day he hammered at a bronze net, whose meshes were fine enough to surround any prey closely but strong enough to be unbreakable. When Aphrodite came back to the palace that she shared with Hephaestus, he pretended that he was going to the island of Lemnos, but he went no

or woman or immortal nymph when she was planning to overpower a god or mortal with sexual desire. As soon as her victims laid eyes on those wearing the golden belt, they would become overwhelmed with sexual desire, unable to control themselves or weigh up the consequences of their passion. Aphrodite, golden goddess of desire, was the cause of many wars.

She even overpowered the mind of Zeus with sexual desire so many times that he finally decided to pay her back with her own technique for trouble. He made her fall deeply in love with a mortal man, Anchises, who was the king of the Dardanians. Zeus's enchantment lasted only one night, and in the morning Aphrodite made Anchises promise that he would never tell anyone that he had shared a bed with her.

Anchises was terrified when he realized that he had made love with a goddess, for he knew all the stories of mortals who had been killed because they had come too close to one of the gods. Aphrodite reassured him that she would never hurt him; after all, she said, she was now pregnant with his son, Aeneas. Anchises soon forgot both his terror and his promise. A few days later, he was drinking with his friends, and they were talking about women as men do when they drink.

"That woman serving the wine," said one of the men, "I would rather sleep with her than with golden Aphrodite. Don't

Above **Aphrodite and Ares.** Aphrodite's husband, Hephaestus, used his expert skills to make her lavish jewelry. The girdle Aphrodite wore around her waist, her weapon that made her irresistible, was made by her husband. He fashioned the belt with finely wrought gold and wove magic into it.

farther than the palace stables. There he hid, while Aphrodite sent word to her lover that it would be safe for him to spend the night with her in her marriage bed. Ares arrived and climbed onto the bed with the goddess, but as soon as they lay down, the bronze net fell onto them. They could not escape, however much they twisted and turned.

Hephaestus called all the other gods to come and see the fine fish that he had caught with his new net. The goddesses stayed away, but in crowded the laughing gods. Instead of sympathizing with the wronged husband, they kept telling Ares what a lucky god he was, and asking if they could change places with him. In the end, Poseidon (Neptune) persuaded Hephaestus to let the lovers go. Ares swaggered off to his latest war, but Aphrodite fled to the island of Paphos until her long-suffering husband forgave her.

Aphrodite and Anchises

Aphrodite's girdle, the golden belt that she wore around her waist, was the weapon that she used against gods and mortals alike. She would lend this golden girdle to some man

Left **Aphrodite.** Over time, Aphrodite developed as a symbol of pure love, in particular wedded love, as opposed to sensual lust. While the perception of the goddess changed, many of her emblems remained constant, including the swan, the dolphin, and the dove.

The planet Mars is named after the Roman god of war, Mars, the equivalent of the Greek god Ares. The god's name lives on in the English language, not only in the name of this planet, but also in the terminology of war, with "martial" and "court-martial." The planet has a reddish color, which was easily associated with the blood shed in battle. Astronomers have named the two small moons of Mars after the sons that Aphrodite (Venus) bore Ares—Phobos and Deimos. Ares was not well liked among the gods of Olympus, but the planet Mars boasts a Mount Olympus of its own, the largest volcano found in our solar system.

Left **The planet Mars.** Ares (Mars) had a reputation for violence. The month of March, named for him, was a time when wars were often started or renewed.

aware that incest was forbidden, and was afraid of the Erinyes, the Furies who come from the under-world to torment criminals with their guilt. But when her mother, Cenchreis, was away celebrating the nine-day festival of Demeter (Ceres), Myrrha gave in to her desires and visited her father's bed-room in secret, in the darkness, pretending to be a serving girl who had fallen in love with the king. She became pregnant on that first night, and came back to his bed the next night, and the next, until he became curious to see her. He brought in a lamp and, to his horror, discovered that the woman in his bed was his daughter.

Cinyras was so distraught and disgusted that he drew his sword and went to kill her. Myrrha fled through the darkness, escaping from the palace and skulking across Arabia as a fugitive. For nine months she hid herself while her womb grew big with the unborn child. Then she began to pray, not knowing which god might listen to her. "If there are any gods who heed those who are truly sorry, I beg them to

Opposite page *Aphrodite and Anchises* by Benjamin Haydon (1786–1846). There are various accounts of the punishment that Anchises suffered as a result of his boasting. Some say he was paralyzed or killed, while others say that he was struck blind by Zeus's thunderbolt.

you agree, Anchises?" Anchises had just enough sense not to offend the goddess by agreeing, but he could not help saying that he was particularly well equipped to judge between the woman and the goddess, for he had shared his bed with both. Zeus heard the boast and instantly threw a thunderbolt at him, but Aphrodite held her golden girdle out to protect Anchises. He did not die from the attack, but was paralyzed, and he had to lie in his bed for the rest of his life with no beautiful goddess to console him.

Right *Aphrodite and Adonis* by Vecellio Tiziano (1487–1576). Aphrodite was completely enamored of Adonis and wanted him with her as much as possible. The infatuation was caused by a wound the goddess received while playing with her son, Eros.

Aphrodite and Adonis

The story of Aphrodite and Adonis begins badly, with a daughter overcome by sexual desire for her own father. It may well have been Aphrodite who inspired Princess Myrrha with her passion for her father, King Cinyras of the Arabian realm of Panchaia. Myrrha struggled with her feelings, well

Above *The Death of Adonis* attributed to Martin de Vos (1596–1678). In one version of the myth, Adonis's tragic death is considered to have been foreshadowed by his birth. The story of his birth has it that after Myrrha was transformed into a tree, a wild boar opened the trunk with its tusks and set the child free.

hear me. I deserve punishment, and I know that I pollute the world of mortal men and women by my mere existence. If I go down to the underworld, I will pollute the world of the dead. Change me, I beg, so that I become neither a living nor a dead human being, so that the pollution ends with me alone, and let the punishment affect me but not the child in my womb who has done no wrong."

The goddess Gaia, bountiful Mother Earth, heard this prayer and held Myrrha's feet fast to the ground. Her toes grew into long roots, traveling deep into the dark earth to support her body, which was gradually lengthening and transforming into the trunk of a tall tree. Her soft skin hardened to bark, and all her human flesh became tree, but she was

still able to weep tears of aromatic sap. This is how myrrh first came into the world.

Myrrha's child Adonis was born from the trunk of the myrrh tree. He grew up to be the handsomest of men, and Aphrodite herself was overwhelmed with desire for him. She wanted nothing but his company, and fretted when they were apart even for a moment. Adonis loved to hunt, and to please him, Aphrodite also took up the hunt, but she wanted to seek out only small creatures without sharp teeth or horns or claws. She entreated Adonis to run no risks, to stay at her side and enjoy her love rather than spend his time hunting savage prey, wild boars or lions or bears.

Adonis seemed to listen and agree, and she felt safe enough to leave him on his own for a day while

she traveled to her beloved island, Cyprus. As soon as her chariot took to the skies, borne by its team of swans, he took up his spear and called his hounds to the hunt. He did not mean to seek out a wild boar, but when the hounds tracked one down by scent, he did not retreat. He cast a spear which wounded the boar on the side. However, the wound was not deep, and the boar easily brushed the spear away. Now Adonis was weaponless, and the boar rushed at him and drove its tusks deep into his groin. He fell to the ground, dying.

Aphrodite heard Adonis cry out and looked down from the sky to see him bleeding to death. She wept and tore at her hair, but she could not persuade the Fates to avert his death. She knelt beside him and touched the blood-soaked earth. "I shall remember you, Adonis," she said, "and so shall all the world. From your blood will grow a flower, quick to blossom in the spring and all too quick to die." The blood of Adonis became the anemone, a flower that no sooner blooms than its petals fall away in the wind.

Hermaphroditus and Salmacis

Some of the nymphs in Greek myth are dryads, each belonging to a particular tree and living and dying with the lifespan of their tree. Others are oreads, nymphs of the mountains, and still others are naiads, nymphs of rivers, streams, and pools. Naiads are at their strongest when nearest to their waters. Salmacis was a naiad, one who treasured her pool so much that she chose to stay close by it rather than joining the other nymphs as Artemis's companion in the hunt.

Hermaphroditus was the son of Aphrodite and Hermes (Mercury) and his name is derived from both his parents, while his alluringly good looks came from his

mother. Hermes was a great traveler, and so too was his son. One day on his travels, Hermaphroditus met Salmacis beside her pool of water. As soon as she saw him, she could not restrain herself from saying, "Are you mortal or god? Surely you are Eros, Aphrodite's son, come to Earth to strike me with a golden arrow. I am so deeply wounded with love that I entreat you to make me your wife, or if you are already married, to take me for your lover."

Hermaphroditus was more than surprised. He was Aphrodite's child, but he knew nothing of passionate desire, and he certainly did not want to marry this nymph. She wrapped her arms around him, and he awkwardly shook them off. She tried to kiss him, and he backed away. "Go away," he shouted, "or do I have to run away myself?"

Salmacis pretended to leave, but she was unable to go far from him. She hid behind a bush, still keeping him in sight while he sat on the ground, resting. Then he decided to bathe in the pool, for the day was hot. He took off his clothes and Salmacis felt her desire flame up, looking at his naked body. As soon as he dived into her pool, she cried out, "He is mine!" and immediately jumped in after him, holding him, kissing him, clinging to him, pressing her body to his, refusing to let him go. "May we always be together," she prayed, and the gods listened to her prayer. The two bodies, so tightly intertwined, began to dissolve together into one body, neither wholly male nor wholly female. What climbed out of Salmacis's pool was neither a man nor a woman but the first hermaphrodite.

Above *Adonis Resting after a Hunt* by Nicolas Cousteau (1658–1733). Adonis is thought to have been originally an Asiatic deity of nature. He was also identified with the Near Eastern god Tammuz.

Below *Ceiling with Hermaphroditus and Salmacis* by Ubaldo Buonvicini (eighteeenth century). Hermaphroditus, shocked at what he had become, prayed to his parents. As a result, Aphrodite and Hermes caused the pool to have a similar effect on all men who bathed in it.

Above **Arachne spinning wool.** Arachne thought that nothing could represent the gods better than to weave the stories of them and their lustful behavior into her cloth. When she proved herself to be equal in skill to Athene, the goddess flew into a jealous rage.

TALES OF OTHER GODDESSES

Greek myths abound in strong women such as Medea, Antigone, Alcestis, and Penelope. These women had some strong role models among the Olympian goddesses. Hera (Juno), the goddess of marriage, frequently defied Zeus (Jupiter), causing trouble for the many mortal women whom he made pregnant, and for their children. Athene (Minerva) was the goddess of the domestic crafts such as

weaving, and she was also a skilled warrior and a friend of heroes such as Perseus. She invented the first ship and chariot. Artemis (Diana) was the goddess of the hunt and also of wild animals, and she was quick to punish any man who intruded on her privacy. Demeter (Ceres) was a gentler goddess, except when her daughter Persephone (Proserpina) was lost to her; then she was as vengeful as any of the other Olympians. Of the Olympian goddesses, only Hestia (Vesta) was completely dedicated to domesticity; peaceful and determined to avoid conflict. The only myth about Hestia is the one that tells the story of the time that Poseidon (Neptune) and Hermes (Mercury) both came wooing her. She was so reluctant to be the cause of conflict between the two that she vowed to stay a virgin forever. It is the other Olympian goddesses, with their enemies and their favorites, who provide rich material for stories.

Athene and Arachne

Like the other gods of Olympus, Athene did not tolerate any insolence on the part of human beings. Of all the Olympians, it was Athene who most appreciated and encouraged the cleverness of human beings, but when her student Arachne boasted that Athene's hands were no more clever than her own hands at weaving, the goddess could hardly believe her ears. Athene visited Arachne in the disguise of an old woman, urging her to talk about her weaving skills to find out just how far her boasts would go. Arachne now claimed to have taught herself all the tricks of weaving and started to boast again that she would beat Athene at any weaving competition. Athene revealed herself as a goddess, casting off her disguise, but Arachne would not apologize or admit that she had told a lie. Instead, she sat down at her loom, picked up the shuttle and started to weave stories of gods and mortals into the cloth.

Athene did the same, the cloth on her loom telling the story of the contest between herself and Poseidon over who was to be the god of a Greek city, which at that point was without a name. On her cloth, Athene depicted the citizens of this nameless city crowded together in the citadel, looking at what the gods were offering them, and deciding which of the two to vote for. As her bid for the citizens' votes, Athene had created the first olive tree for the city, while Poseidon had offered a miraculous spring of water on the rocky heights of its acropolis. All the men were looking with interest at the water, recognizing how useful it would be in times of siege, and all the women were praising the olive tree, noting its many uses in the household. There was one more woman than man in the picture, as in the competition itself. Athene did not bother to show her victory, for everyone knew that she had won by a single vote, and the city was called Athens in her honor.

Arachne was too much carried away with pride and insolence to heed the warning implied by the goddess's weaving, the demonstration that Athene always wins. She took it as a challenge rather than a threat, and responded by weaving into her cloth the many stories of the gods' deceptions, showing how they changed shape to seduce mortal women.

When the tapestries were finished, no one could decide whose cloth was the finer. Athene tore up the girl's weaving and started to beat her with the wooden shuttle. In desperation, Arachne took hold of a rope and tied it around her neck, then looked around for a roof beam to hang herself from. "Hang yourself all you like," said Athene, "you will never die from it, nor will your children, nor the children of your children. You will suffer for your insolent folly for the rest of your life." She struck Arachne once again and as a result the girl's body began to grow smaller and smaller until her head seemed to almost disappear. No ears, no hair, no nose, nothing but stomach and legs, Arachne was

Left **Athene in armor.** As a goddess of war, Athene is represented in full armor with a helmet, spear, and shield. Over her breast she is often seen wearing the "aegis," a breastplate made of goatskin with tassels. The Gorgon's head is painted on the aegis, or sometimes on her shield.

Below *Arachne* by Walter Crane (1845–1915). Just as Arachne condemned herself to hang, so did Athene. The goddess transformed the girl into a spider so that she may hang on a thread and spin forever. The spider retained Arachne's skill as a weaver.

GODDESS PRAYER CHART

WHICH GODDESS	COULD BE PRAYED TO FOR:
APHRODITE (VENUS)	IRRESISTIBLE GOOD LOOKS
ARTEMIS (DIANA)	EASY CHILDBIRTH; SUCCESS IN RUNNING
ATHENE (MINERVA)	CLEVER STRATEGIES; DOMESTIC SKILLS; PRACTICAL WISDOM
DEMETER (CERES)	FERTILITY
HECATE	WEALTH; MAGICAL POWERS
HERA (JUNO)	FAITHFULNESS IN MARRIAGE
HESTIA (VESTA)	PROTECTION AT THE HOME AND HEARTH
MUSES	INSPIRATION IN POETRY AND MUSIC

Above *Actaeon Metamorphosing into a Deer* by Francesco Albani (1578–1660). Another version of the Actaeon myth is that he offended Artemis by claiming to be a more skillful hunter. Yet another version is that Artemis destroyed him because he wanted to marry Semele.

Right *Eos* by Jean-Simon Berthelemy (1743–1811). Eos had countless love affairs with mortals and gods. As well as the four winds and the stars, she gave birth to Emathion, who became king of Arabia, and Memnon, who died in combat with Achilles.

transforming into a spider, and her many eight-legged descendants can still be seen in the corners of the ceiling spinning their intricate webs of the finest gossamer thread.

Artemis and Actaeon

Artemis was a virgin goddess who did not enjoy the company of men. She and her many virgin companions, nymphs of the trees, mountains, and streams, lived together in the woodlands, and their favorite sport was the hunting of wild animals. When they were hot and weary from the hunt, they would cool off by bathing together in a pool in the valley of Gargaphie.

One hot day a huntsman became lost in the woods. Actaeon was a prince, grandson of Cadmus who founded the city of Thebes, but his royal blood did not deter the goddess from taking a savage vengeance when he wandered into Gargaphie. Artemis was being washed in the cool waters by one of her nymphs, while another tied up the goddess's hair and a third waited beside the pool with her cloak and sandals. The rest of Artemis's companions were washing themselves clean from the dust of their morning hunt. All were as naked as the goddess.

The nymphs shrieked with dismay and anger when they noticed that a man was looking at them in all their nakedness. Artemis stood up, her cheeks red with anger, as her companions hurried to cover her with their own bodies. Her bow and arrows had been put aside, to protect them from being splashed while the goddess was bathing. Now she longed to have them in her hands, so that she could shoot the intruder dead at once.

There were other ways, though, for a god to punish a human being. Artemis scooped up water from the pool and threw it in Actaeon's face and hair, saying, "Now you can tell all the world, if you are able, just what it was like to see the goddess of the hunt without her clothes on." Where the water fell on his forehead, horns began to sprout. He fell toward the ground with arms outstretched to break his fall, but instead of human hands, sharp little hooves landed on the ground, and at the same time his arms began lengthening into slender legs to match his new hind legs. He had become a stag.

As a man, Actaeon had been frightened of the goddess and her nymphs, but as a stag he became terrified of everything. He ran and wept, not knowing where to turn for help. Suddenly he heard the yelps of hunting hounds. His own dogs had caught his scent and they were eagerly rushing toward him. "Melampus," he tried to call out, "Ichnobates, Dromas, Laelaps, I am your master, Actaeon," but he could say nothing. The dogs leapt up at him, tearing at his flesh and pulling him down. Some of them looked around, puzzled that their master was not with them to urge them on. Then Actaeon's friends ran up, shouting for him to join them at the kill as he lay there bleeding before them. No one realized until too late that the magnificent stag whose antlers they were taking home as a trophy was their friend and leader, the prince of Thebes.

Eos and Her Lovers

Eos (Aurora), daughter of the Titans Hyperion and Theia, was the goddess of the dawn. Poets praised her rosy fingers that colored the sky in readiness for the sun god's chariot to set out on its daily path. Eos gave birth to the four winds, the North Wind Boreas, the East Wind Eurus, the West Wind Zephyrus, and the South Wind Notus, with Astraeus (whose name in Greek means "starry") as their father.

Eos looked down every morning on the world of mortals, and she took particular notice of handsome young men. Her first lover was Ares, but the goddess

Below *Death of Actaeon* by **Francesco Parmigianino (Parmigiano) (1503–1540).** The Centaur Cheiron created a statue of Actaeon to soothe his dogs afterward.

ATHENE'S OWL

There are many different kinds of owl. Athene's (Minerva's) owl is the Little Owl, and it is so strongly associated with the goddess that the scientific name for this owl is *Athene noctua*. Athene was the patron goddess of Athens, and the coinage of Athens in classical times used to be stamped with the picture of a Little Owl. Athene herself is described as having "owl eyes" as a mark of wisdom and perceptiveness. Not all owls are birds of wisdom, however. The Short-eared Owl was once a man, Ascalaphus, meta-morphosed by Demeter (Ceres) to punish him when he revealed that her daughter Persephone (Proserpina) had eaten the pomegranate seeds that kept her from wholly returning to the upper world.

Left **Athene, Poseidon, and other gods.** The sea eagle, the cock, the serpent, and the olive tree were sacred to Athene, but above all she was most identified with the owl.

Below *Cephalus and Procris* by Jean-Honore Fragonard (1732–1806). Thinking he was hunting an animal, Cephalus hurled his spear and killed his unfortunate wife. The grieving husband was subsequently charged with murder and sentenced by an Athenian court to a lifetime of exile.

Aphrodite (Venus) became very jealous because she regarded Ares as hers, and she punished Eos with an insatiable hunger for young men. Clitus was one man whom Eos saw and desired, and she carried him away to her palace for a while. Clitus enjoyed his time with the goddess, but Cephalus was less fortunate. He was the son of Hermes and Herse, happily married to the princess of Athens, Procris. Cephalus was out hunting when Eos noticed him and began to long for his love. She told him that his wife was unfaithful to him, and then, to prove what she was saying, she sent him to Procris in disguise to tempt her with rich gifts; Procris quickly agreed to share her bed with the stranger, and then Cephalus revealed who he was. Procris ran away to Crete in

shame, and Artemis allowed her to become one of her companions in the hunt even though she was certainly not a virgin. The goddess even gave her a spear that always found its target, and a dog that ran as fast as the wind. Procris's husband joined Eos for a while as her lover, but eventually he returned to the world of mortals.

He was out hunting once more when he met a strange woman. It was his wife, Procris, but he did not recognize her. He saw her dog running as swiftly as the wind, and her spear hitting its target each time it was cast, and longed to own both of them. Cephalus offered to share his bed with the woman if only she would give him her dog and spear. Procris laughed and told him who she was. Cephalus went red with shame, and begged for her forgiveness. "Let us forgive each other," she replied, "for we have each betrayed the other equally." Cephalus and Procris were reconciled, and for a time they lived together happily.

But Procris was a jealous woman, and when she heard that her husband kept calling for "Aura" when he was out hunting, she thought he was summoning some nymph to make love to. All that he was doing, though, was to summon the breeze, "aura" in Greek, to cool him down. Procris hid in the bushes to catch her husband in the act, and as Cephalus ran past with his hounds, she made a rustling noise. He thought that some wild animal was hidden there, and threw the spear that could never miss its mark. It found its way to Procris's heart. Cephalus had killed his wife

endlessly, but he could never shed his human years to regain his youth.

Jealousy and doubt proved to be powerful weapons mastered by Eos when snaring Cephalus. In some versions, Cephalus remained with Eos for eight years and she bore him a son, Phaethon.

Selene and Endymion

Selene was the daughter of the Titans Hyperion and Theia, and was the goddess of the moon. Sometimes she is identified with Artemis, the virgin huntress and sister of the sun god Apollo, but unlike Artemis, Selene clearly enjoyed the company of men and was no virgin. One night she looked down from the sky and saw a very handsome young man asleep in a cave. He was Endymion, the son of Zeus and the nymph Calyce, and Selene took him as her lover. They are said to have had 50 children, a story that suggests that he lived many years in her company, but he is also said to lie in perpetual sleep, never ageing from the handsome young man that she first fell in love with. Was his sleep a punishment, brought upon him by the king of the gods, Zeus, because the mortal's beauty might have tempted his wife Hera, or was it an offering from the love-struck Selene, wanting to keep him forever young and beautiful? Did Endymion ask to remain in ageless sleep so that he could avoid old age, or was it the goddess's way of restraining her lover from making passionate love? After giving birth to 50 children, perhaps she was quite simply too tired of becoming pregnant over and over again. Whatever the truth, Endymion is said to be still sleeping with the moon continuing to shine lovingly down upon him.

with her own spear. Some say that this was Artemis's revenge on both husband and wife for bartering her gifts in order to buy sexual favors.

Tithonus was another of the lovers of Eos. He was young and desirable, and Eos was so pleased with him that she asked Zeus to grant him immortality. Zeus agreed, but as the years went by, Eos's immortal lover began to look older, then to become less supple and energetic, and then to become very thin and frail. The goddess had forgotten to ask Zeus to give her beloved Tithonus eternal youth. She entreated Zeus to restore Tithonus's youth, but the only gift he would now give was to change the aged man into a cicada. This was a mocking gift, for cicadas renew their bodies every year by shedding their outward husks. Tithonus could renew his cicada form

The goddess of the moon had an astonishingly white face, which made the stars seem pale in comparison. She is sometimes portrayed with horns to symbolize the crescent moon. As Artemis came to be identified more and more with the moon, Selene was forgotten.

Above **The goddess Persephone.** Persephone and her mother, Demeter, were celebrated in many rites, notably the Eleusian Mysteries and the Thesmophoria. In these rituals, Persephone's name was not uttered, she was instead referred to simply as "Kore" (maiden).

Opposite page **Demeter.** The great earth goddess was particularly revered by women, for example at the festival of the Thesmophoria, which was a ceremony for women who prayed for fertility for themselves and their city.

Right *The Abduction of Persephone* by Gian Bernini (1598–1680). Some versions of the myth have Zeus ignorant of Hades' intentions, while others do not. Some say that Hades fell in love with Persephone and sought permission from Zeus to marry her. Zeus said nothing. If he gave his consent, Demeter would be heartbroken, but to withhold it would offend his brother.

PERSEPHONE

Demeter (Ceres) is one of the goddesses of ancient Greece of whom little is told. She was the goddess of the crops, especially the grain harvest, and was responsible for the fertility of the world. She played little part in the battles of mortal men or the sexual entanglements of the gods of Olympus.

The daughter of Demeter and Zeus (Jupiter) was called Persephone (Proserpina) and she grew up to become a beautiful maiden who enjoyed gathering flowers—though she outshone any flower in beauty. The Greeks thought of her as perfection in a young girl, and she is sometimes named simply Kore, maiden. One day she was picking flowers, some say in Crete, or else in the fields of Sicily near Enna, when the black horses of Hades (Pluto), the god of the underworld, hurtled out of the ground pulling the chariot in which Hades himself was standing. He had decided that Persephone was to be his queen, and without a word he pulled her into the chariot and urged his horses to race down to the depths of the earth again, to the world of the dead. Some say that Hades had been wounded by the arrows of the mischief-making Eros (Cupid), son of golden Aphrodite (Venus), seeking to put all the gods of Olympus under the control of his mother and himself.

No one could tell Demeter where her daughter had vanished to—no one, that is, who was prepared to tell her. All-seeing Zeus was well aware of what had happened, but even though Persephone was his own daughter, he did nothing to help her. Zeus did not want to offend his brother, who was angry enough with him already. Hades always resented the division of the world among the three brothers Zeus, Poseidon, and himself, after the overthrow of Cronus (Saturnus). Poseidon (Neptune) enjoyed his sea kingdom and Zeus was lord of all the world, but Hades had to live underground and his subjects were the dead. If Zeus were to make a ruling that Persephone must be returned to her grieving mother, Hades' resentment might turn to uncontrollable anger.

*And I will sing
how sad Proserpina
Unto a grave and gloomy
Lord was wed*

OSCAR WILDE (1854–1900),
"THE GARDEN OF EROS"

The Wanderings of Demeter

Demeter wandered the world searching for her lost daughter. While she was searching, she set aside her duties as goddess of the harvest and fertility. The crops failed. The people began to starve. There were no births anywhere in the world, among the birds or the fish, the insects, the animals, or the human beings. Fewer and fewer people came to the temples to worship the gods and there were fewer animals to give in sacrifice to the gods. Perhaps it was the dwindling number of sacrifices that eventually forced Zeus to help Demeter, as much as the sufferings of the human beings calling out to the gods of Olympus for help.

But before Zeus was ready to tell Demeter that her daughter was now queen of the underworld, before the harvests totally failed, before people's cries to the gods became so loud that someone had to listen, Demeter found her way to the royal household of King Celeus in Eleusis. A baby prince, Demophoon, had just been born, and she was employed as a nursemaid. No one recognized the woman weeping for her lost daughter as the great goddess Demeter. Each night, secretly, she would touch the baby's skin with ambrosia, the food of the gods, and then put him into the middle of the fire for a few moments. When she lifted him out, he was unharmed. One day a frightened servant told the queen that the nursemaid was torturing the baby. The next night the queen rushed into the kitchen and found the nursemaid once more calmly putting the baby into the fire. The poor mother shrieked and pulled him out, but the flames had not hurt him at all. He even seemed to glow with good health. Demeter sighed at the folly of human beings. She revealed herself as a goddess and explained that if only she had been left alone, she would have given the baby the gift of immortality in the flames.

The Return of Persephone

Demeter wandered on, once again searching for her daughter. Now the crops failed entirely and everything that lived was suffering along with the

goddess. It began to seem as though the whole world was dying. At last Zeus decided that Demeter's grief must be healed and her daughter given back, or else all that lived on Earth would perish and the gods would receive no more sweet-smelling sacrifices to enjoy. Reluctantly, he sent the messenger of the gods, Hermes (Mercury), to tell Demeter the story of how the earth had opened and the black horses and chariot of Hades had emerged, how the god had driven onto the spring meadow, had leaned out from his seat and put his huge arm around the maiden's waist and pulled her to him. The horses

Above *Demeter Mourning for Persephone* **by Evelyn De Morgan (1855–1919).** In some versions of the myth, it was not Zeus, but the sun god Helius who revealed the truth to the grieving Demeter.

Right **Persephone and a pomegranate.** Persephone came to be represented in two different ways. As a beautiful young virgin, she usually had a cornucopia and a sheaf of wheat, but as the queen of the underworld, she often held a torch or a pomegranate in her hand, symbolizing death and rebirth.

being from ever returning to the world of mortals. Persephone did not eat much—only a few seeds from a pomegranate—but this would be enough to keep her in the underworld of her uncle and bridegroom, Hades.

Zeus was faced with a problem. He had to give Persephone back to her mother, or else the world would come to an end with no harvests and no mothers giving birth ever again. At the same time, he needed to placate his brother Hades, who already felt that all the other gods had pleasures that he could never share. Zeus ruled that Persephone could return to her mother, so that the crops could come to harvest once more, so that babies could once more be born and there would still be people in the world to give sacrifices to the gods. But Persephone would also have to go back down to Hades' kingdom each year, for just as many months as the number of pomegranate seeds that she had eaten.

had plunged back into the darkness, the chariot and Hades and Persephone all disappearing into the ground, which closed up behind them. This was why Demeter had found no trace of her daughter anywhere on Earth.

Hermes promised Demeter that her daughter would be returned to the bright upper world, to feel the sun and enjoy the fresh air, if only Demeter would agree to look after the harvest again and allow new life to be born on Earth. He added, as an afterthought, that Persephone would, of course, be free so long as she had not eaten any of the foods of the underworld.

Hermes is a trickster god, and perhaps he already knew perfectly well that Persephone had eaten some of the food of the underworld. After all, it had been weeks and months since she had disappeared, and even gods need to eat now and then. Centuries later, in medieval stories, the warning was often given that if anyone were to be kidnapped by the fairy folk, they should not eat or drink anything, however fine the feast and however hungry and thirsty they became, for a single taste would keep a human

Rape or Renewal

The number of seeds varies in different retellings of the story of Persephone. Sometimes it is three, or four, or even six. This reflects the climate of the region where the story is being told, and how short the growing season is there; for the story of Persephone is a myth that explains how the seasons came into being and why the crops sprout from the soil after a period each year when nothing seems to grow. In the northern regions, the myth of Persephone is an explanation for winter. When Persephone goes down to Hades' kingdom, winter arrives, and when she returns, so too does the spring. The story of Persephone is usually understood as explaining the seasons of winter and spring, but in warmer climates, it is in the scorching summer that nothing grows. Here the myth speaks to its listeners about the ending of the hot season and the coming of the cool months when everything revives again. Where the icy winter or scorching summer is short, Persephone is said to eat only a few seeds from the pomegranate,

THE MYSTERIES OF ELEUSIS

The mysteries of Eleusis are one of the best-kept secrets of ancient Greece. Demeter (Ceres) found kindness when her wanderings led her to Eleusis, where she was employed as the prince's nursemaid, and when she had regained her daughter, she thanked the people of Eleusis who had given her food and shelter by telling them how she wished to be worshipped. No one knows for certain all that happened in the rituals of Eleusis, but they were based on the story of Persephone's (Proserpina's) descent into the world of the dead and her yearly return to the world of the living. The mysteries offered the promise of a life

to come that was much more appealing than Hades' (Pluto's) gray kingdom where the dead simply endured and existed, or else suffered for the evils they had committed while alive. This promised life after death was not available to all, but only to those who were initiated into the mysteries. For centuries the mysteries continued to be celebrated, and for centuries no one did more than hint at what really happened there.

Below **Eleusian Mysteries.** The three stages of induction were initiation *(meusis)*, perfection *(teleth)*, and beholding *(epopteia)*.

and where the harsh months are long, she is said to eat more seeds.

This, then, is an etiological myth, one of those myths that gives an answer to a question that perplexed the science of the time—why do the seasons exist and why are there times in the year when nothing grows? Persephone is a distant cousin of the Mesopotamian goddess Inanna, who also went down to the world of the dead and came back. Inanna was a strong-willed goddess who knew quite well how to look after herself. Persephone, in contrast, was something of a victim, needing to be rescued by her mother who did not know how to help her daughter except by threatening the whole world with extinction, no longer doing her duty as goddess of the crops and goddess of fertility.

Or was it quite so simple? Was Persephone really a victim of rape, as so many poets and painters have depicted her? In some lesser known myths, Persephone seems to be quite happy to be queen of the underworld, and very ready to protect it from invaders. When two mortal heroes, Theseus and his

Thou makest me remember where and what Proserpina that moment was when lost Her mother her, and she herself the Spring.

DANTE ALIGHIERI (1265–1321), THE DIVINE COMEDY, "PURGATORIO," CANTO XXVIII

friend Peirithous, drank too much and dared one another to go down to the underworld and bring back Persephone as their prize, she set out to trap them with a table covered with good food and tempting wine, and two golden thrones. Clearly Theseus and Peirithous had learned nothing from the story of Persephone and the pomegranate seeds, because they sat down on the golden seats and began enjoying the food and drink. Suddenly they noticed that they were stuck to their seats. Theseus was eventually rescued when Heracles (Hercules) came down to Hades' realm in quest of the three-headed dog, Cerberus. Heracles tore him from the throne, but he left most of his skin behind. Neither Hades nor Persephone could do anything to prevent Heracles, son of Zeus, from carrying off either Cerberus or Theseus, but at least Hades' queen had the satisfaction of keeping Peirithous stuck to his golden chair forever.

So perhaps Persephone was not such an unwilling bride. European art has depicted her as the victim, taken by surprise, dragged down to a dark kingdom full of horrors; but perhaps she came to love her new husband, her new realm of death, and her new powers. Although at every new growing season she returned to her mother, perhaps she was not altogether sorry to go down once again to her kingdom, her husband, and her darkness. After all, it is out of darkness that the new life of spring emerges, out of the dark soil that the spring bulbs send their green shoots, and out of the hidden womb that the babies push their way. The story of Persephone is usually told from the point of view of her desperate mother, Demeter; but what would Persephone say?

FLOWER AND PLANT MYTHS

There are many Greek myths about the origin of various trees, flowers, and other plants. Most involve the metamorphosis of a human being into a form of vegetation; occasionally a nymph like Daphne is also transformed into a plant. These metamorphoses are irreversible. It is very rare in Greek myth for metamorphosis into a plant to function as a reward, as in the story of Baucis and Philemon. Much more often, the creation of a new plant is the occasion for bitter-sweet celebration. Even the gods, in Greek myth, cannot restore a mortal life once lost, but sometimes, as a last resort, they commemorate their beloved friends and lovers forever in the form of some new plant.

Sometimes transformations of people into plants occur as a punishment, even a self-imposed punishment, as in the case of Narcissus. In his case, the misguided human being wasted his precious life, which could not be restored to

him. The narcissus flower, which grows anew each year, mocks at his foolishness at the same time as it commemorates his beauty.

Echo and Narcissus

Narcissus was the son of a naiad, Liriope, and a river god, Cephisus, the god of the same river where Deucalion and Pyrrha purified themselves before becoming the parents of a new human race after the flood. At Narcissus's birth, Teiresias the soothsayer prophesied that he would live long, provided that he never came to know himself. No one knew what this prophecy meant, but it became clear all too late, when he was just between boyhood and manhood.

Narcissus was the most handsome of young men, and many felt the stirrings of sexual desire for him, but he responded to no one's advances. He kept aloof, preferring to hunt wild animals than to enjoy the company of humans or nymphs. One day the nymph

Above *Echo and Narcissus* by John Waterhouse (1849–1917). Another version of this myth sees Echo as the object of the god Pan's unrequited love. Pan cursed her with the power of repetition. The shepherd people grew so infuriated at her habit that they tore her to pieces, scattering her body all over Earth. This is why Echo's voice can still be heard everywhere.

Left **Dish depicting the story of Narcissus from the workshop of Francesco Durantino (sixteenth century).** Narcissus found it impossible to look away from his own reflection. From his name comes the word "narcissism," meaning "self-love."

Above *The Death of Hyacinthus,* Italian School (seventeenth century).

The angry actions of Zephyrus were unlike him. Of the four winds, he was generally considered to be the most mild and gentle.

"You can still chatter," Hera told her, "but nothing you say will be your own."

Echo longed to tell Narcissus how much she loved him, but she had to keep silent until she could echo someone else, hoping that they would voice her desires for her. Narcissus heard a rustling among the trees and called out, "Is someone in the bushes?" Echo answered, "In the bushes." He said, "Come out and let me see you," and she replied, "Let me see you." Then she came out into the open, boldly walked up to him and wrapped her arms around him. For a moment Narcissus was too surprised to do anything, but the next moment he pushed her away, saying, "Keep your hands off me! You disgust me! Never, ever, touch me like that!" All that poor Echo could say was, "Touch me like that."

Echo pined away for love of Narcissus. She stopped eating, she hid away from all the other nymphs, and eventually her body simply disappeared. All that was left of her was the voice that still repeats the last thing that someone has said. Narcissus just did not care about the miseries of Echo, or of the hundred others whose love he had rejected. One day, someone who sighed for Narcissus grew angry and prayed to the gods that the sulky boy would fall in love

Echo met him, and fell in love with him on the spot. She was a nymph then, and had been cursed with the habit of saying nothing new, but only repeating the last part of whatever someone else said in her hearing. This curse was laid on her by Hera (Juno), queen of the gods, because the chatterbox Echo had diverted her too often from noticing her wayward husband enjoying himself with the other nymphs.

and be treated as badly as he had treated others.

One day Narcissus went out hunting, as usual, and began to feel thirsty in the heat of noon. He found a pool and knelt down to drink, but he caught sight of his own reflection in the still waters and fell instantly in love. He tried to convince himself that the face he saw in the pool was that of someone else, someone who kept mocking him by duplicating all his actions. Narcissus would put out his hand to touch the beloved boy in the water, and the boy would put out his hand in response, but instead of warm fingers, all he could feel was the water. He tried to kiss his beloved, but though the face in the water drew close, it was only water that met his lips. Narcissus could not eat, he could not sleep, and he could not leave the pool. He knew that he was in love with his own reflection, but his heart ignored anything that he told himself. He wished to separate himself from himself, so that he could love himself as he longed to do. Narcissus pined away as Echo had done, until he was on the point of death.

Then Echo came back to the pool, listening to her beloved Narcissus for the last time. "I am so miserable," he groaned, and Echo replied, "I am so miserable." Narcissus moaned, "My love is futile," and Echo responded, "My love is futile." He had no more strength to speak, and soon he was dead. The nymphs wept over his wasted body and prepared it for the funeral rites, but when they were ready, the body was no longer there. It had become a pale yellow and white flower with trumpet-shaped petals, that blooms in early spring. That is how the first narcissus came into being.

Apollo and Hyacinthus

Those mortal men and women whom the gods desire usually die young, sometimes because they reject a god's advances and sometimes because another jealous god decides to punish them. Hyacinthus died because two gods fell in love with him at the same time. He was the son of King Amyclas and Queen Diomede, and became famous throughout Laconia for his beauty. Apollo fell in love with him, and so did the god of the west wind, Zephyrus. One hot summer's day, Hyacinthus and Apollo were playing a game of quoits, when Zephyrus interfered with the game. He blew at the quoit that Apollo was throwing, so fiercely that it hurtled toward Hyacinthus. The quoit struck him on the head so hard that he died. Apollo wept over the body of the beautiful boy, and changed the blood that soaked the ground into a flower, the hyacinth. On its petals can be seen the letters "AI," which in Greek are the sound of lamentation. When the boy Hyacinthus died, the god could not bring him back to life as a human being, but the hyacinth plant dies

THE FIRST CYPRESS TREE

The cypress tree was once a beautiful young man, Cyparissus, who was loved by Apollo. Cyparissus loved his pet stag to the point of obsession, and wanted to do nothing except care for this animal. He did not go hunting with the other young men, he did not go chasing after women, nor did he pay any attention to Apollo. One day he accidentally stabbed his beloved stag with his javelin, and then he pined away with grief. "If you love me," he sobbed to Apollo, "grant that I may mourn for my stag forever." The god granted his unusual prayer, and Cyparissus changed from human shape into a cypress tree, the tree of mourning.

Right *Cyparissus* **by Burney (1823).** In some stories, Cyparissus was a Cretan youth who found himself fighting off Apollo's advances. As the young man tried to flee, he was turned into a cypress tree.

down in each scorchingly hot summer, as though it had been killed by the sun, and then revives again in the spring of the following year.

Apollo and Clytie

Aphrodite (Venus) decided that Apollo had been prying into her affairs too much. It was Apollo who had told her husband, Hephaestus (Vulcan), about her love for Ares (Mars), and as a punishment she told her son, Eros (Cupid), to shoot an arrow of love into the sun god. After being struck by Eros's arrow, Apollo immediately fell in love with Leucothoe, princess of Persia, and disguised himself as her mother. Then he ordered the servants to leave the room and revealed himself to Leucothoe as a god. What else could she possibly do except submit and weep?

Leucothoe's sister, Clytie, desired Apollo just as passionately, but the sun god was only interested in his beloved Leucothoe. That night, as soon as she realized that Apollo cared nothing for her, Clytie ran to her father, King Orchamus, in a jealous rage and told him that Leucothoe had a secret lover. The king sentenced Leucothoe to be buried alive immediately under a huge pile of sand. The following morning, Apollo looked down from his chariot and saw what had happened. He scattered the sand, but it was already too late. Leucothoe

Left *Apollo and Hyacinthus* **by Cellini Benvenuto (1500–1571).** Apollo was distraught at the death of Hyacinthus. The god decreed that Hyacinthus be honored in an annual festival, called the Hyacinthia, held over three days during July at Amyclae.

Right *Philemon and Baucis* **by Arthur Rackham (1922).** Philemon and Baucis were simultaneously transformed into a linden tree and an oak tree respectively. It is said that passing strangers hung wreaths on them in memory of the piety the couple showed the gods.

lay crushed and dead. All that the god could do was to transform her lifeless body into a new plant, the frankincense tree whose sap was burned for its aromatic smoke in his temples.

Clytie had daydreamed of Apollo falling in love with her now that her sister and rival was dead, but he hated her for what she had done. Clytie could not eat or drink, she could not sleep, and all she could do was to weep all night and sit in the sunlight all day, turning her head to keep looking toward Apollo in his chariot. After nine days, her legs grew into roots and her thin body metamorphosed into a tall, thin stalk, while her head became a golden flower. She had become the first sunflower, a plant whose flowers follow the steps of the sun.

Baucis and Philemon

The gods often liked to disguise themselves as human beings, to investigate crimes, give advice to heroes, and test people's devotion to them. One day Zeus (Jupiter) and his son Hermes (Mercury) came down to Earth, to Phrygia, disguised as ordinary people, and started to ask for a place to stay the night. It was the duty of every Greek to offer hospitality to strangers, but the two gods tried many houses until they found one that would let them in. It was the poorest of houses, built of mud, thatch, and reeds, and was beginning to collapse back into the swamp in which it stood. An elderly couple opened the door to their home and immediately invited the gods to come in, while at the same time apologizing for their poverty. The old woman, Baucis, took down a piece of the long-hoarded fletch of bacon that had been hanging from the ceiling, and cut off a generous portion for her stew. The old man, Philemon, used all his firewood to build up the fire, and then went into his garden and started picking all the vegetables and fruit that he could find, to add to the stew. Then the couple gave the gods water to wash in, and

put their much-mended festival cloths onto their only couch, in the hope that their unexpected guests would feel welcome.

The table was shaky, the couch was dilapidated, and their festival cloths were worn, but Baucis set about wiping the table with mint and putting out all the food in the house—eggs, fruit, cheese, and fresh vegetables, and then the bacon and vegetable stew. She brought out the wine and watered it well, and when all had been eaten, she then offered the gods nuts and berries, dates and apples, and honey just taken from the hive. She was concerned that her guests would still be hungry and thirsty at the end of the meal, but there was nothing more in the house that she could give them. Then she noticed that the wine pitcher was somehow still full, even though Philemon had refilled the guests' cups several times already. She fell onto her knees, and Philemon knelt beside her, praying that their divine visitors would accept such a humble meal.

Philemon had a sudden idea. The goose that guarded their cottage, warning them of the arrival of visitors with its incessant cackling, could be killed and cooked in honor of these exalted dinner guests. Philemon then went out to catch the bird, but old age slowed him, and the goose quickly ran indoors and took refuge on the lap of the great Zeus himself. "Do not kill your faithful guard," said the god, "and do not stay here any longer. We intend to take vengeance on all those people who turned us away and violated the law of hospitality to strangers, but

Below *Baucis and Philemon* **by Walter Crane (1845–1915).** The elderly peasants Philemon and Baucis were a shining example of kindness and hospitality. By showing the "strangers" such generosity, the couple were rewarded in their human lives and ever after.

you deserve to live. Climb up the mountain with us, and do not look back until you are at the top."

It took Baucis and Philemon a long time to climb the mountain, and when they finally reached the top and looked back, they saw that the whole country-side was flooded. Only their little cottage in the marshes still stood, but it was no longer a cottage. Instead of mud and reedy thatch, it had become a marble temple with a roof of gold. Zeus offered Baucis and Philemon any gift that they desired. "Let us serve you," they replied, "as priest and priestess of your temple. Then, when it is time for us to die,

grant that we die in the same instant, so that neither of us has to grieve for the loss of the other." Zeus was very happy to grant both their wishes.

For years afterward the old couple lived on as priest and priestess of Zeus, until one day they were standing in front of the marble temple and found that they could no longer walk. Their four legs had become firmly rooted to the ground, and their bodies started growing leaves. Zeus had granted their special wish, that they should leave their human life together, and they continued to live on as intertwining trees in front of the temple.

Above *Clytie Transformed into a Sunflower* by **Charles de Lafosse (1636–1716)**. A different version of the legend reveals Clytie as one of Apollo's former lovers. Devastated that she had been abandoned, Clytie revealed the god's identity to her rival's father—with disastrous results.

73

Above *Landscape with Hermes and Apollo as a Shepherd* by Claude Lorrain (1600–1682). Although he was the god of prophecy, healing, and music, Apollo was the protector of flocks and herds. He was often referred to as Lycius, the wolf god.

HERMES AND OTHER MUSICIANS

Hermes (Mercury) was the son of Zeus (Jupiter) and the nymph Maia. He was one of the two messengers of the gods; the other was Iris, goddess of the rainbow that joins sky to earth. Hermes and Athene (Minerva) were the two Olympians who best loved humankind, enjoying rather than resenting their trickery. Like Athene, Hermes was calculating and

clever, and he was worshipped as the god of all those who buy and trade, the god of thieves, and the god who presides over mining what lies hidden beneath the earth. Hermes was also the god of roads and travelers; if something valuable or unusual was picked up on the roadway, it was called a gift from Hermes. Hermes was also responsible for looking after land boundaries, and he showed the newly dead the way to the underworld.

being done, but a nymph at the entrance to the cave told them that she was looking after an extraordinarily clever and talented baby called Hermes, who had invented the first musical instrument from the shell of a tortoise and the guts of a cow, and was playing it to help his mother go to sleep.

The satyrs pricked up their hairy ears when they heard the word "cow," and then they noticed two cow skins stretched out in front of the cave, in the process of becoming leather. "Apollo, here is the thief," they shouted, and very soon Apollo joined them, ready to punish the criminal. He marched into the cave and woke Hermes' mother, Maia, demanding the return of his cows. "My son is a mere baby," said Maia, and showed Apollo the little child who was doing his best to seem asleep. "He was born only three days ago—how could he have walked that distance and driven a whole herd of cows back here?"

But the hides outside the cave were definitely those of Apollo's cows, and the god was determined to have the culprit punished. He seized the baby in his arms and carried him up to Olympus, to the throne of Zeus. It was there that Hermes finally admitted that he was the thief, and agreed to hand back the herd—all 18 of them. "But there were 20 cows in the herd," complained Apollo, "and I want all 20 of them back."

"Brother," said Hermes, looking up sweetly into his half-brother's face, "you saw the two hides outside the cave. Those two cows were the ones I cut up and sacrificed to the 12 gods of Olympus." Zeus and Apollo were both taken aback. They knew of only 11 Olympian gods: Who was the twelfth, and how did the baby know so much about the pantheon? Hermes pretended to be embarrassed as he explained to them that he was the new twelfth god of Mount Olympus, but he was feeling secretly triumphant.

Even when he was a baby, Hermes could outwit his half-brother Apollo almost without effort. He could hardly walk, but he managed to wander far away from his mother, getting halfway across Greece. As Hermes looked down from the top of a hill, he discovered Apollo tending a herd of cows. Hermes' first thought was to steal the cows. Noticing that their hoof marks showed which way they were walking, he deceived Apollo by making shoes for the cows from tree bark and putting them on back to front, so that the tracks led one way while the cows were walking in the opposite direction.

Apollo could see no trace of his cattle, and no sign of where they had disappeared to. There were plenty of fresh hoofprints leading into the field, but none going out. He searched the world from his sun chariot, but even from the sky he could see no sign of the cows anywhere. In the end Apollo offered a reward for his lost herd, and the satyrs, who were followers of Pan, started to search for them in hidden places.

Some of the satyrs went looking in Arcadia, and there they heard a very strange sound coming from a cave. It was the first music ever to be played. They could not see how it was

Ah, leave the hills of Arcady, Thy satyrs and their wanton play, This modern world hath need of thee.

OSCAR WILDE (1854–1900), "PAN: DOUBLE VILLANELLE"

Apollo and Marsyas

Apollo remembered the story that the satyrs had told him, about the strange noise coming out of Hermes' cave, and he asked to see the new instrument. With its cow-gut strings stretched over its tortoise shell, it was the first lyre, and Hermes plucked the strings skillfully and sang a lyric poem that he had just composed in honor of

Left **Apollo playing a cithara.** As the patron god of music, dance, and poetry, Apollo earned the epithet of "Musagetes," the leader of the Muses. It was believed that the goddesses danced with Apollo and the other deities, the Graces and the Hours, at different festivals on Olympus.

Below **The god Hermes.** Hermes had many duties to fulfill, and not all of them were pleasant. One such duty was having to lead the souls of the living to the world of the dead. In this capacity he was known as "Psychopompos," which means "guide of souls."

75

Above **Musical competition.** Not content to be pronounced the winner of the competition over Marsyas, Apollo flayed his opponent alive. For a very long time Apollo refused to allow the flute to be played in his presence, but he finally allowed one to be played at Delphi on special occasions.

Right *Arion Preserved by a Dolphin* by Bernard Picart (1673–1733). The myth of Arion was based on an historical figure Arion, the likely son of Cycleus of Methymna in Lesbos. This Greek poet and singer is said to have invented the dithyramb—a choral song or poem of wild character and irregular form.

the great sun god. Apollo was so delighted with the music and the words that he forgave the child. He was even willing to leave the cows with Hermes if only he could have the lyre. Hermes was happy to agree, and at once he began inventing another musical instrument. This time, he made a pipe from some reeds. Again Apollo asked for the instrument, offering his shepherd's staff in return. If Hermes took the staff, he would become the god of all who herded cattle or sheep or goats. Hermes was already very skilled at bargaining. He said that the staff was not enough; he wanted the art of augury as well.

Apollo hesitated at this candid and self-assured suggestion. He wanted to become the god of music, to excel with the lyre, but he was lord of Delphi and was reluctant to give his oracle over to Hermes, however sweet the pipe.

"I will teach you how to prophesy from pebbles," he proposed, and that was good enough for Hermes. The new god not only practiced the art of auguring from pebbles in water, but he also invented the game of knucklebones and a technique for telling the future from the bones. Zeus was pleased with his astonishingly clever little son, and made him the gods' herald, the first negotiator and smooth-tongued diplomat in the world.

Hermes was not the only god ingenious enough to invent a new musical instrument. The flute was invented by Athene, but when she puffed out her cheeks as she played it, the other gods laughed at her. It was the satyr Marsyas who took up the flute and practiced until he played to perfection. He was so proud of his flute playing that he challenged Apollo to a musical competition, the

PAN AND PANIC

The word *pan* means "everything" in Greek, but the god Pan was not one to claim supreme power. He did not care to live in Olympus, preferring a simpler life in the Arcadian countryside where he helped herdsmen and hunters and the keepers of bees. Yet Pan can be a terrifying god. The word "panic" derives from Pan, referring to the sudden terror that is inflicted on those who intrude into solitary places, when the god does not wish to be disturbed (especially when he is enjoying an afternoon sleep).

Above **Detail of wall showing Pan playing pipes by Franz von Stuck (1863–1928).** Pan passed the time by either playing his pipes or resting. Pan liked to have a sleep in the middle of the day and would frighten anyone foolish enough to disturb his slumber. Knowing this, shepherds did not play on their pipes at midday.

flute against the lyre. The nine Muses were the judges, and Marsyas was the loser. Apollo flayed him to death for his insolence in challenging a god.

Pan and Syrinx

Syrinx was one of the dryads of Arcadia. She was an eager companion of Artemis (Diana) in the hunt, and like Artemis she had vowed herself to chastity. She dressed like Artemis and was armed just like her, except that the goddess carried a golden bow and the nymph carried a bow made of horn.

One day the god Pan met Syrinx as she was returning from the hunt. Instantly he felt an overwhelming attraction toward her, and he put out his hand to stroke her. She recoiled, then fled, and he chased after her on his fast goat hooves. As she ran, Syrinx prayed to any god who was listening, to help her escape, and when she saw the River Ladon in her way, she begged the river god for aid. Pan had almost caught up with her, reaching out his arms to grasp her waist, but as he embraced her, he found in his arms only a bundle of reeds. Syrinx had become the reeds that grow in shallow waters and marshlands. Pan sat disconsolately by the river, looking at the reeds and longing for the nymph. As he sat there, he heard the thin music that reeds make when the breeze plays through them. He broke off reeds of different lengths and tied them together, making the first panpipes. From then on, the pan-pipes were called *syrinx* in Greek.

Some say that it was the god Pan who invented the first musical instrument in the form of the pan-pipes. Hermes' pipe, the one that he traded with Apollo in exchange for the art of prophecy and lordship over herdsmen, was only a copy of Pan's pipes, which he had left behind one day in the fields.

Arion

Arion was the son of Poseidon (Neptune) and the nymph Oneaia. He lived in Corinth, and the ruler of Corinth, the tyrant Periander, loved to hear him sing

Pan himself,
The simple shepherd's
awe-inspiring god!
WILLIAM WORDSWORTH (1770–1850),
THE EXCURSION, BOOK IV

and play on the lyre. Arion went to Sicily to compete in a musical competition and won. He gained not only the victor's wreath to bring back to Corinth, but also money and other gifts from those who had heard him play the lyre so well.

He boarded a ship with all his treasures, but the sailors did not intend to take him home to Corinth. When the ship was far from land, they stood around him and explained politely that he would have to die, because they could not risk stealing his treasure and letting him live. Arion begged for one last favor, to sing a final song.

He stood at the very front of the ship, singing in praise of the gods, then leapt overboard. The sailors looked over the side and could not see him. He had saved them the trouble of killing him, or so it seemed.

But Arion was not dead. A school of dolphins had heard his wonderful singing and swam all around him, nudging him until he climbed onto the back of the largest of them. Then they all went speeding through the water, overtaking the ship on its way to Corinth. Arion arrived days before the ship, and the dolphin made sure that everyone had time to witness his arrival, plunging through the sea like a prancing horse. Arion told his story to the tyrant Periander, who waited for the ship to arrive and then sent for the sailors. "Where is my dear Arion?" he asked them. "He is still in Sicily," they replied, "and he asked us to tell you that his beautiful songs are so well liked there that he intends never to leave the

Above **Orpheus.** Many believe that Orpheus was a more ancient poet than Homer. He is credited as the author of many poems, hymns, prayers, and mystical books. Orpheus is also said to be the founder of a religious sect who called themselves the Orphics.

place." Periander then confronted the men with the living Arion, and passed a sentence of death on them.

Arion lived a long and happy life, and according to some stories, the gods placed the Lyra constellation in the sky at his death to commemorate his truly wonderful talent with the lyre.

Orpheus

Orpheus was the finest musician who ever lived. When he made music, everyone and everything listened. People fell silent, animals clustered around him, and even the trees drooped their branches so that they could hear with every leaf. Playing the lute, he could enchant even the wildest of beasts—hungry lions and tigers—and he could charm the fish out of the sea with his singing. It was the Iron Age of

humankind, and evil ways tempted everyone alive; but when Orpheus played, people's hearts grew calm, and when he sang, their hearts filled with joy.

Orpheus traveled with Jason and the Argonauts, but his greatest adventure was one that he had to face without help. The story of Orpheus and Eurydice begins in happiness, with a wedding. The marriage feast of Orpheus and his bride Eurydice was nearing its end, and some of the guests had drunk too much wine. Aristaeus was so drunk that he forgot all the respect due both to his host and to a married woman. While Orpheus was busy with his other guests, Aristaeus began to attack the bride, trying to rape her. Eurydice fled into the garden and, as she ran, a poisonous snake bit her on the foot. Within a moment she was dead.

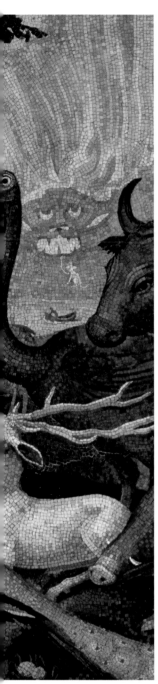

Orpheus laid aside his lute and could think of no reason why he should ever sing again. He could not bear to stay at home, so full of memories of his lost Eurydice, and so he began wandering the world. Wherever he wandered, though, he could not escape his thoughts, and his longing for his dead bride. In the end he remembered the myth of Persephone, the maiden who had been raped and abducted from the upper world, whose mother had grieved so strongly that Zeus was moved to allow the girl to return to the world of life. Surely Persephone would understand his grief, if he could only go down to the underworld and sing to her. Perhaps, like the goddess Persephone, his beloved Eurydice would be allowed to return from the realm of death. Since his magnificent song could enchant every creature on earth, Orpheus was willing to risk his life on the chance that he could also enchant the god and goddess of the world below.

ORPHEUS IN THE
UNDERWORLD

It was easy enough for him to find his way down to the palace of Hades, easy to pay the ferryman with a song and charm the three-headed dog Cerberus to sleep. It was not easy to sing before Hades and Persephone, for all his hopes lay in this moment. He felt the pain in his heart and sang to Persephone about her longing for the daylight and the heart beating with life. He felt his longing for the bride he had lost on their wedding day and sang to Hades about his loneliness, condemned to a world of shades. He sang to both god and goddess about the heart glowing with love, melting away all pain and isolation and loneliness.

The shades of the dead had long forgotten the pains and pleasures of life, but now they crowded close around, like birds huddling together in the winter for warmth. When Orpheus sang, the Furies,

THE BIRTH OF PAN

Pan was the son of Hermes, but no one except Hermes knows for sure who his mother was. Some say that she was a nymph, and some that she was Penelope, wife of the hero Odysseus (Ulysses), and others wonder whether she might have been the goat Amaltheia. Pan was born half-goat, half-man, with little goat horns and a tail, a goat beard and sturdy little goat legs. Hermes took his son to Olympus where the gods all laughed at him, but later he was a true friend to Athene, helping her people, the Athenians, to win the battle of Marathon by making the Persian invaders panic.

Below **Pan from the *Book of Hours*** (mid-sixteenth century). Pan was a peculiar and sometimes frightening-looking god. Later, the medieval image of the Devil was derived from his strange appearance.

the pitiless voices of tormenting guilt, learned how to weep, and the tortures of the wicked came to a pause. His marvelous song moved the goddess Persephone to take pity on him, and she thereby decreed that he could take Eurydice back to the world of the living. The only condition was that he must walk ahead, without turning around, keeping silent, until they reached the upper air. Orpheus caught one glimpse of his dead wife among the clustered shades, and then turned to walk the long path back to the world of the living.

Left **Orpheus and Cerberus**. The father of Orpheus by some accounts was Oeagrus, the king of Thrace, but by others, it was Apollo. When Apollo gave Orpheus the seven-stringed lyre, it is said that Orpheus added another two strings in memory of the Nine Muses, one of whom was his mother, Calliope. The gentle music he played and the beauty of his voice were enough to soothe savage beasts.

Above **Orpheus and Eurydice.** When Orpheus returned to Thrace without his beloved wife, he resolved to spurn the love of all women. While this is seen as the reason behind his murder by the Maenads, some authors believe that each of the raging women wanted Orpheus for herself and tore him apart in the ensuing struggle.

Right **Death of Orpheus.** The Muses were overwhelmed with grief over the loss of Orpheus. They gathered the pieces of his body and buried them at Mount Olympus. It is said that the nightingales there sing more beautifully than anywhere in the world.

As he walked, he began to doubt Persephone's warning. Was Eurydice really there, following him, or was this merely a malicious trick on Persephone's part? Surely, if Eurydice was walking close behind him, he would be able to hear something, some footfall, some sound of her breathing, but all remained silent. He kept on walking until light began to glimmer ahead, where the long path climbed to the upper world. With only a few steps to go, he could no longer bear the silence and the uncertainty, and quickly turned to look back. There was his beloved wife Eurydice, tears streaming down her cheeks, with a wind of death blowing her away from him. She held out her arms to him, and he reached out for her, but already she was far away, silently calling out to him with her eyes. Orpheus would have gone back into death's kingdom for his bride, but Charon the ferryman would not let him pass.

FINAL DAYS

He wandered the world restlessly until his death. In Thrace he met the Maenads, the wild followers of Dionysus, who attacked him with spears and stones, and when these weapons refused to hurt the marvelous musician, they wrenched his body apart. He may have intruded unknowingly upon their sacred rituals in honor of the god, or else they were taking vengeance for his rejection of women.

Since the double loss of his wife, he had not been able to consider marrying again. The Maenads tore off his head, and it kept singing as it floated down the River Hebrus, and across the Mediterranean to the island of Lesbos. There it was buried with proper funeral rites, and the shade of Orpheus traveled the familiar route down to the underworld, where he could at last be together again with his bride Eurydice.

MYTHS OF TRANSFORMATION

Metamorphosis was one of the favorite themes of Greek myth. The gods changed themselves into many forms when in pursuit of new sexual partners, and they liked to take on the forms of human beings when speaking to their favorites. When Athene (Minerva) helped Odysseus (Ulysses), for instance, she often took the form of a surprisingly helpful stranger. Some of the lesser gods had a small repertoire of shapes that they could assume, but a god like Zeus (Jupiter) could choose any form that he wanted. In contrast, human beings were at the mercy of gods who chose to transform them, and this transformation was rarely of benefit to the one who endured it.

Midas and the Golden Touch

One day the old satyr Silenus, the unruly companion of the god Dionysus (Bacchus), drank too much wine, as usual, and was taken captive by some Phrygians working in the fields. He offered no resistance, and so they tied him up with chains made from flowers and led him to their king. When King Midas saw the satyr tottering toward him, garlanded with flowers around his neck, wrists, and hooves, he instantly recognized him as Silenus, and celebrated his arrival with a festival, including plenty of watered wine. Then he gave the satyr back to Dionysus, who offered the king in return anything he could wish for. "I wish that all I touch would turn to gold," Midas eagerly replied. "Are you quite sure?" asked Dionysus, and Midas assured him that the touch of gold was exactly what he wanted.

Midas was delighted to find that the god had granted his wish. He touched a flower, and it became solid gold. He picked up a pebble, and it shone golden. He ran his hands up the sides of trees, and they became a golden avenue fit to welcome a god. Midas imagined transforming his whole palace into gold, wearing cloth of gold, and heaping up gold treasures for himself. His dream of golden glory lasted until his mealtime. Out came the bread and the roasted meat, piled high on his plate, but when he tried to break off a piece of bread, it all turned to gold, and when he speared a piece of meat on his golden dagger, it turned to gold as soon as his lips touched it. He lifted his cup to his mouth, and the wine turned to molten gold. Midas was beginning to starve amid splendor. He did not dare to touch his wife or children, and he bitterly regretted the wish that he had made.

King Midas prayed to Dionysus, humbly acknowledging how foolish he had been, and the god was willing to take back his gift. "Go to the River Pactolus where it rises in the mountain," he said to Midas, "and dip your whole body into it,

Left **Sleeping Silenus.** Silenus, teacher and companion of Dionysus, was almost always in a state of drunkenness. He was considered to be very wise and if captured by mortals, could reveal a great number of secrets.

Below *King Midas* by **Nicholas Tournier (1590–1638).** Although Dionysus warned Midas about the danger of his wish for "the golden touch," Midas would not listen. In some myths, he even accidentally killed his daughter by turning her to gold when he touched her.

Above *The Judgment of Midas* by Domenico Zampieri Domenichino (1581–1641). Midas, who was a follower of Pan, was punished by Apollo by having his ears changed to ass's ears. Midas was so embarrassed by the gossip of his people, he ran away from Phrygia forever.

part in a competition to determine who was the better musician, and Apollo proved overwhelmingly superior, Midas dared to disagree with the verdict. In his opinion, the peasant song that Pan played on his pipes outshone anything that Apollo could produce on his lyre.

Apollo punished Midas for both his presumption and his poor taste in music, by transforming his ears into the ears of an ass, while the rest of him stayed just as it was. Midas was ashamed and embarrassed, and tried very hard to keep his new ears a secret by wrapping a huge turban around them. He deceived everyone except his barber. When he realized that the barber had noticed his enormous gray ears, Midas swore him to secrecy. The barber longed to tell someone, anyone, this choice piece of gossip. If only he could speak to someone about it!

The barber could not bear to remain silent, but he wanted to keep his oath to the king. He went out into the fields and dug a little hole. He put his mouth close to the earth that he had dug out of the hole, and he whispered to it, "King Midas has ass's ears!" Then he filled in the hole and went away,

so that the clean water can wash away the power of gold." Midas did as he had been told, and from then on, flecks of gold could be found in the Pactolus River.

feeling much better. The earth sprouted reeds, and when they were fully grown, they sighed in the wind, "King Midas has ass's ears." Someone heard, and ran to tell someone else, until the whole of Phrygia was full of gossip and laughter.

Midas and the Ass's Ears

It is never safe for a mortal to intervene in a dispute among the gods, as Troy found out when Paris judged which of the goddesses was the fairest, and Teiresias found out when he adjudicated between Zeus and Hera (Juno). When Pan and Apollo took

Tereus and Philomela

Tereus, the son of Ares (Mars), was a king of Thrace, and he married Procne, the daughter of King Pandion of Athens. Their son was called Itys. When Itys was five years old, Procne asked her husband to invite her sister, Philomela, for a visit. Tereus went to Athens to escort Philomela back to Thrace, and as soon as he saw her, he lusted after her. He urged her to go with him, telling her how ardently his wife desired her company, but it was his own ardor that made his words so urgent. Philomela was overjoyed at his invitation, and she set off for Thrace in his ship. All went well on the voyage, under the eyes of the sailors, but when they reached the coast of Thrace, the king invited her into his chariot and, instead of making for the city, drove her to a hunting lodge long abandoned in the forest. There he raped her.

As soon as she could speak, Philomela hurled reproaches at Tereus, evil king, evil husband, evil brother-in-law. She threatened to accuse him before his wife and his people, and to entreat King Pandion of Athens to take revenge for her rape. She also promised that she would accuse him before the gods if he kept her imprisoned in the forest. Her speech was bold, but she did not have the strength to resist Tereus when he seized her again, tying her arms behind her back. Fearful of what she might say, he cut off her tongue with his sword and left her imprisoned in the hunting lodge, keeping her alive for his sexual pleasure but making sure that she could not escape. He went home to his wife and told her that Philomela had died on the journey, weeping as he spoke. "Tereus, you are the best of men," said his weeping wife, and Tereus secretly gloated while he was pretending to lament.

Philomela recovered from her wound and longed to tell the world what had been done to her. She had been silenced, but her hands could still weave a story. There was a loom and spun thread in the hunting lodge, and she spent her long days weaving a white cloth with the story of her rape set out in red. Then she persuaded a servant, with gestures and tears, to take the cloth to the king's wife, as a gift.

Procne looked at the scene woven in red and understood her sister's message. She was too angry to weep, instantly casting her mind around for a means of revenge. It happened to be the time of the Bacchic festival, when women left their cities dressed in fawn skins, garlanded with vine leaves, and carrying spears. After some time, Procne pretended to be overcome with Bacchic ecstasy and ran to the hunting lodge where she found her sister. Procne dressed Philomela in festival costume and covered her poor face with vine leaves and ivy, so that she would not be recognized. Then the two sisters ran back to the palace to take their revenge.

Procne wanted to hurt Tereus as badly as he had hurt Philomela. She told Tereus that she wanted to practice a ritual of her own country, where the wife, not the servants, cooked and served a meal to her husband. When he agreed, she took her small son into the kitchen and forced herself to kill him. Then the sisters cut up his body and cooked the pieces, boiling some and roasting others. Tereus enjoyed his meal, and when he had finished, he called for his son. "Itys," he called, "come here to your father." "He is already here," replied Procne, and Tereus looked around the room for him. Out sprang

Left **The sisters' revenge.** Procne and Philomela plotted a dreadful revenge on Tereus, killing Itys, his son. Exacting revenge on one family member by harming or killing an innocent relative rather than the wrong-doer was common practice in Greek myth.

Below *Tereus Confronted with the Head of His Son Itys, Whose Flesh He Has Just Devoured* by Peter Paul Rubens (1577–1640). As in a number of myths, revenge was made complete with the presentation of the child's severed head to his father. In Greek myths, taking revenge was more acceptable for men than for women.

Opposite page *Pyramus and Thisbe* by Lucas Cranach the Elder (1472–1553). Pyramus, believing Thisbe to be dead, was overcome with grief and stabbed himself with his sword. Thisbe asked him to wait for her and then plunged the sword into her heart. So, they died together. William Shakespeare's play *Romeo and Juliet* is said to have been based on the story of Pyramus and Thisbe.

Philomela, smeared with the boy's blood, panting with her eagerness to accuse the king but unable to speak. She was carrying the head of Itys, and pointing to the meat.

Tereus howled with fury and ran after the sisters, ready to impale them both on his sword. The gods intervened, changing Tereus to the bird called a hoopoe, with a great beak like a sword and a crest of feathers like a crown. They changed Procne to a swallow, her feathers red as if stained with blood, and voiceless Philomela they changed to the sweetest singer among the birds, the nightingale. From that day the nightingale has sung "Tereu! Tereu!" accusing the king with every note that she utters.

Pyramus and Thisbe

Pyramus and Thisbe were neighbors in the city of Babylon, and the houses that they lived in were separated only by a wall. They fell in love and wished to marry, but their parents refused to allow this. Some old disagreement between the neighboring families had festered into a feud. Pyramus and Thisbe could not talk to one another in public, but they found a little hole in the wall and whispered words of love through it, Pyramus telling Thisbe how much he longed for her, Thisbe telling Pyramus how she longed to be closer to him. They often talked to the wall, reproaching it for not opening wider

*As at the name
of Thisbe oped his lids
The dying Pyramus, and gazed upon her,
What time the mulberry became vermilion*

DANTE ALIGHIERI (1265–1321), *THE DIVINE COMEDY*, "PURGATORIO," CANTO XXVII

for them, so that they could reach through to one another. They used to kiss the wall each night, because their lips could come no closer than this.

One day, they whispered to each other that they could no longer endure being separated. They decided to run away that night, and planned to meet under the mulberry tree that grew by the tomb of Ninus. Thisbe was the first to creep outdoors, at midnight, and she sat under the mulberry tree, waiting for Pyramus. As she waited, a lioness came to drink at a stream that flowed past the tree. Thisbe crept away fearfully into a cave, and the lioness paid her little attention. She had come to drink after making a kill. Thisbe had dropped her veil, and the lioness played with it, tearing at it and staining it with blood from her earlier kill, before she ambled off into the night.

By the time Pyramus arrived, it was dawn. There was light enough for him to see the lioness's paw prints, and the bloodstained veil that he recognized as Thisbe's. In despair, certain that she was dead, he killed himself with his sword. His blood spurted onto the mulberries, which at that time were white. Thisbe now felt brave enough to creep out of her cave and look for Pyramus. She came back to the mulberry tree and saw her dear Pyramus lying there in his blood. Thisbe lifted up his head, and he opened his eyes for the last time to see her beloved face. Then he died, and Thisbe cried out her futile reproaches to the deceiving veil and the lioness. Words gave her heart no ease, and she ended by picking up the sword stained with Pyramus's blood and using it to stab herself through the heart. Her blood, like that of Pyramus, spurted onto the berries. Since the death of Pyramus and Thisbe, all mulberries have been colored a deep blood-red.

THE PERFECT WIFE

Pygmalion was a sculptor who looked in vain for a woman to suit him as a marriage partner. He was a hater of women, finding some fault in all of them, but he carved an ivory statue of his ideal woman, as true to life as he could make it. So realistic was it that he fell in love with his own creation, naming it Galatea, kissing and stroking it, and he longed for the ivory to turn into human flesh. He prayed to the goddess Aphrodite (Venus), and she granted his prayer. That night Pygmalion kissed the statue, and as he did, the ivory became a human woman. He had found his perfect wife.

Left **Pygmalion.** Aphrodite brought the statue of Galatea to life because she thought it looked like herself. Pygmalion and Galatea happily paid homage to Aphrodite for the rest of their lives.

Right **Dionysus with satyrs and Maenads.** Dionysus is the god of wine, intoxication, and creative ecstasy. Orgies held in his honor began in Rome around 200 B.C. These parties were outlawed by the Roman Senate in 186 B.C.

TALES OF DIONYSUS

The Greeks talked about Dionysus (Bacchus) as though he were the newest of the gods, arriving as an adult from Asia long after Zeus (Jupiter) and the rest of his family had established themselves on Mount Olympus. Archaeological evidence indicates, however, that he was one of the oldest of the Greek gods, and that it was really the Olympian gods who were the newcomers. According to myth, he was a son of Zeus, born long after Artemis (Diana) and Apollo, Athene (Minerva) and Hermes (Mercury). Zeus disguised himself as a mortal man in order to seduce Semele, the daughter of King Cadmus of Thebes. His jealous wife, Hera (Juno), found out as usual what her husband was up to, and took a nasty revenge. She too disguised herself as a human being, this time as Semele's old nurse. She told the girl that her lover was hiding his true identity. If he truly

Below *God Zeus and Goddess Semele Dying from his Love* by Luca Ferrari (1671–1753). The Orphic version of this myth sees Dionysus originally as the child of Zeus and Persephone. The child, then named Zagreus, was devoured by the Titans, but Zeus saved his heart and served it to Semele in a drink, causing her to fall pregnant. When the child was born, Zeus named him Dionysus.

loved her, he would show her who he really was. Semele was six months pregnant with her lover's child— surely he could not refuse her now.

That night, Semele asked Zeus for a gift, to prove that he loved her, and he promised to give her whatever she asked for, sealing his promise with an unbreakable oath by the River Styx. "I want to see you as you really are," she said, and the king of the gods was dismayed, for no mortal can look on Zeus in his glory and live. He tried to persuade her to change her mind, to ask for jewels or a palace of her own or a kingdom for her son to rule, but she kept saying the same words, until he was forced to yield to her.

Zeus discarded his human disguise and showed himself in his splendor, intolerably bright to mortal eyes. Semele was burned to ashes, but Hermes was hovering close by, ready to rescue the unborn child. He seized the child from her womb and sewed him into Zeus's thigh, where he grew for the next three months. Then Hermes helped Zeus cut himself open again and delivered the baby. That is why Dionysus is called the twice-born god.

Hera was still angry, and ordered the Titans to capture the baby and kill him. They tore him into tiny pieces and boiled them in a cauldron. From his blood sprang up the first pomegranate tree. Zeus's mother Rhea noticed what the Titans were doing with her grandson, and put together all the scraps of flesh so that Dionysus could live once more. After surviving this dismemberment, Dionysus might well have been called the thrice-born god!

The God of Wine

In order to hide the baby from Hera, Hermes metamorphosed him into a baby goat and asked the nymphs of Mount Nysa to care for him. They hid him in a cave and fed him on milk and honey and, as a reward, Zeus placed the nymphs among the stars as the Hyades. When Dionysus was a little older, he was turned back again into the form of a god. He then began experimenting with the juice of the grapes that grow on Mount Nysa and had soon invented wine. Ivy and grape vines were always associated with the god of wine; he and his followers each carried a staff called the thyrsus, entwined with ivy and tipped with a pinecone.

Dionysus never settled on Mount Olympus. He traveled the world with his riotous, hard-drinking, and lecherous companions, the goat-legged, goat-horned satyrs, and his especial friend, Silenus.

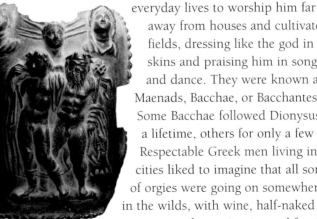

Silenus was the son of Hermes and the oldest of the satyrs, with a bald head and a bulging stomach, and he was perpetually drunk. Dionysus was also accompanied by women who left their ordinary everyday lives to worship him far away from houses and cultivated fields, dressing like the god in fawn skins and praising him in song and dance. They were known as Maenads, Bacchae, or Bacchantes. Some Bacchae followed Dionysus for a lifetime, others for only a few days. Respectable Greek men living in the cities liked to imagine that all sorts of orgies were going on somewhere in the wilds, with wine, half-naked women, sexual promiscuity, and feasts on raw meat torn from living animals, but there are also stories of these women peacefully singing in praise of the god, with songs that could charm savage beasts to tameness.

Above **Dionysus.** Like other gods, Dionysus had a number of icons attributed to him. These include his drinking cup, an ivy wreath, grape vines, and the thyrsus. Some accounts describe the thyrsus as being a long fennel stalk topped with ivy leaves.

Left **Dionysus and Silenus.** Silenus was the faithful tutor and companion of Dionysus. In his consistently drunken state, Silenus was often seen being propped up by satyrs, or being carried by a donkey.

Above *Pentheus and Dionysus* by J. Briot (c. 1610). Pentheus opposed the cult of Dionysus. After the king discovered that the Theban women had gone out to worship Dionysus on the mountain, Pentheus retaliated and imprisoned Dionysus and the women. Later, he found that the walls of the jail that held them crumbled of their own accord and they were set free.

Right *Pentheus Torn Apart by Maenads* by Berlin Painter (c. 500 B.C.– 460 B.C.). The Maenads, also known as Bacchantes or "Frenzied Ones," sometimes painted or tattooed their faces and arms to disguise themselves. They were endowed with great physical strength, which enabled them to tear apart wild beasts. Pentheus was no match for them.

Dionysus and his followers traveled to Egypt and across North Africa to Libya, revealing the secrets of winemaking everywhere they went. They reached India, with some difficulties along the way. At the River Euphrates, a local king tried to stop their progress, but Dionysus killed the king and then sent ivy and grapevines twining across the river until they were strong enough to serve as a bridge. Everywhere that people welcomed Dionysus, they experienced not only revelry but also good government, for he founded cities and restored order, but where he was opposed, he brought riot, madness, and death.

Lycurgus, the Thracian king of the Edonians, sent his army to stop these dangerous foreigners from invading his land. He captured all of Dionysus's followers, but the god escaped by jumping into the sea. Perhaps Dionysus and his satyrs put up little resistance because they were exhausted from their drinking the night before. His grandmother, Rhea, was ready once more to help, this time by taking vengeance on the king. She drove Lycurgus mad, and he started to hallucinate that he was pruning a grapevine. When he struck with his ax, it was no grapevine that he severed, but the neck of his own son, Dryas. Then he kept on cutting at the vine, or so he believed, but it was hands and feet that he was really pruning from his dead son's body. This deed so horrified the gods that they cursed the land of Thrace. Nothing would grow there, they decreed,

Bacchus, that first from out the purple grape Crush'd the sweet poison of misused wine.

JOHN MILTON (1608–1674), "COMUS"

until the criminal was punished. The Edonians did not want the blood-guilt of killing him themselves, and so they took him to a mountain where he was killed by wild horses.

Pentheus and the Bacchae

Pentheus was the king of Thebes and the nephew of Semele. When Dionysus arrived in Thebes, disguised as a mortal man, Pentheus thought that this fellow claiming godhead could only be an imposter, and his band of Bacchae could bring only trouble into the city. The king found it impossible to believe that Dionysus, the son of his own aunt, could be a god, for surely, he thought, all the gods had existed long before people came into the world. Even when the blind seer Teiresias told him that Dionysus was telling the truth, Pentheus refused to accept him as a god. He found it ridiculous that Theban women had gone out to worship this charlatan, and told Cadmus and the seer Teiresias how idiotic they were when they dressed themselves in fawn skins and took up the thyrsus, ready to join the Bacchae outside the city. He did not laugh, though, when he found that his own mother, Agave, had gone to join the Bacchae on the mountainside.

Dionysus stood in front of Pentheus, daring him to keep on disbelieving despite the consequences, but all that Pentheus could see was some ridiculously dressed troublemaker.

Even when Dionysus caused an earthquake to shake the palace walls, Pentheus would not believe. The god was determined to be honored in his own city, and to make sure that his mother, Semele, also received due honor. He put the idea into the king's head that Agave was disgracing herself and the royal house with scandalous orgies on the mountainside, along with the other women of Thebes. "It would

be sensible," Dionysus suggested, "for you to spy out what exactly they are up to, and you will have to dress as a woman to escape their notice. Everyone knows that they will tear apart any man who intrudes on their antics." Pentheus was now deeply under the god's influence, and he agreed to the whole plan. Dionysus dressed him as a woman and sent him on his way by night to spy on the so-called orgies of the Bacchantes.

The god then made the women of Thebes hallucinate as though they were drunk or drugged. They spotted Pentheus as he crept up the hill that night in his woman's clothing, but what they thought they saw was a mountain lion. They were fearless, intoxicated with the god's presence, and they took hold of Pentheus's body and tore it to pieces, believing that they were killing a wild animal. Agave tore off the head and proudly led the parade

DIONYSUS AS HUSBAND

Despite his reputation for orgies, Dionysus (Bacchus) was the only one of the gods except, perhaps, for the equally unlikely god of love, Eros (Cupid), to be totally faithful in marriage. He found Ariadne weeping on the island of Naxos, where Theseus had abandoned her. Dionysus married Ariadne and they had many children. She was made a goddess at their marriage, and Zeus (Jupiter) took the crown that she was wearing and set it in the sky as the Corona Borealis constellation.

Above *Dionysus and Ariadne* by Vecellio Tiziano (1487–1576). Ariadne was propelled into Dionysus's world of endless celebration.

back to Thebes, to show the men just how capable and strong the women had been. When Agave reached the palace, Dionysus lifted his hallucination from her mind and she saw what she had done. In her arms was no lion head, but the severed head of her own son, Pentheus. Agave cried out with grief and horror. Thebes had learned all too well that Dionysus was indeed a god.

Above **The triumph of Dionysus.** In many tales, as in the story of the sailors, Dionysus was associated with lions, panthers, lynxes, and tigers. He, too, is often dressed in the skin of a wild animal, with his head crowned with a wreath of ivy or vine leaves.

Dionysus and the Sailors

A Lydian ship was sailing for the island of Delos, when it ran short of fresh water. They were passing the island of Chios, and so they rowed to the shore and went looking for a spring. The captain went one way and his men went another. The captain found a stream and called his sailors to join him, but when they arrived, they brought with them a stranger. In both face and dress this person could have been either a young man or a young woman, but when he began to speak, there was no doubt that he was a man, or rather a boy. They had found him asleep in a field, and he was still half-asleep, smelling of the wine that he had been drinking.

The captain looked at the boy with awe, for he was as beautiful as any of the immortal gods, and his clothes were finer than any woven by mortals on a loom. He must be a god, the captain thought, and he started to pray, asking for forgiveness and help with their voyage. The sailors thought that this was ridiculous behavior. To them the boy was no more than a captive, a lucky find that they could put up for sale as a slave. They would not listen to the

Come, thou monarch of the vine, Plumpy Bacchus with pink eyne!

WILLIAM SHAKESPEARE (1564–1616),
ANTONY AND CLEOPATRA

captain when he forbade them to take the god on board. "A curse will fall on the ship and all of you," the captain began to say, but one of his men hit him in the stomach to keep him quiet. Then the crew set sail for Delos again, threatening to throw their captain overboard if he tried to stop them.

Dionysus woke up properly when the ship was out at sea, and asked where he was and where they were taking him. The sailors all put on friendly faces and swore that they would take him anywhere he wanted to go, but they had no intention of keeping their sacred oath. The captain refused to help in any way with the ship's voyage, fearing what would happen when the beautiful boy decided to punish his captors.

Before he showed himself to be a god, Dionysus tested the sailors, giving them one last chance to change their minds. He wept and begged them to pity him, saying that he was only a child and had done them no injury. They paid no attention to any of this, and just sailed on. Then the ship suddenly stopped dead in the water, even though some of the sailors were rowing and a breeze was filling the sails. The oars became too bulky and heavy to move through the water, for ivy twined thickly around them, and more ivy weighed down the sails. The boy seemed no longer a boy, but a grown man adorned with a wreath of vine leaves and grapes. It seemed as though he were surrounded by panthers and tigers and lynxes, all lying at his feet.

The sailors took fright and jumped overboard, and as they hit the water, their bodies changed, their skin grew dark, and their backs arched, their arms disappeared and their feet stretched out into the shape of a curved tail. They were now dolphins instead of men. Only the god-fearing captain lived on as a human being to tell his story.

90

Left **Io and Isis.** Io was forced to wander the land in the form of a white heifer. It was only when she reached Egypt that Zeus finally interceded and restored her to her natural form. Although she is shown here being received by the goddess Isis, the Egyptians worship Io and Isis as one and the same.

THE HOUSE OF CADMUS

The tale of Dionysus (Bacchus) about his mother, Semele, and his father, Zeus (Jupiter), and the death of his cousin, Pentheus, comes in the middle of a series of tales about the kingdom of Thebes and the shifts in fortune within the house of Cadmus that ruled it. Like many Greek myths, the story of the house of Cadmus goes back many generations, with the gods moving in and out of the tale. Many of the Greek myths about a family's fortunes, such as the stories about the house of Tantalus, begin with horror and end with almost everyone dead. The stories about the house of Cadmus are different, because after each catastrophe, things seem hopeful for a while, until the next disaster. The house of Cadmus always seems to gain a little breathing space before its next ordeal.

The Daughters of Danaus

The story goes back as far as Io's troubles with Zeus, when she wandered the earth in the form of a cow and eventually became a goddess. The son of Zeus and Io was called Epaphos, and he married the nymph, Memphis. Their daughter was called Libya, and she became the lover of the god Poseidon (Neptune), giving birth to twin boys, Belus and Agenor. Then Belus became the father of two boys, Danaus and Aegyptus. Many of these names relate to territories in North Africa: Egypt, Libya, and the Egyptian city of Memphis. Clearly, after Io's wanderings, the family flourished royally, and by the time Danaus and Aegyptus were born, Belus had two kingdoms at his disposal—Egypt, which he gave to Aegyptus, and Libya, which he gave to Danaus.

Things were not quite as harmonious as this, however, because Belus did not want to divide his kingdom. Indeed, his first idea was not to divide his kingdom into two parts, Libya and Egypt, but to arrange for his twin sons to share the rule of the whole, taking it in turns to be king. The twins balked at the idea, each suspicious that the other intended to oust him. Danaus married and fathered 50 daughters, while Aegyptus married and fathered 50 sons. It seemed obvious to Aegyptus that the way to trust and peace was to pair all these sons and daughters in marriage. The daughters of Danaus did not like the idea at all. If they married,

Below **Dionysus.** The festival of Dionysus is celebrated over two days, 16–17 March. The Greek god is equated with the Roman god Bacchus, and with the Italian god, Liber.

Above *The Rape of Europa* by Francesco Zuccarelli (1702–1788). Zeus and Europa became lovers, and as a result of their union, Europa bore three sons. In exchange for these children, Zeus gave Europa three gifts: Talus, a bronze man who guarded her island; a dog that never missed its prey; and a spear that never missed its mark.

they would lose their property rights to their husbands, so that Aegyptus and his sons would be the only winners.

Then Danaus began to suspect that the sons of Aegyptus might be planning to kill their brides as soon as they were married, to make absolutely sure that the kingdom of Libya would pass to their family. When an oracle confirmed his suspicions, he did not know how to resist the 50 strong warrior sons of his twin brother and enemy, about to arrive for their weddings. He prayed to Athene (Minerva) for help, and she advised that he and his daughters should flee from their home immediately. They sailed

> *Jupiter himself was turned into a satyr, a shepherd, a bull, a swan, a golden shower, and what not for love.*
>
> ROBERT BURTON (1577–1640), "ANATOMY OF MELANCHOLY"

to Argos as suppliants in a ship that Athene had helped Danaus to build. There they begged King Pelasgus to save them from the sons of Aegyptus, who would no doubt be on their heels.

Pelasgus was reluctant to help, not wishing to bring trouble on his own people by helping strangers. The Danaids, the daughters of Danaus, were desperate for his help, and they threatened to hang themselves in the temples of Argos if he tried to turn them away. Such an act would have polluted the land and infuriated the gods. Pelasgus had no choice but to help the women, and he promised that he would not let the sons of Aegyptus marry them by force.

THE SIEGE

Soon the 50 sons of Aegyptus were besieging King Pelasgus's city, and very soon after that, the city ran out of water. The people of Argos would die of thirst if they did not surrender or hand over the Danaids. "You must marry your cousins," Danaus told his daughters, "but let it be a fake marriage. They were planning to kill you once the marriages were celebrated; learn from your delightful bridegrooms how to conduct yourselves as married women. Here are some knives—use them well tonight."

The Danaids agreed to their father's plan, and the 50 sons of Aegyptus came into the city ready to celebrate their marriages. The women gritted their teeth as they kissed their new husbands, and once each pair was in bed and the man was falling asleep, the bride took out her hidden knife and slit his throat. So died 49 of the sons of Aegyptus. The fiftieth son was a kind and honorable man, called Lynceus, and he was married to the gentlest and kindest of the Danaids, Hypermnestra. She could not bring herself to kill him, just as he had resolved that he would never kill his new wife.

Eventually Danaus became king of Argos, and later still, Lynceus and Hypermnestra succeeded him as rulers of Argos. The other 49 daughters were polluted by blood-guilt, and though Hermes (Mercury) eventually purified them for the remainder of their lives on earth, they received an everlasting punishment when they died and went to the kingdom of Hades (Pluto). There they were forced to draw water in sieves, so that their task could never be completed. In the world of the living, however, it seemed as though family troubles had worked themselves through to a happy ending.

Zeus and Europa

The Danaids' grandfather, Belus, had a brother called Agenor, who was also the son of Poseidon, the god of the oceans. Agenor was king of Phoenicia and his children were not prone to quarreling or plotting against each other. Trouble came to them through Europa, Agenor's beautiful daughter. So remarkably beautiful was she, that she caught the eye of Zeus himself. Europa was never far from her brothers, and Zeus decided to pursue her with cunning as well as brute force. He ordered his son, Hermes, to drive all King Agenor's cattle down to the fields that bordered the sea. Then Zeus transformed himself into a bull, the most magnificent of animals, huge but seemingly gentle.

Europa could not resist patting the bull's head, then stroking his neck, hanging garlands on him, and feeding him with flowers. Finally, when he knelt down before her, she climbed onto his back. Zeus stood up and began to pace across the meadow toward the sea, then gently waded into the water, deeper and deeper, until he was swimming far out to sea. By the time Europa noticed, it was too late for her to escape. Zeus swam on with the speed of a god until he reached the island of Crete. There he took the form of an eagle, the bird of Zeus, and took the girl's virginity by force. She gave birth to three children from this rape, Minos, Sarpedon, and Rhadamanthus. The continent of Europe was named after her, while the constellation Taurus

Above *Danaids Punished by Bernard Picart (1673–1733)*. The 49 Danaids who killed their husbands escaped punishment during their lifetime; their father eventually found them new husbands by offering them as prizes in a footrace. Punishment after death, however, was another story.

THE NAME "PALLAS ATHENE"

Athene (Minerva) was a prudent goddess, a trait inherited from her mother, Metis (meaning "prudence" in Greek), but early in her life she once acted without thinking and regretted the outcome forever. She and her mortal friend Pallas were playing together, trying out their strength as warriors by casting spears at each other. Pallas protected himself with a shield, but the goddess's strength was too much for him and she struck him a killing blow with her spear. Athene bitterly regretted his death, and in his memory, she called herself from then on Pallas Athene, to remind herself in future to be more mindful of the difference between mortal men's puny powers and the immortal strength of a goddess.

Left *Pallas Athene*, Fontainebleau School (sixteenth century). Though famous for her armor, Athene was more than just the goddess of war. She was also the goddess of wisdom, the arts, industry, and skill.

commemorates Zeus's disguise as the bull. Europa's son, Minos, became king of Crete, and it now seemed for a while that this branch of the family had found its way to happiness.

Cadmus and the Founding of Thebes

Europa's family were left on the shore, watching helplessly as the bull carried her far out to sea. Her father, Agenor, ordered his sons Cadmus, Phoenix, Cilix, Thasus, and Phineus (the same man who was later harassed by Harpies), to scatter across the world in search of their sister, and not to return without her. Not knowing which direction to choose, Cadmus went first to Rhodes, then to Thera, but he could find no trace of Europa. In the end he consulted the oracle at Delphi, and was given some

enigmatic advice: "Abandon your quest for your sister. Find a milk-white cow that has never been put to the plow, and let her roam freely. Follow her until she falls to the ground, and that is the place where you must build a city." Cadmus could not understand why the oracle told him to abandon his search for Europa. He had no intention, however, of ignoring the god's advice, and so he wandered the lower slopes of Mount Parnassus until he found a milk-white heifer that had never been put to the plow. He came close and she ran away. He followed and she trotted onward, until finally, she fell to the ground in exhaustion. On this spot, Cadmus knew, was the place to build his new city.

Cadmus was well aware of the right way to found a city. The first thing to do was to sacrifice to the gods, and the white cow seemed just the right animal to offer them. A sacrifice needed not only a fine animal but also fire and water. Cadmus sent his men upstream in search of a spring, so that he could honor the gods with the first and freshest outpourings from the earth. They followed a stream back toward its source, into a cave where a monstrous serpent was waiting to attack them. The stream belonged to the god of war, Ares (Mars), and he was not at all willing to let strangers wander in and take its water without asking.

The serpent reared up and struck out with its fangs, again and again, until Cadmus's men were all dead. Then Cadmus himself went into the cave to find out why they were taking so long to fetch the water. Luckily, he was still wearing his armor and carrying his spear and shield. It took all of Cadmus's agility and strength to kill Ares' snake, and this killing offended the god of war still more. "Agenor's son has killed my snake," Ares' harsh voice rang out, "and I demand compensation. Turn to snake, Cadmus, and take over the guarding of my cave."

Cadmus glanced down at his body, expecting he would never see it again in human form, but the goddess Athene whispered in his ear, "No t[ime] for that! Go to the dead snake and pull out its t[eeth] as fast as you can, then sow them in the field." Cadmus recognized the goddess's voice. He did understand what she was telling him to do, but was quick to obey. The goddess helped him bre[ak] apart the serpent's jaw, showering the ground w[ith]

falling teeth. Everywhere a tooth fell, it sank into the ground and the earth began to bulge. By the time he finished, the mounds of earth were breaking apart and out of them were stepping warriors in full armor. It was a whole army, and they were all threatening Cadmus. He prayed to Athene for help, and heard her whisper in his ear, "All you need to do is to throw a rock toward them."

The warriors did not notice the rock until it hit one of them, and then they started to blame one another. One of them hit the man next to him, then a couple more hit him, and soon the whole army was fighting itself with spear and sword. Cadmus watched as one after another, the men fell down dead. There were only five men left standing when Athene called out, "Stop!" Once they realized that a goddess was helping Cadmus, these five men agreed to help him build the city as the oracle had prophesied. This was how the city of Thebes was founded.

Above *Cadmus and the Dragon* by Francesco Zuccarelli (1702–1788). Cadmus first tried to crush the serpent with a huge stone, but it made no impression. Eventually he killed it with his spear. Some say that the serpent was the offspring of Ares.

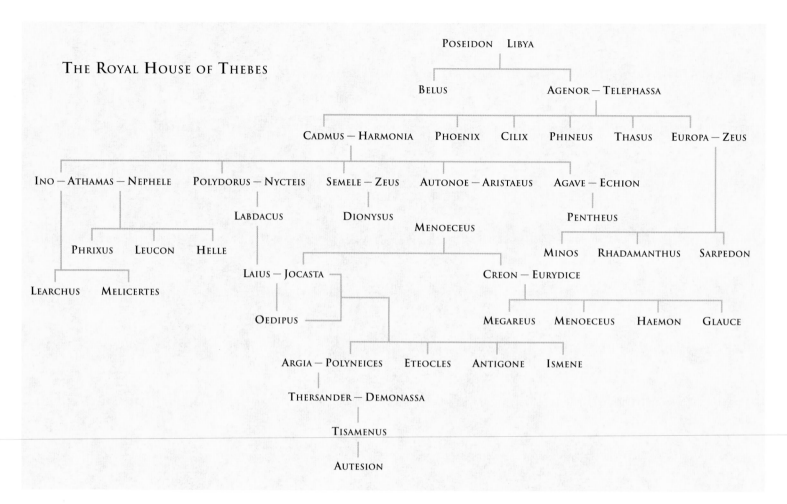

THE ROYAL HOUSE OF THEBES

POSEIDON — LIBYA

BELUS · AGENOR — TELEPHASSA

CADMUS — HARMONIA · PHOENIX · CILIX · PHINEUS · THASUS · EUROPA — ZEUS

INO — ATHAMAS — NEPHELE · POLYDORUS — NYCTEIS · SEMELE — ZEUS · AUTONOE — ARISTAEUS · AGAVE — ECHION

LABDACUS · DIONYSUS · MENOECEUS · PENTHEUS

PHRIXUS · LEUCON · HELLE · MINOS · RHADAMANTHUS · SARPEDON

LEARCHUS · MELICERTES · LAIUS — JOCASTA · CREON — EURYDICE

OEDIPUS · MEGAREUS · MENOECEUS · HAEMON · GLAUCE

ARGIA — POLYNEICES · ETEOCLES · ANTIGONE · ISMENE

THERSANDER — DEMONASSA

TISAMENUS

AUTESION

Disasters for the House of Cadmus

At first all went well in Thebes. Cadmus served Ares for eight years as a punishment for killing his serpent, and then married Harmonia, the daughter of Ares and Aphrodite (Venus). All the gods of Olympus came to the wedding, and it seemed as if the house of Cadmus would now flourish in harmony, befriended by all Olympus. Harmonia was given wonderful wedding presents by the gods. Aphrodite presented her with a golden necklace made by Hephaestus (Vulcan), which gave its wearer a beauty that no man could resist. Athene gave her a golden robe that invested her with the dignity of a ruler. Hermes gave her a lyre, and Demeter (Ceres) gave the gift of fertility by frolicking in the fields with her new lover, Jasion. Some of the wedding guests thought that Demeter's behavior was scandalous, but it did lead to plentiful harvests in the fields and a wealth of children for Theban families. The king and queen had four daughters, Autonoe, Agave, Ino, and Semele, and one son, Polydorus. Then the troubles began again.

Autonoe's son was that same Actaeon whom Artemis (Diana) turned into a stag when he came upon her bathing naked after the hunt. Semele was the woman who demanded that her mysterious lover reveal his true identity, and was burned to ashes when Zeus was forced to show himself as a god in divine glory. Then came more troubles when Cadmus handed over the kingship of Thebes to Agave's son Pentheus. The new king sneered at the twice-born son of Semele, Dionysus, and the god drove Agave mad, so that she tore off her own son's head, believing that he was a lion. Cadmus was prudent enough to worship Dionysus as soon as he appeared in Thebes, and so there was no reason for the god to punish him. But Cadmus remembered Ares' anger when he had killed the serpent long ago, and kept wondering if all the disasters that his children and grandson endured could be traced back to that well-meant intrusion into Ares' cave for water. Cadmus offered himself up to Dionysus as a willing victim, and his wife Harmonia did so too, in order to put an end to the miseries befalling their house. The god transformed them into snakes. And so, years after Cadmus's fight with the serpent, Ares' curse had come true, but not in anger. When Cadmus and Harmonia died in their snake form, Zeus sent them to the Elysian Fields to live forever among the blessed dead.

Right **Cadmus, Harmonia, and Apollo.** The gods left the comfort of their home on Mount Olympus to attend the wedding of Cadmus and Harmonia. As a wedding present, the gods gave Harmonia a robe, and a necklace specially wrought for the occasion by Hephaestus.

THE HOUSE OF OEDIPUS

After the founding of Thebes by Cadmus, and after the follies of Pentheus in not accepting Dionysus (Bacchus) as a god, the troubles of Cadmus's family were still not ended. Pentheus was succeeded as king by his son, then his grandson, and it seemed as if the gods were no longer paying attention to this royal house. But then came the turn of Laius to become king, and a fresh brew of troubles began. Laius married Jocasta, and when they had no children, he asked the oracle of Delphi for advice. The oracle responded with a message that, for once, seemed unambiguous. Laius's son would kill his father.

Laius was beside himself with grief and anxiety when he heard this, and his worries grew when he returned to Thebes and found that Jocasta was pregnant. The royal pair decided that if this child were a boy, he would have to die, to avert the oracle. However, oracles are impossible for human beings to circumvent. The king and queen did not want the blood-guilt of killing their child, or of ordering him to be killed, and when a son was indeed born to Jocasta, they ordered him to be taken to Mount Cithaeron and exposed to the elements. Everyone believed that this meant certain death, but there was always the remote possibility that such a child might be rescued and adopted by someone else. Thus there was no actual blood-guilt for the miserable parents.

The unlikely happened. The baby was taken to Mount Cithaeron to die, but first his ankles were pierced through with iron rods. That is how he

Left **Consulting an oracle.** The priestess sat on a tripod, which was positioned above a fissure in the floor of the temple. Strange, hallucinating vapors rose up from the floor, and in a state of trance, the priestess would mumble her answer.

Below *The Finding of Oedipus,* French School (seventeenth century). Overwhelmed with pity for the baby, the herdsman did not abandon Oedipus, but instead gave him to the care of a Corinthian peasant. Oedipus was saved from dying from exposure on the hillside.

Above **Detail from a crater showing Oedipus and the Sphinx, attributed to the Painter of the Birth of Dionysus.** The Greek Sphinx was an evil creature of death, destruction, and general misfortune. She struck fear into the hearts of everyone except Oedipus, who managed to outwit the beast.

Right *Sibyl* **by Lorenzo Ghiberti (1378–1455).** "Sibyl" was the name given to those prophetesses who prophesied while in a state of ecstasy inspired by the god Apollo. Two of the most famous Greek Sibyls are the Cumaean Sibyl and the Erythaean Sibyl.

himself might all have been averted. But the oracle chose to tell Oedipus about his future, not his past. He would be the most accursed of mortals, he was told. He would marry his own mother and kill his own father.

The Oracle Comes True

Oedipus was distraught. He swore to himself that he would never return to Corinth. If he kept away, he would be in no danger of marrying Merope or killing Polybus. All might yet be well. He was hurrying down the road to a place where three roads met, a place of ill luck sacred to the goddess Hecate. Coming toward him was a chariot, and the driver and the passenger rudely demanded that he step aside and let them pass. Oedipus was not about to yield to rudeness. He stood in the middle of the road, refusing to budge. The driver swore at him, and then the passenger, an elderly man, struck out at him with a staff. Oedipus struck back, and killed the passenger, the driver, and all their companions except one, a man who ran away.

Oedipus walked on, a long and weary journey, until he was close to the city of Thebes. The people that he met on the road were full of the city's bad news. Its king, Laius, had just been killed by some villains, while he was far away on a journey, and a monster, the Sphinx, was attacking and killing everyone who tried to get in and out of the city. Queen Jocasta had promised that whoever killed the Sphinx would become king of Thebes and gain her as his wife.

The Sphinx was a monster with the head and upper body of a woman and the lower body of a lion, and she liked to play with her victims. She offered not to kill and eat them, if they could answer a riddle. The road past Mount Phicion, where the Sphinx waited for her next victim, was covered with bones of men who had failed to find the right answer. Oedipus decided that he would try his wits with the monster, and walked along the road

received his name, Oedipus, which in Greek means "swollen foot." The Theban shepherd who took him to the mountain did not abandon him there, but gave him to a Corinthian shepherd, who took him to his king and queen, Polybus and Merope. This pair were longing for a baby to adopt, since they could not bring one into the world themselves. Merope treated the child as her own, and in a little while everyone seemed to have forgotten that he was not the royal heir of Corinth by blood.

It was not until he was nearly grown up that Oedipus heard the story that he was not the true son of Merope and Polybus, and when he asked the king and queen for the truth of the matter, they swore that he was their son by blood. But then he heard another rumor that he was an adopted child, and he determined to find out the truth. If he could not be sure who among mortals was speaking the truth, surely the oracle of Apollo at Delphi would not lie. It was a long journey from Corinth to Delphi, and when he arrived, the oracle did not even answer his question. If only it had told him what he asked, the miseries that befell his family and that passed by Mount Phicion. There the Sphinx was waiting for him, and once he was in earshot, she asked, "What goes on four feet in the morning, then two at noon, then three in the evening?" Oedipus did not panic, like those who had left their bones on the hillside. He thought for a moment and answered, "A human being, for people go on four feet when they are babies, then on two feet as adults, and then, when they are old and infirm, they use a walking stick as a third foot to balance them." This was the correct answer. Enraged, the Sphinx threw herself down the mountainside and died on the rocks below. Oedipus had won for himself the kingship of Thebes and its queen for his wife.

Oedipus the King

All went well for King Oedipus for a while, and his mother-wife Jocasta gave birth to four children by her son-husband, two sons, Polyneices and Eteocles, and two daughters, Antigone and Ismene. Oedipus was loved by his people, and regarded as the wisest of rulers. Years passed, and then a plague came to Thebes, making the whole countryside barren. Crops failed, and there were no new births of children or animals. Such a disaster

meant that the gods were displeased with the city; someone must be polluting Thebes by their presence. Oedipus sent a servant to the oracle at Delphi to ask for its advice. When the servant returned, he brought the answer that it was the murderer of Laius who was at fault. The city would not be healed until the murderer was punished.

Oedipus turned to the blind Teiresias to help find the murderer, for he was famous throughout Greece for his supreme skills as a prophet. Teiresias refused to help him, saying that he would not bring pain on the king, but Oedipus insisted, anxious to fulfill his duty as a king and punish the murderer of Laius.

THE OEDIPUS COMPLEX

Sigmund Freud developed a theory about the early life of children in which they find and organize satisfaction in a variety of ways. In what Freud called the Oedipus complex, a boy chooses an object of satisfaction based on his mother, who has satisfied such basic needs as feeding and nurturing. This love of the mother brings him into rivalry with his father. Girls have to overcome their initial attachment to the mother to form an affectionate relationship with their father, and then relate to the mother as a rival. Freud believed that the myth of Oedipus, as dramatized by Sophocles, held the key to this organization of sexual difference and satisfaction. For Sigmund Freud, this powerful Greek myth spoke one of the most formative truths of the human unconscious mind.

Right **Oedipus kills his father.** Unaware that King Laius, who was one of the travelers in a group Oedipus met on the road, was really his father, Oedipus killed him after a heated argument.

Above *Oedipus* by **Ernest Hillemacher (1818–1887).** Overcome with the horror of his crimes, Oedipus punished himself by stabbing his eyes until he was blind. That way he was unable to look at the misery he had caused.

Eventually Teiresias revealed that the murderer was Oedipus himself. Oedipus was a wise king, but when he heard this revelation, he could not accept the gods' truth. He cast around for someone to blame. Teiresias must have lied, Oedipus reassured himself, and Jocasta's brother Creon must have conspired with him because he wanted the kingship for himself.

Still the king fretted over the oracle, for the plague still tormented the land, the animals, and the people of Thebes. He decided to investigate the murder of Laius to the best of his ability. The only

thing of which he could be certain was that the murderer was not himself, for everyone knew that Laius had been killed by a group of rogues, while the murders that Oedipus had committed near Delphi, he had done without help. He tried talking his thoughts over with Jocasta, but what she said did not comfort him at all. She wanted to reassure him by telling him of an oracle that she and her previous husband, Laius, had thwarted years ago. The oracle had said that Laius's son would kill his father, yet the child had been exposed on the mountain and died.

It was some completely unrelated villains who had lain in wait at the intersection of three roads near Delphi and ambushed Laius's chariot.

OEDIPUS DISCOVERS THE TRUTH

Oedipus could hardly bear to listen to this. It was at the intersection of three roads near Delphi that he had killed the elderly man and his servants. He began to dread the unfolding of the truth, but he knew that for the sake of his people, he must not stop investigating who had killed Laius. Now he sent for the herdsman who had exposed the baby and who, it turned out, was also the man who had run away from the fight where Laius had died. Oedipus was horrified when the servant admitted that it was just one man who had killed the king of Thebes, and that the story about a crowd of villains was only an exaggeration to excuse his cowardice in running away. Oedipus heard all this with difficulty, and his wife begged him to stop the investigation then and there. Then she ran out of the room, as she realized that he was on the point of discovering all the truth. The servant admitted that the baby he had been ordered to expose on Mount Cithaeron had been taken by a Corinthian shepherd to be adopted by Merope and Polybus. Oedipus could not escape

the chain of evidence. It was he, Oedipus, who had killed his father and married his mother, while trying so hard to avoid any contact with them. It was he, Oedipus, who had brought plague on his people. His sons and daughters were the product of incest. His mother-wife—and there he stopped thinking and ran after her—Jocasta had killed herself, hanging herself by a rope from the roof beam of the royal bedroom.

Oedipus vowed that he would never again look on the miseries of his family, his wretched wife and children. He took up the brooches from Jocasta's garments and stabbed his eyes blind. "Bring up my children well," he implored Jocasta's brother Creon, "for you must be regent in Thebes until my sons are old enough to take the throne. Let me be led to Mount Cithaeron, where I should have died as a baby, and perhaps the gods will finally be willing to take my life now." Creon agreed to all of this, and the great King Oedipus left his kingdom, the most wretched of men.

Oedipus at Colonus

Oedipus did not die quickly after he had blinded himself and stumbled out of Thebes. He lived for many years, treated by the kings of neighboring city-states with a mixture of honor and dread. Here was a most unfortunate man, one whose deeds had broken the laws of gods and men, guilty and yet blameless for what he did. No one wanted to call down the wrath of the gods for sheltering someone so accursed; no one wanted to be the gods' target

Below *Antigone from "Antigone" by Sophocles* by Marie Stillman (1844–1927). Antigone was determined that the body of her brother would be treated with respect. Defying the king's orders, she secretly performed a ceremonial burial by sprinkling dust on him. Some versions of the story say she burned his body on a funeral pyre.

for not protecting a suppliant. When he was close to death, Oedipus was summoned by Apollo to Athens, where the just and merciful King Theseus ruled. Just outside the city, at Colonus, the blind man entered the sanctuary of the Erinyes, the Furies, whose secret place all other people feared to enter. Finally, Oedipus found peace of heart in the sacred grove dedicated to those dreaded beings whose task is to punish the minds of the guilty. He had transcended human shame and guilt, and was now favored by the gods. Oedipus was said to be buried in the sanctuary

For the gods, though slow to see, see well, whenever a man casting aside worship turns folly.

SOPHOCLES (C. 496 B.C.–C. 406 B.C.), *OEDIPUS COLONUS*

at Colonus, but the only person to know his final fate was King Theseus. The Athenians believed that his bones were buried there, or that he had descended to the underworld from Colonus. His body had the power to protect the place of his death, and the Athenians long prided themselves on being the one state to welcome Oedipus on his sorrowful wanderings.

The Sons and Daughters of Oedipus

Once again, things went well for a while. Creon ruled well and justly until Eteocles and Polyneices came of age. They agreed to share the kingship in alternating years, one year for Polyneices and the next for Eteocles. Polyneices ruled well for his first year, and then handed over the kingship to his brother, but at the end of the next year Eteocles would not relinquish the crown. Polyneices was forced into exile, where he found allies in the exiled Tydeus of Calydon and King Adrastos of Argos. They assembled a mighty army of Argives, divided into seven smaller armies under seven commanders, to attack the seven gates of Thebes.

Creon advised Eteocles not to attempt full-scale battle but to send out seven champions to fight in single combat at the seven gates, against the seven battle leaders of Polyneices's army. Polyneices himself did not die there, but the six other commanders did. One of them, an Argive called Capaneus, was killed by Zeus (Jupiter) himself. Capaneus was an insolent fellow, who swore that he would win through even if Zeus were to try to stop him. He brought a ladder to climb the wall surrounding Thebes, and he was just about to jump into the city when Zeus's thunderbolt knocked him back to the ground and killed him. Now Polyneices's Argive army retreated a little way, and a general battle began. Eteocles called out in a loud voice, "Men of Argos, do not die for a cause which is not yours! Let the issue be decided in single combat between Polyneices and myself." Polyneices was eager for the fight, and the two brothers fought until both were streaked with blood and sweat. The end came quickly, Polyneices stabbed through the stomach by Eteocles, Eteocles mortally wounded by Polyneices. They fell dead almost in one another's arms.

CREON AS KING

The armies disbanded; the war was over. The new king of Thebes would be Creon, Jocasta's brother. His first decree as king was that Eteocles should be buried as befitted a king of Thebes, but that the rebel Polyneices should be left in the dust as food for the dogs. Creon's second decree as king was that anyone caught trying to bury Polyneices would be put to death. So began the next round of troubles for the children of Oedipus.

One of Oedipus's daughters, Ismene, was a pliant young woman who wanted nothing more than to live a quiet life, and she was determined to obey the new king, Creon, and leave her brother to rot outside the walls of Thebes. His other daughter, Antigone, was as firm-minded as her father-brother Oedipus. She planned to bury her brother, if only symbolically, by scattering a little dust over his corpse. She made her way out that night, and succeeded in reaching the body and pouring a handful of dust over it, but the next day the furious king ordered the body to be brushed clean again. Anyone who disobeyed and was caught would die a very unpleasant death. Again Antigone went out, took up a handful of dust, and sprinkled it on the body. This time she was caught.

Above **Burial denied.** King Creon forbade the proper burial of the rebels. He commanded that the bodies be left on the battlefield as dog's fodder. This decree was offensive to his people and the gods.

Below **Antigone, Eteocles, and a woman carrying a hydria to the tomb of Oedipus.** When he died, Oedipus was finally at peace. Some myths say that his daughters remained faithful to him throughout his wanderings.

Creon found himself in a painful position. Antigone was only doing her duty by her dead brother, and every Greek could sympathize with a sister wanting to help her beloved brother to go to the underworld, rather than have him linger as an uneasy ghost. Yet she had disobeyed the first edict of the king of Thebes by giving succor to someone who had invaded the kingdom with an army. As a king, Creon felt that he could not yield his authority to a girl. As a father, he had a still more difficult decision to make. Antigone was soon to be married to his own son, Haemon. It would have been possible to forgive her, Creon thought, if only the wretched girl would promise not to try to bury her brother a third time; but Antigone would not consider such a promise. Instead, she swore that she would keep on trying to bury her brother properly until Creon had her executed.

In exasperation, the king ordered her to be buried alive. As so often in Greek myth, he was trying to avoid the blood-guilt of actually ordering her to be killed, in the knowledge that lack of air or starvation would soon enough kill her for him. Antigone went to her death in triumph, knowing that what she had done would please the gods. Haemon pleaded with her to change her mind, and then, when she would not listen, secretly joined her in her prison.

ANTIGONE'S DEATH

While Antigone was still on her way to her place of entombment, the blind prophet Teiresias came to give Creon a last chance to change his mind. Teiresias told the king that what he was doing offended the gods and would mean the ruin of his family line. Creon blustered and then suddenly gave in, ordering his men to run after the guards who had been leading Antigone to her death,

and countermand his order. It was too late. There in the burial chamber, she had already hanged herself, and when Creon himself arrived, his son Haemon despairingly committed suicide next to his beloved Antigone. The king knew that his own wife would be the next to kill herself out of grief for her dead son.

This is how the line of Cadmus came to an end. Perhaps Ismene lived on, perhaps she married and had children, but those of Oedipus's children who most resembled him, his stubborn sons and daughter Antigone, were all dead. Jocasta's bloodline was coming to an end as well, with the deaths of Creon's wife and son. The long-drawn-out story of Oedipus and his children is characterized by themes of obstinacy, defiance, and readiness to face death. The larger sequence of myths about the house of Cadmus lurches between times of good rule, prosperity, orderliness, and quiet, and times of trouble that strained sufferers beyond the limits of their humanity. But what else could Antigone have done, and still been true to herself? What else could Oedipus have done, or his parents, other than trying to avert the prophecy? Their tragedy was inescapable, and yet it was also the opportunity for Oedipus, tormented seeker after truth, and Antigone, dauntless honorer of the gods' law, to achieve heights of heroism to which none of the Greek warriors came close.

GANYMEDE

Ganymede, the son of King Tros of Troy, was an exceptionally handsome young man. Zeus (Jupiter) found him desirable, and changed himself into the form of an eagle to abduct him from Troy. He snatched Ganymede into the air with his claws and carried him to Olympus, much to the annoyance of his wife Hera (Juno). Annoying Hera further, Zeus made Ganymede cupbearer to the gods, a task which had previously been carried out by Hebe, the daughter of Zeus and Hera. Zeus went further still, commemorating his love for Ganymede in the constellation Aquarius, the waterbearer.

Left *Ganymede* by **Benvenuto Cellini (1500–1571).** Zeus's liaison with Ganymede saw Zeus infatuated and Hera outraged once more. The affair is believed by some to be a religious justification for homosexuality within the Greek culture.

Above *Danae* by **Francesco Primaticcio (1504–1570).** Not even an impermeable brass tower could dampen Zeus's desires. By transforming himself into a shower of gold pouring down into Danae's lap, he fathers Perseus.

Left *Danae and the Brazen Tower* by **Sir Edward Burne-Jones (1833–1898).** Hoping to change his fate, the king imprisoned his daughter Danae. In some stories the prison is described as a bronze tower, while in others, it is an underground chamber.

the tower, Acrisius did not find out about Danae's son Perseus until he was four years old. Perseus grew up to be an active child, making so much noise that he could be heard even through the tower walls, and that was how Danae's secret became known. Acrisius was beside himself with anger and perplexity. How had any lover found his way to Danae? And how could he destroy Perseus without incurring blood-guilt? Acrisius ordered a large wooden chest to be built, and the mother and baby to be put inside it. Then it was cast adrift on the sea, where the king hoped that the pair would die.

Almost all oracles come true, however hard people fight against them. Perseus and Danae survived their time in the wooden chest, which was caught in a net by a fisherman near the island of Seriphus. The fisherman, Dictys, took the child and his mother to the court of King Polydectes, who was very much attracted to Danae. For years he courted her, but she kept refusing him, saying that she was devoted only to her son. One day the king invited Danae to a feast along with Perseus, who was by now a young man. All the guests ate and drank well. Polydectes asked each man present to give him a horse, pretending that he needed them for his courtship of a distant princess. Perhaps the wine went to Perseus's head, for after admitting that he had no horse to give, he found himself promising that he

PERSEUS

Acrisius was the king of Argos, and his life was made miserable by an oracle, which prophesied that his grandson, the child of his daughter Danae, would kill him. In order to thwart this prophecy, he kept his daughter indoors, virtually in prison, shut up in a tower of brass. This was no obstacle to the king of the gods, Zeus (Jupiter), who manifested in Danae's lap in a shower of gold. Soon she became pregnant by the god, but because she was hidden in

Right *Medusa* by Glen Vause. Some people believe that the mythological beheading of the Gorgon Medusa symbolizes the domination of patriarchal society. "Medusa," which means "sovereign female wisdom," had been silenced, and her powers had been brought under the control of the male order.

Below *Study for Perseus and the Graiae* by Sir Edward Burne-Jones (1833–1898). The three Graiae or "gray ones" were sisters. They were guardians of the Gorgons. Gray-haired from birth, the siblings were Deino ("dread"), Enyo ("horror"), and Pemphredo ("alarm").

would do anything to please the king. He would even kill the monster Medusa. That was just what Polydectes had been hoping to hear, to give him an excuse to get rid of the inconvenient young man, and instead of treating it as the wine talking, he promptly accepted Perseus's kind offer.

Athene (Minerva) and Hermes (Mercury) liked young Perseus, and were waiting for him next morning with good advice and gifts. Athene gave him the equipment he needed to fight Medusa—a bag, a shield burnished as bright as any mirror, and a helmet that had once belonged to Hades (Pluto), the god of the underworld. This helmet made its wearer invisible. Hermes gave him a curved sword like a sickle and a pair of sandals with wings, rather like his own ankle wings. Athene told him to try out his wings by flying to the kingdom of Night, to the home of the Graiae, the only ones who knew just where to find Medusa.

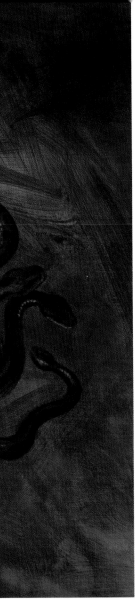

ancient deities who shared a single eye that they took in and out of their empty eye sockets, and a single tooth that they took in and out of their gummy mouths. Perseus was ready to fight them, but Athene urged him to use cleverness, not force. He waited just by the entrance to their cave with Hades' helmet on his head, to make him invisible, but the Graiae could feel that someone was there. "Give me the eye, sister," insisted one of them, and blindly stretched out her hand. The one with the eye reluctantly eased it out and for a moment, all three Graiae were blind. In darted Perseus, grabbing the eye out of her hand. Then he waited for one of the panic-stricken goddesses to take out their one tooth, to pass it to the next, and immediately grabbed it as well. Once they were at his mercy, he told them that he would give them back their precious tooth and eye only on one condition: that they would tell him where to find Medusa. The Graiae had no choice but to mutter the directions that he asked for. In some accounts he gave the eye and tooth back to the sisters, but some say that he threw them into the depths of a lake, leaving the Graiae in despair.

Medusa

Medusa was one of the three Gorgon sisters. They were the daughters of a sea god, and lived far from the lands of mortal men and women on an island in the remotest ocean. Two of these Gorgons, Euryale and Stheno, were immortal, but their sister Medusa could be killed. In some versions of the story, however, Medusa was not the immortals' sister by birth, but a mortal woman who had been punished by Athene for intruding on her mysteries, or

the virgin goddess's temple. Athene did not take away Medusa's beauty, but turned her hair to a wild tangle of snakes and condemned her to lurk in the darkness, unable ever to be intimate with a man. Anyone who looked at her with love in his eyes would instantly turn to stone. In many accounts and many works of art, Medusa is represented as hideously ugly, with a fat tongue protruding from her mouth, but she is sometimes portrayed as a serenely beautiful woman whose snakes are regal ornaments on her head, rather than loathsome disfigurements.

Perseus used the helmet of invisibility to make his way into the cave where the Gorgons were sleeping, and he used the mirrorlike shield to look for Medusa indirectly, staring at her reflection as he came closer and drew his sickle sword. The Gorgon's snaky hair writhed, sensing danger, but she could see nothing to strike at. Out of nowhere flashed the sword, and cut off her head. Even in death, the terrible head had the power to turn to stone anyone who looked directly at it. Perseus thrust the bleeding thing into his bag and flew away. He needed all the swiftness and agility of his winged sandals to outfly the other Gorgons, but eventually they were left behind, thrashing about and wailing in the darkness.

As soon as he had cut off Medusa's head, out of her severed neck sprang the winged horse, Pegasus, and a fully grown human warrior, Chrysaor, her children by Poseidon. Medusa's blood dripped from the bag as Perseus flew onward over the deserts of Libya, and each drop turned into a different kind of snake. Eventually the hero became tired and wanted to rest, but when he tried to land in northwest Africa, the Titan Atlas pushed him back into the sky, because an oracle had once told him that he would be robbed by a son of Zeus. When Atlas would not let him land, Perseus pulled the head out of the bag, and the gigantic Titan was robbed of life and turned into an even more gigantic mountain range, the Atlas Mountains that to this day hold up the sky with their summits.

Below **Perseus and Medusa.** The Greek Medusa is an import from Libya where she was worshipped by the Libyan Amazons as their Serpent Goddess. Originally symbolizing wisdom, female mysteries, and the cycles of nature, she was eventually made instead into an evil monster.

Left **Gorgon.** The Gorgons' powers were greatly respected. The Gorgon mask symbolized fierce strength and power. These masks were often used in temples and sanctuaries and even in battle on the armor of the warriors.

Styx was one of the six rivers of the underworld, and an oath by the waters of Styx was the most binding oath that a god could take. When an oath was sworn in Olympus by the Styx, the goddess of the rainbow, Iris, sped to the river to fetch its water in a golden cup. Those who drank the water and swore a false oath were punished with a year of sickness and silence, starved of nectar and ambrosia, and were then banished from Olympus for another nine years.

Opposite page *Crossing the Styx* by Joachim Patenir (Patinir) (c. 1485–c. 1524). The Styx is said to wind around Hades nine times. The other rivers of Hades are Acheron, Cocytus, Phlegethon, Lethe, and Aornis.

Andromeda and the Monster

Perseus flew on, delighting in the speed with which he could travel to the farthest north and then the south. As he flew across the sea to the coast of Ethiopia, he saw a huge rock on the beach with a naked young woman chained to it. She had been struggling, for her arms and legs were bruised from the chains, but now she was rigid with terror, looking out to sea where a monstrous serpent was riding the waves toward her.

Below *Perseus and Andromeda* by Pierre Puget (1620–1694). Perseus swooped down from the sky to rescue Andromeda from the sea monster. Some say his winged sandals were a gift from Hermes, while other accounts name the Graiae as the gift-bearers.

The woman in chains was Andromeda, daughter of King Cepheus and Queen Cassiopeia. This queen was as foolish as Niobe, daring to set herself up as equal to the gods in beauty and, as with Niobe, her boasting ended in tears. Cassiopeia claimed that she was more beautiful than any of the sea nymphs, more beautiful than Hera (Juno) herself, and the sea god Poseidon retaliated by laying the country waste with floods of water and sending a sea serpent to attack the people. Cepheus consulted the oracle of Zeus to find out how to save his country from flood and monster, and was told that only the willing sacrifice of his own daughter would placate the god of the sea. That morning, the wretched parents had walked in tearful procession to the sacrificial rock to chain down their weeping daughter, just as Psyche's parents wept when taking her to a marriage with death.

Perseus flung himself downward, sickle sword in his hand, and tore gashes in the serpent's coils until it died. Then he slashed Andromeda's chains apart and carried her back to her parents, though he longed to keep her in his arms. What could the king do but consent to Perseus's marriage with his daughter, even though she had already been promised to her uncle, Phineus?

Andromeda did not want to marry her uncle, but he very much wanted to marry her, and at the wedding feast he and his men started to cause trouble. Perseus knew just how to silence their angry tongues; he took the dripping head of the Gorgon out of its bag, and as Phineus and his men looked at it, they turned to stone. Some say that Cassiopeia also objected to her daughter's marriage, and like Phineus, was turned to stone. It seems more likely, though, that she was overjoyed with her daughter's rescue, for Poseidon eventually forgave her and commemorated her in the night sky as a constellation, close to the constellation Cepheus that commemorated her husband. Poseidon's sea monster can also be found in the sky as the constellation Cetus. Perseus and Andromeda were also given constellations as a memorial at their death, with the star Algol representing the head of Medusa in Perseus's hand.

LATER YEARS

It was many years before Perseus and Andromeda grew old and died. Before they could settle to a happy marriage, Perseus had affairs to resolve with two kings. First he took vengeance on Polydectes, the king who had tried to send him to his death. He flew back to Polydectes' palace and told the king that he had killed Medusa, as promised, but Polydectes accused him of idle boasting. The king summoned all his people to the marketplace, to put the liar to public shame. No one would believe Perseus's claim, except for his mother, Danae, and the fisherman, Dictys, who had rescued both of them from the sea. "Cover your eyes," Perseus told Danae and Dictys, and then he pulled Medusa's head once more from the bag and held it up high,

so that everyone could see. In that instant, the marketplace became full of stone statues instead of living people.

After that mass extermination, Athene decided that the head of Medusa was too potent for any mortal to use as a weapon, and she took it for herself. It adorns her aegis, the goatskin that she wears when she goes armed into battle. Perseus gave back the helmet of invisibility and the winged sandals, but he still had one task to accomplish, seeking out and forgiving King Acrisius who had forced Danae into the tower and then sent mother and son out onto the sea in a wooden chest to die. Acrisius was hiding in the city of Larissa, assuming that Perseus was coming to kill

The Gorgon's head
its leaden eyeballs rolled,
And writhed its snaky horrors
through the shield

OSCAR WILDE (1854–1900),
"CHARMIDES"

him. Even when he discovered that the head of Medusa was no longer in Perseus's bag, he found it hard to believe that his life was not in danger. Perseus suggested a ritual of reconciliation, and then joined in an athletics contest being held in Larissa. He entered the discus competition, and when he hurled the discus, it somehow flew the wrong way and hit Acrisius on the foot. The king was an old man by then, and the pain and shock killed him. The oracle had come true, and he had died by the hands of his own grandson. Was it an accident, though, with the discus just happening to slip sideways as Perseus threw it, or did it fly true to his feelings, if not his conscious intent?

Above **The wounded Chimaera.** The Chimaera, offspring of Typhon and Echidna, was a ferocious fire-breathing monster. It was believed that the Chimaera represented a volcanic mountain of the same name in Lycia, the peak of which was the home to lions, the middle part was where goats resided, and the foot was the home of serpents.

Opposite page *Mount Helicon with God Pegasus and Centaur Cheiron and Fountain Hippocrene with Zodiac Sign Sagittarius by Giovanni Falconetto (1458–1534).* Mount Helicon was part of a range of mountains in western Boeotia, not far from the Gulf of Corinth. Both the Hippocrene and Aganippe springs began here, and it was the abode of the god Apollo, leader of the muses.

Right **Poseidon.** Poseidon was the god of the sea and earthquakes, and was associated with dolphins, horses, and bulls. In art, Poseidon was usually represented as a tall, bearded, powerfully built man in the prime of his life. It is often difficult to distinguish his figure from that of Zeus.

TALES OF REVENGE

Both gods and humans frequently sought revenge in Greek myth. Taking revenge was a normal and acceptable action for a man in Greek myth, but not for a woman. In the story of Jason and Medea, for instance, Medea was regarded with a mixture of sympathy and horror for her extensive revenge on Jason and all close to him. For men in Greek myth, standards were different. If a king was overthrown or killed, for example, it was expected that his son or grandson would eventually seek revenge on the usurper. The gods also took revenge, avenging insults to themselves by killing the insolent human being responsible, and sometimes extending their vengeance to a family, however innocent its other members may have been (as in the story of Niobe and her children). The stories of Bellerophon and Orion tell of heroes, those favored by the gods, who became impertinent and presumed the gods' good will, and thus became the objects of divine revenge.

Bellerophon

No one knows the true name of the man called Bellerophon, who was the son of Poseidon (Neptune) and the sea goddess Eurynome. "Bellerophon," meaning "slayer of Belleros" in Greek, was his nickname, and the story goes that he murdered a Corinthian man called Belleros and fled to Tiryns, to the court of Proetus. Proetus was the brother of Acrisius, who was the father of Danae and brother of Perseus's grandfather. The twin brothers had quarreled even before they were born, and they had fought over the kingship of Argos, but by the time Bellerophon arrived seeking sanctuary, that quarrel at least had been resolved. The kingdom was split, and Proetus ruled over his share from the city of Tiryns.

It was not King Proetus but his wife, Stheneboia, who quarreled with the new-comer, Bellerophon. He suffered a fate like that of the biblical Joseph or Theseus's son Hippolytus, as Stheneboia became infatuated with him and tried to seduce him. When he refused her, she could not restrain her

Oh for a beaker full of the warm South, Full of the true, the blushful Hippocrene! With beaded bubbles winking at the brim, And purple-stainèd mouth.

JOHN KEATS (1795–1821), "ODE TO A NIGHTINGALE"

feelings, but they had changed from longing to fury. She forced herself to weep and then ran to her husband to show him her tears, crying out that Bellerophon had tried to seduce her. Bellerophon protested, but in the uproar, no one paid him any attention beyond throwing him into a dungeon.

Proetus did not want to be directly involved in the death of this wicked young man, because Bellerophon had come to Tiryns seeking sanctuary, and the gods looked sternly on anyone who violated sanctuary by killing the suppliant. So the king sent Bellerophon to his wife's father, Jobates, in Lycia, carrying a wax tablet bearing the message that Bellerophon had tried to seduce Stheneboia and must be put to death for it. Either Bellerophon was a remarkably honorable messenger or he was unable to read. Without reading its contents, he brought the tablet to Jobates, who was reluctant to acquire blood-guilt by killing a guest. Jobates came up with what he thought was a very clever solution. He would send Bellerophon to his death against the monster that was troubling his kingdom, rather than simply kill him on the spot.

BELLEROPHON AND THE CHIMAERA

Jobates sent Bellerophon to kill the Chimaera, a horrifying monster that breathed fire. The first third of its body was that of a lion, the middle was a goat, and instead of back legs it had the coils of a serpent. Some say that the Chimaera had the heads of a lion, goat, and serpent, with the goat's head coming out of the middle of its back and the serpent's head attached to the end of its tail.

Athene (Minerva) and Poseidon favored Bellerophon, and suggested to him that he travel to the fountain of Peirene in Corinth. There he saw a wonderful winged horse, stooping to drink. This was Pegasus, the son of Poseidon and Medusa, born from her dead body after Perseus had put an end to her. Pegasus usually lived on Mount Helicon with the Muses. A spring emerged at the spot where he struck the ground with his hoof, and it was named the Hippocrene spring (Hippocrene meaning "horse fountain" in Greek), much invoked by later poets seeking inspiration. Today, though, the gods had inspired the winged horse to leave his mountain spring and fly

to the citadel of Corinth, where Bellerophon was waiting with a golden bridle, the gift of Athene.

Soon the winged horse was tamed, all the more easily because Bellerophon was his half-brother. Pegasus learned to trust his rider enough to face the fiery breath of the monstrous Chimaera with him. They swooped around the monster faster than it could twist and turn its unwieldy body, and Bellerophon aimed and shot the lion, goat, and serpent parts of the monster's body full of his arrows. Then he used his spear for the first time. He had tipped it with lead, and when he plunged it down the Chimaera's lion throat, the monster's flames melted the lead. That is how the creature killed itself, seared to death by the hot lead that its own fire had made into a lethal weapon.

Then Jobates sent Bellerophon to war against the Amazons and their allies, the Solymians, and again the hero won with the help of Pegasus. Jobates was becoming afraid of the young man who seemed to be invincible, and organized an ambush to greet him on his return, but again Bellerophon was triumphant. Confronted with armed men, he prayed to his father Poseidon, who sent a torrent of water to drown his enemies on the Xanthian plain. It was only when the Xanthian women came out naked that Bellerophon called back the flood; he was always very shy in the company of seductive women.

IN THE COMPANY OF THE GODS

After Bellerophon killed the Chimaera, Jobates knew that he was assisted by the gods, and made the sensible decision to welcome him back. He sought out the truth of what had happened at Tiryns, and discovered that Bellerophon was totally innocent of seduction there. Then he offered the young man his daughter in marriage, and made him the heir to Lycia. Bellerophon became foolishly proud because of all his good fortune, and dreamed of flying to Olympus, like a god, with the help of Pegasus. He mounted the winged horse and began the flight upward, but Zeus (Jupiter) sent a gadfly to attack Pegasus, who reared up until Bellerophon dropped to the ground. In his fall, he hurt his legs and lost the sight of both eyes, and he lived on in great misery until his death. Pegasus, however, was welcomed into the company of the gods where he sometimes hauls thunderbolts for the king of the gods and sometimes carries Eos (Aurora), goddess of the dawn.

THE EVIL EYE

Both the Greeks and the Romans (like many Middle Eastern peoples) believed in the evil eye, a magical power that some people were supposed to possess, usually without being aware of it. Those with the evil eye were often not intentionally evil but looked too attentively, were too fond of what they saw, and so brought bad luck. The Greeks and Romans used amulets, such as the horseshoe, to turn away the evil eye's influence. Any amulet with this power is known as apotropaic. The face of Medusa in its own right causes death to anyone who looks upon it, and when worn by Athene (Minerva) it turns away evil influences that might threaten her.

Right **Apotropaic eye.** The use of amulets for protection was called phylakterion. Objects used to make amulets were believed to have special powers. Often a stone or piece of metal was used, usually with an engraving on it.

Orion the Hunter

Orion was the son of Poseidon and Euryale. He was a famous hunter, and when he visited the island of Chios, he fell in love with Merope, the daughter of Oenopion, who was the son of the god Dionysus (Bacchus) and his wife Ariadne. Like many other rulers in Greek myth, Oenopion felt threatened by a visiting hero and planned to kill him off by sending him out on a dangerous quest. The king promised that he would give his daughter to Orion if the hunter would free the island from all the wild animals that plagued it. Day after day, Orion piled up the skins of slaughtered animals in the palace, but Oenopion kept telling him that there were still more creatures lurking in caves and among the rocks. He did not want to keep his promise; monstrous though it sounds, he was overcome with desire for his own daughter.

One night, Orion drank too much and could not restrain himself from raping the unfortunate Merope. The next day, Oenopion pretended that he knew nothing of his daughter's rape, but he called on his father Dionysus for revenge, and the god provided him with more strong wine. Oenopion (whose name in Greek means "plenty of wine") insisted on filling Orion's cup time and time again with the strong wine that had not been watered down. After a very short time Orion collapsed into a heap on the floor, drunk and completely helpless. Oenopion quickly came forward and gouged out both of his eyes and threw him out of the palace. Orion stumbled blindly to the shore of Chios, praying to the gods for help.

Opposite page *Bellerophon Riding Pegasus Fighting the Chimaera* by Peter Paul Rubens (1577–1640). The winged horse Pegasus roamed the sky and land and refused to let any man approach him. It is said that Bellerophon enlisted the help of the seer Polyeidus, who advised him to spend the night on Athene's altar, whereupon he was rewarded with a dream in which Athene offered him the magic bridle.

Left **Bellerophon on Pegasus.** Before the lovely Medusa was transformed into a Gorgon, Poseidon had seduced the young maiden. It was not until after she had been killed and her head cut off that the offspring of this union were born—Chrysaor and the winged horse, Pegasus.

Right *Orion Killed by Scorpion* by Burney (1816). There are many different accounts of the death of Orion. While the tale of the scorpion is widely known, another version is that Orion was in amorous pursuit of the Pleiades, the daughters of Atlas, and that Zeus placed all of them in the sky as stars. This is why the Orion constellation appears to be hunting the Pleiades in the night sky.

The gods helped him by sending a prophecy that he could regain his sight if he traveled far to the east and looked—if eye sockets can be said to look—toward the point where the chariot of the sun first rises above the horizon. Orion groped along the shore until he laid hands on a boat, and rowed it out into the Mediterranean, to the utmost east, where the goddess of the dawn, Eos of the rosy fingers, prepares the night sky for the horses of the sun. There he regained his sight, and the goddess fell in love with him.

For a while Orion stayed with Eos as her lover, but he ached for vengeance, and soon returned to Chios looking for Oenopion. The king was nowhere to be found (in fact he was hiding in a secret room underground), and Orion kept traveling, determined to track him down. Meanwhile Apollo was planning vengeance on Orion himself, for he was not pleased that Eos had taken him as her lover on Delos, the island sacrosanct to Apollo himself. Apollo's concern was not only for the violation of his island, but also for the chastity of his sister Artemis (Diana). He had heard that Orion had joined Artemis's band of hunters, from which men had always

previously been barred, and he started to wonder whether she might be planning to abandon her vows of chastity and take the mortal as her husband. Nor did Apollo like Orion's foolish boast that he would free the whole world of wild animals. It is always a mistake for a mortal man to pretend to have the powers of a god.

Apollo went to Gaia, the goddess of earth, and informed her that Orion had threatened to kill off every animal in the world. Gaia wasted no time in sending a huge scorpion to kill the hunter before he destroyed any more of her children. Orion could not kill the scorpion, and dived into the sea to escape. Apollo then begged his sister Artemis to shoot the swimming man, claiming that he was a wretch who had just tried to seduce one of her nymphs. Artemis could not make out the swimmer's identity, but she sent an arrow through his brains. Then she discovered that her brother's story was a lie, and that she had shot her own dear companion in the hunt. She begged Asclepius (Aesculapius) to bring the dead man back to life. It was then that Zeus destroyed Asclepius for interfering with Death's proper prey. Artemis could not restore Orion to life, but he is commemorated in one of the most easily recognizable star patterns in the northern sky, the Orion nebula, with three stars representing his sword belt, while the scorpion forever shines close by as the constellation Scorpio.

Acis and Galatea

Galatea was a nereid, a nymph of the sea, who loved Acis, the son of Faunus and Symaithis, and he loved her in return. The Cyclops Polyphemus, son of Poseidon (the same one-eyed giant who eventually met a sorry fate at the hands of Odysseus) also longed for Galatea, and followed her around the countryside. Galatea shrank from Poly-phemus, but nothing that she said or did could dis-courage him from pursuing her. Polyphemus tried his hardest to please her. He worried about his clothes, tried to smile whenever he thought she might be look-ing, and even trimmed his beard and washed his face.

One day Polyphemus had the idea of pleasing his beloved Galatea by serenading her. He made a colossal pipe of a hundred reeds and blew it so loudly that it could be heard several mountains away. He bellowed a love song, piling together all the images

Below *Acis and Galatea* by I. Briot (c. 1610). The giant Polyphemus, like the other Cyclopes, was said to draw sustenance from the flocks of sheep he kept, as well as the occasional human. Like all the gods of woods and fields, Polyphemus filled his lonely hours and days by playing music.

of love that he could think of. Galatea was an unplucked rose, he sang, a bud yet to spread its petals, as sweet as honey, as intoxicating as unwatered wine, lovely as the morning, but as elusive as the wild deer, and as cold as ice. "If only," he roared, "you would melt in my arms, my dear." Then he played his pipe for a while before bellowing out the whole song again.

Meanwhile Galatea was lying on the Sicilian shore in the arms of her lover, Acis, laughing at the giant's love song. She laughed too much to notice that Polyphemus had stopped singing. Suddenly he was standing over her, shouting with anger instead of love. "No more kissing and fondling for you!" he yelled, and Galatea rushed into the water to hide. Acis tried to follow, but the giant grabbed at the hillside and threw most of it at him. Acis fell down under an avalanche of rocks, crushed to death.

Galatea did not have the power to bring her lover back to life as a man, but she could at least transform his blood into water. Faster and deeper the new stream flowed to the sea, and then the hillside that Polyphemus had torn apart began to gush with springwater that mingled with Acis's blood. In a few moments, a river was formed, and out of its depths rose Acis, transformed into a new river god. As a god, Acis could still be the lover of the sea nymph Galatea, and they clung together as closely as the fresh waters of the River Acis, perpetually intermingling with the sea.

Above *Coastal Landscape with Acis and Galatea* by Gellée Claude (1600–1682). While most versions of the myth tell of the love and sorry fate of Acis and Galatea, there is another account that has a completely different outcome. In this version, Polyphemus wins the heart of the nymph and she bears him three children—Galus, Celtus, and Illyrius.

115

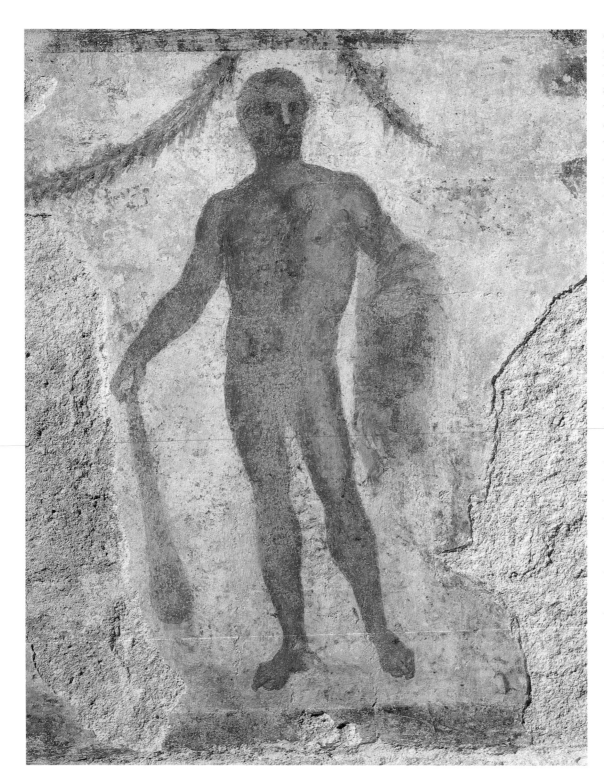

Above **Heracles holding his club.** Heracles was worshipped throughout the Mediterranean world. Every town, city, and village wanted to be associated with him in some way, and often added some act or exploit to the legend of Heracles, which would identify him with their people.

HERACLES

Heracles (Hercules) was the son of Alcmene and Zeus (Jupiter). Alcmene's story begins with Perseus and Andromeda, whose children ruled over golden Mycenae, Tiryns, and Midea in Argos. Electryon ruled in Mycenae, and his rule was threatened by Taphian raiders who stole his cattle and killed seven of his sons. Electryon's nephew, Amphitryon, found the cattle safe in the fields of the king of Elis, and bought them back from him. When Electryon found out that his own cattle had to be paid for again, he

quarreled furiously with his nephew. Amphitryon threw his stick at one of the cows and it hit and killed his uncle by accident, or so he claimed in his defense. He was judged to be polluted by the killing, and his punishment was to be banished from Argos and prevented from having sexual relations with his new wife, Electryon's daughter Alcmene, until he had avenged the deaths of his uncle's seven sons.

Alcmene and Amphitryon traveled to Thebes, where Creon was king. There the uncle-killer was cleansed of his pollution, and he soon avenged his cousins' death by going to war with the Taphians and conquering them. One night, while her husband was on the road home to Thebes from this war, Alcmene lay in bed worrying about him, hoping that he would come home safe and unwounded. In walked someone who certainly looked just like Amphitryon and sounded like him, full of news about the war, but he was really Zeus in disguise. He was carrying a finely carved golden beaker as well as a magnificent golden necklace, gifts for the bride from the gods. That night, Alcmene conceived a son by Zeus. The next night, her real husband returned home from his war and shared her bed for the first time, and she conceived a second son. Nine months later, she gave birth to twin sons, Heracles, son of Zeus, and Iphicles, son of Amphitryon.

A day before Alcmene was due to give birth, Zeus had been boasting to the other gods that the child about to be born, a descendant of Perseus, would rule all the other descendants of Perseus. Hera (Juno) was already angry with Alcmene for sharing her bed with Zeus, and these boastful comments drove her to vengeful action. She went to Argos, where the wife of

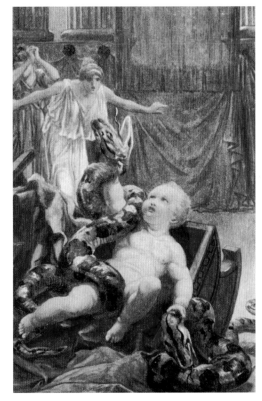

King Sthenelus (another of Perseus's sons) was also pregnant but not yet due to give birth. Hera hastened her labor, so that her son was born prematurely, and prolonged Alcmene's labor, so that Heracles came into the world later than Zeus had intended. Now Zeus's prediction would have to be applied to little Eurystheus instead of little Heracles. It would be Eurystheus instead of Heracles who would become king of Mycenae and Tiryns in Argos, and the son of Zeus would be forced to serve the son of Sthenelus until he had accomplished 12 mighty labors.

The Childhood of Heracles

Alcmene left her newborn sons alone for a few moments in their cradle. When she came back, she saw two snakes poised to sink their fangs into the children's faces. Alcmene ran over, ready to put her body in between the snakes and her sons to protect them, but before she could reach the cradle, the baby Heracles had taken hold of the snakes, one in each hand, and was strangling them to death. This was the first of many occasions when Hera tried to have Heracles killed, and when he won glory from her actions. The name Heracles means "glory of Hera" in Greek, and it seems an inappropriate name for the hero because of Hera's enmity toward him. Some think that originally, Heracles was the son of Hera and Zeus, and the stories of her anger were later inventions. But perhaps the "glory" in his name can be understood as the glory that Hera evoked, time and time again, by providing him with so many monsters to overcome.

As a child, Heracles had an ungovernable temper. He had many tutors, and while he enjoyed learning the arts of war, he would not put up with the tutor who tried to teach him how to read and write. One day he attacked this teacher, Linus, with the nearest weapon to hand, the chair that he was sitting on. When he heard about this outburst of temper, Heracles' stepfather, Amphitryon, thought that it would do the boy good to spend time on the mountains herding sheep. Heracles soon heard from the other shepherds about a lion that was attacking the sheep on Mount Cithaeron and Mount Helicon. He provided himself with a club and a massive wild olive tree that he pulled out of the ground, and easily killed the lion. Perhaps this lion was the one that provided the lion skin that Heracles is usually shown wearing, draped

Hercules was the strongest man on earth and he had the supreme self-confidence magnificent physical strength gives. He considered himself on an equality with the gods.

EDITH HAMILTON (1867–1963), MYTHOLOGY

around his neck, with its head showing on top of his own head.

Heracles' next heroic deed was to help Creon, the king of Thebes. Like Athens in the time of King Minos of Crete, Thebes was a defeated kingdom owing tribute to its conqueror, the king of Orchomenus. Heracles met the men from Orchomenus who were coming to collect the tribute and picked a quarrel with them, then defeated them all and cut off their ears and noses, saying, "Take these bits of your bodies back to your king. That is all the tribute he will be getting out of Thebes." In response, the people of Orchomenus gathered an army to enforce the tribute, but Heracles overcame them with absolute ease. King Creon proposed a marriage between the hero and his only daughter, Megara, and, when Heracles agreed, offered him the kingship of Thebes as well. All seemed to be going well for the young hero, but Hera's vengeance was about to unleash itself.

Zeus had boasted that the next descendant of Perseus to be born would rule the others, and now Eurystheus, the king of Tiryns and Mycenae, had demanded that Heracles should perform and finish 12 labors for him, as a servant of the king.

The First Labor

The first task that Eurystheus gave Heracles was to destroy the Nemean lion, a creature that could not be killed by club, sword, spear, or arrow. The lion may have been brought to Nemea by Hera, or it may have been the one that Selene, the moon goddess, gave birth to and threw down to Earth.

Heracles soon discovered that his weapons were useless against the lion, for all the good that they did was to force it to retreat into its den. He decided that the only way to kill the lion was to move in closely, risking its teeth and claws, so that he could wrestle it to death. Into the narrow opening of the den he

Left **Head of Heracles.** Heracles was the symbol of strength, energy, and heroism. The stories of his valor, spirit, generosity, and pity for the weak saw Heracles become the most famous and popular of all Greek heroes.

Above **Infant Heracles by Innes Fripp.** Many believe that it was his stepfather, Amphitryon, not Hera, who placed the snakes in Heracles' cradle. It is thought that he wanted to settle, once and for all, which of the boys was really his own son, and which was the son of Zeus.

crept—not the best way to start a wrestling match—and as the lion leaped at him, Heracles caught hold of its front legs with one huge hand and its back legs with another, forcing its body backward until he broke its spine. This lion is another possible contender for providing the massive skin and head that Heracles usually wore over his head and shoulders. He carried the carcass back to Mycenae and threw it down at Eurystheus's feet. The king was both disgusted and frightened, and immediately commanded Heracles never again to bring his trophies back into the city, but he changed his mind with the labors still to come, demanding to see with his own eyes evidence that Heracles had really done as he had been ordered. Zeus commemorated this first labor of Heracles by putting the lion in the sky as the constellation of Leo.

The Second Labor

Eurystheus now sent Heracles on a more tricky mission, to kill the Hydra of Lerna. Lerna is a swampy area on the sea coast, full of streams that sometimes open into bottomless depths. There lived the Hydra, a water snake whose breath was poisonous. Heracles knew that she had many heads, at least nine and possibly a hundred. Few had seen the Hydra and lived to tell their story, and with each story the number of her heads increased. All but one of these heads was mortal, and if Heracles wanted to kill the Hydra, he would have to find a way to cut off the immortal head. Otherwise, she would simply grow twice as many new heads to replace those that he cut off.

Heracles took his nephew, Iolaus, son of his twin brother Iphicles, as a helper. Iolaus busied himself building a huge fire, while Heracles started to attack the Hydra. Down in one of the deep pools of Lerna lived a huge crab, one of Hera's creatures, which helped the Hydra by biting Heracles' foot. He turned his attention to the crab and killed it; this is the crab that shines in the night sky as the constellation Cancer. Then Heracles fought on. Each time he lopped off one of the Hydra's heads, he called to Iolaus to cauterize the bleeding neck in order to slow down its regrowth. Eventually, he fought his way to the immortal head and chopped it off. The whole body of the Hydra collapsed in a dramatic turn of events, and Heracles proceeded to return to Mycenae

Opposite page *God Heracles Kills Hydra of Lerna* by Giovanni Falconetto (1458–1534). The Hydra was half-sister to the Nemean lion. Heracles buried the head beside the road from Lerna to Elaeus.

in triumph, after dipping his arrows in the poisoned blood of the vanquished Hydra.

Eurystheus complained that Heracles had not carried out this labor by himself, but Heracles paid no attention to this. He was well aware that Eurystheus hoped that he would die during one of these labors. The king was terrified of Heracles, expecting that he would finish his 12 labors by killing the man who had imposed them on him. Eurystheus was so frightened that he took to hiding underground in a huge bronze jar whenever Heracles was in his palace.

The Third Labor

Now Eurystheus changed his mind about banning Heracles' trophies from his city. He hankered after the hind of Ceryneia, a young deer that Artemis (Diana) cherished. She had given it golden antlers, and Eurystheus longed to have the hind for himself. It seems an easy enough task to catch a young deer, but this hind had the intelligence of a goddess. She was once the Titan Taygete, and had been metamorphosed into a deer to protect her from the amorous advances of Zeus. When Heracles came hunting for her, she led him to the ends of the Earth. First she ran through Arcadia, in northern Greece, then farther north to the land of the Hyperboreans, the northernmost land which human beings inhabit. There he finally caught the deer, put her over his shoulder, and started to carry her back to Mycenae. Artemis came hunting for Heracles, ready to take revenge for the murder of her companion, but he showed her that the deer was not dead and explained that he was only carrying out the decree of their father, Zeus. Artemis accepted this explanation, and stored up her anger against Eurystheus instead.

The Fourth Labor

The next labor that Eurystheus demanded from Heracles was to fetch him the boar of Erymanthus. The hind had been much too easy a prey, the king thought. It would be far riskier for Heracles to catch a savage wild pig alive, and then

Left *Heracles and the Nemean Lion* attributed to the Amasis Painter (c. 550 B.C.–530 B.C.). Some say that after Heracles strangled the ferocious lion with his bare hands, he then skinned it and dressed himself in the pelt, with the head and scalp serving as a sort of hood. The hide of the animal was so tough that arrows could not pierce it.

Below *Heracles and the Arcadian Stag* from the workshop of Giambologna (1529–1608). It is thought that Heracles pursued the young deer for up to a year before he eventually captured it. Stories vary as to how the hero finally caught her. Some say that he crept up on her as she slept, some say that he used a net, while still others say that he wounded the creature with a shot from his bow.

Above **Sagittarius**. Each of the 12 signs of the zodiac symbolizes a myth, legend, or constellation. The Centaur Cheiron, known as the constellation Sagittarius, was wounded in battle by mistake. It seems that he was wounded in one of two ways—by either dropping a poisoned arrow on his own foot, or by his friend Heracles accidentally shooting him.

Right **Heracles and the Erymanthian Boar** by Giambologna (1529–1608). The great Heracles captured the wild boar quickly and easily. Heracles waited outside its lair and shouted loudly until it came rushing out into the snow, whereupon Heracles cast his net over it.

transport it across Greece. Eurystheus did not consider that Heracles would run any risks in going to the region of Erymanthus, because the Centaurs who lived there were friendly to human beings. But it was the Centaurs who caused Heracles the most grief in this labor. It was easy enough for him to catch the boar and take it back to Mycenae, and it was not the fight with the boar that littered the countryside with dead Centaurs. The trouble started when Heracles visited the cave of Pholus and was welcomed with a banquet.

The Centaur tried to provide food and drink suitable for a human guest, and opened a jar of wine that Dionysus (Bacchus) had given him. This was the first time that any Centaur drank wine, and it went straight to his head. Then the other Centaurs smelled the wine, galloped up, and started drinking. Soon the banquet turned to a brawl, and Heracles started to shoot down those who were attacking him. His arrows were tipped with the Hydra's poison, and killed most of the drunkards, but he also wounded the Centaur Cheiron by mistake. Cheiron was the wisest of the Centaurs, and a great healer, and he had been granted immortality by the

gods. He could not die, but he could do nothing to cure the wound that Heracles had inflicted. Cheiron did eventually die, centuries later, bargaining his life for Prometheus's freedom, but when Heracles abandoned Erymanthus with the boar, it seemed as though the Centaur was doomed to an eternity of pain. When Cheiron did finally die, he was commemorated in the starry heavens as the constellation Sagittarius.

The Fifth Labor
The next labor of Heracles concerned the Birds of Lake Stymphalus. Stymphalus was more of a swamp than a lake, and its host of birds were creatures of Ares (Mars), the god of war. They were part-human creatures with the claws of birds and the heads of women, and their favorite food was human flesh. Instead of shooting arrows, they shot their feathers, which were sharp enough to slice open a human hand, and they rampaged among the people of Arcadia, wantonly destroying their farmlands and killing anyone who tried to stop them. Heracles was only required to drive these birds away from the lake, not to kill them, and this task was the easiest of his labors. All he needed to do was to alarm them with the sound of a bronze rattle, and they flew off to the Black Sea to torment people there.

The Sixth Labor
Eurystheus was now so frightened of Heracles that he could not control his bowels when the hero was in the palace. Perhaps it was this embarrassment that gave him the idea of the next labor, cleansing the stables of Augeias. King Augeias of Elis had herds of cattle whose dung had piled up in the stables for years, and Eurystheus required Heracles to clean it up in a single day. If he failed, he was to stay there

for the rest of his life as a stablehand and dung raker. Augeias was so confident of the task's impossibility that he promised to give Heracles a tenth of his herds, if the stables were cleaned in one day. Heracles could wield a rake as forcefully as he wielded sword or club, but even he could not rake the stables clean in a day. He looked around and noticed that the palace had been built between two rivers. A couple of trenches would be enough to lead the waters into the stables. Within a day, the rivers were running in their new course, straight through the stables, and all the dung had been washed away. The king tried to

wriggle out of his promise, refusing to give Heracles a tenth of his cattle, arguing that it was the rivers, not the man, that accomplished the task. Heracles went back to Mycenae, nursing a grievance against Augeias. Eurystheus jumped at the chance to postpone the day when Heracles would be a free man again, and he too claimed that this was not to be counted as a genuine labor.

The Seventh Labor

After the Augeian stables were cleansed, Eurystheus cast about Greece to find another peril for Heracles

Above *Heracles and the Stymphalian Birds* by **Albrecht Durer (1471– 1528).** Heracles shook the bronze rattle so violently that the huge, pestilent birds took off in fright. The hero was then able to shoot a great number of them with his arrows. The rattle had been forged by Hephaestus and given to Heracles by Athene.

121

Above *Heracles and the Cretan Bull* by Alexander de La Borde (1813). Heracles had no trouble capturing the Cretan bull. King Minos is believed to have even offered to help the hero with his task as he was so eager to rid the island of the animal. It was not only an embarrassment to him, but it was wreaking havoc and destroying all the crops on the land.

Right *Theseus Abducting Antiope* attributed to Myson (c. 480 B.C.). Heracles was sent to fetch the girdle of Queen Hippolyta in order to bring it back for Admete, the daughter of Eurystheus. The belt was a gift from the queen's father, Ares. The plan was running smoothly until Hera stepped in, resulting in the death of the queen and the abduction of Antiope.

from the sea and which King Minos had failed to sacrifice. The god punished the king firstly by making his queen become infatuated with the bull, and then, after the Minotaur had been conceived, by driving the bull completely mad. Heracles was by this time an expert at dealing with wild animals, and he managed to subdue the bull with his club and take it across the sea to mainland Greece, where Theseus eventually killed it.

The Ninth Labor

Eurystheus decided that it was not profitable to keep sending Heracles after wild animals, for he always managed to dispose of them without effort. The gods seemed not to care, either, when their creatures were killed or tamed by this son of Zeus. If wild animals could not kill Heracles, the king thought, perhaps wild women could. He asked for the girdle of Queen Hippolyta of the Amazons, the belt that she wore around her waist to tie up her garments for battle. The Amazons were a race of women who sent all their boy children out for adoption, and only tolerated the company of men for the purpose of becoming pregnant. They cut off their right breasts, so that they could use their bows with complete freedom.

Heracles took several other heroes with him on this expedition, including Theseus. At first the Amazons were friendly, and it seemed that he might acquire the girdle simply by asking, but Hera made sure that there would be trouble, spreading a rumor that he was there to kidnap the queen. A fight broke out, and in the melee, Heracles killed Hippolyta. That was the fight in which Theseus abducted Antiope, who became the mother of Hippolytus. The quest for the girdle of Hippolyta brought glory to neither man.

The Tenth Labor

Eurystheus sent Heracles farther and farther abroad for each successive labor. When the king asked for the cattle of Geryoneus, Heracles had to travel to the utmost west, crossing the wide stream of

to face. He decided upon the mares of Diomedes, the king of Thrace. Diomedes was the son of Ares, and had inherited his father's bloodthirsty nature. His mares were meat-eaters, and like the gruesome, part-human birds of the Stymphalian lake, their favorite food was human flesh. Along the way to Thrace, Heracles decided to visit his friend Admetus, and it was then that he rescued Alcestis from the death that she had invited upon herself.

Then he traveled on to Thrace, to the palace of Diomedes. The king was always happy to see strangers at his door, fresh food for his horses, but this time it was Heracles who marched the king over to his stables and left him to the teeth of his mares. Then, when their stomachs were full of food and they were less savage, Heracles led them in a line, bridled and roped together, to Mycenae, to give Eurystheus a problem of his own. Eurystheus liked the mares, however, and their offspring could still be found in the kingdom of Mycenae until the period of Alexander the Great.

The Eighth Labor

It was at this time that Jason and the Argonauts set off on in quest of the Golden Fleece, and since Eurystheus could not instantly think up another labor, Heracles joined the Argonauts for a short time, until the death of Hylas. Then he returned to Thebes, sure that the king had something nasty in store for him. This time, he was ordered to fetch the bull of Minos, the same bull which Poseidon (Neptune) had sent

Opposite page *Diomedes Devoured by His Horses* by Gustave Moreau (1826–1898). Some say that Heracles just fought the grooms and took the horses.

Above *Heracles Slaying Cacus* by Hendrik Goltzius (1558–1617). Heracles was hailed as hero once more when he defeated Cacus. The giant and thief, surrounded by the skulls and bones of his victims, was crushed to death by Heracles. One version has it that Cacus's own sister fell in love with Heracles and she told him where her brother could be found.

Right *Heracles Wrestling Antaeus* by Euphronios (fl. c. 520 B.C.–500 B.C.). Heracles almost met his match in the giant Antaeus. Shrewd as well as strong, Heracles overcame the giant. Afterward it was said that he subdued all of Libya and put it under cultivation.

5. Tartessu

6. Erytheia

Journeying on to the west, Heracles passed through the north of Libya, and there he met Antaeus, a belligerent giant who insisted on challenging him to a wrestling match. Antaeus was the son of Gaia and Poseidon, and whenever he touched the ground, he was filled with the strength of a god. In the past, Antaeus had always won the wrestling matches that he forced on strangers, and he had decorated his father's temple with the smashed skulls of his many victims. Heracles was a very skilled and strong wrestler, and kept throwing Antaeus to the ground. Any other wrestler would have suffered broken bones, at the very least, but Antaeus just kept on lumbering back to his feet and attacking Heracles again and again, gaining fresh strength with every fall. Heracles could hardly believe that a mere giant was in danger of beating him, when he had just sent some of the immortal gods scurrying back beaten to Olympus. He was very nearly overpowered by Antaeus during the wrestling, but eventually he made the connection that Antaeus's strength seemed to leave him when his feet left the ground. Then Heracles stopped using his wrestling throws, and tried holding Antaeus up off the ground at the full stretch of his arms. The giant grew feebler and feebler while he was held aloft, and so Heracles easily broke his neck and killed him.

Oceanus to the island of Erytheia. There a two-headed dog, kin to Cerberus and the Hydra, guarded the cattle of Geryoneus, the grandson of Medusa and son of the warrior Chrysaor. Geryoneus had two legs just like other people, but from the waist up, his body branched out into three trunks, with six arms and three heads. Eurystheus ordered Heracles to overcome this monster of a man, take the cattle, and bring them to Mycenae.

In order to get to the island, Heracles needed to find a ship. He went to Pylos, but its ruler, Neleus, barred the city gates against him. The gods of Olympus took an interest in this conflict, and some went down to fight alongside Neleus, others to support Heracles. On the side of Heracles were his father, Zeus, and his half-sister, Athene (Minerva). Against him were Hera, of course, and Ares, Apollo, Hades (Pluto) the god of the underworld, and Poseidon. Heracles struck out at the immortal gods and wounded Ares in the thigh, Hades in the shoulder, and Hera in the breast. Not even the gods could save Neleus and his sons (all except Nestor, who was away from home) from death at Heracles' hand.

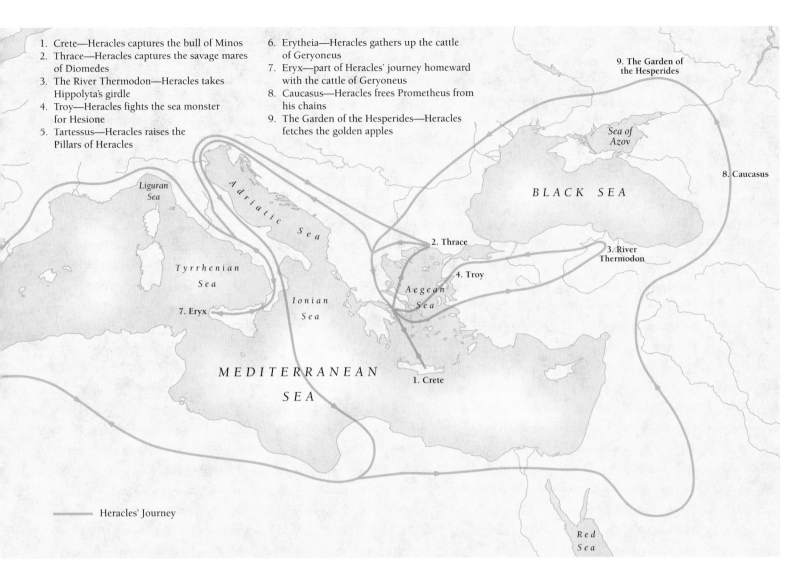

1. Crete—Heracles captures the bull of Minos
2. Thrace—Heracles captures the savage mares of Diomedes
3. The River Thermodon—Heracles takes Hippolyta's girdle
4. Troy—Heracles fights the sea monster for Hesione
5. Tartessus—Heracles raises the Pillars of Heracles
6. Erytheia—Heracles gathers up the cattle of Geryoneus
7. Eryx—part of Heracles' journey homeward with the cattle of Geryoneus
8. Caucasus—Heracles frees Prometheus from his chains
9. The Garden of the Hesperides—Heracles fetches the golden apples

Liguran Sea

Adriatic Sea

Tyrrhenian Sea

Ionian Sea

7. Eryx

MEDITERRANEAN SEA

1. Crete

2. Thrace

Aegean Sea

4. Troy

BLACK SEA

Sea of Azov

9. The Garden of the Hesperides

8. Caucasus

3. River Thermodon

Red Sea

——— Heracles' Journey

Heracles then passed the narrow waters of the Mediterranean, where Africa almost meets Europe, and there he raised the Pillars of Heracles. On he went to the island of Erytheia, where he killed first the two-headed dog and then the three-headed owner of the cattle. It was easy to win the cattle by force, but considerably less easy to bring them back to Mycenae. Along the way Heracles encountered another three-headed creature, Cacus, who could breathe fire. Cacus was the son of Hephaestus (Vulcan), but he possessed the cunning of Hermes (Mercury). When Cacus he decided to steal some of Heracles' cattle, he pulled them backward by their tails so that their footprints all pointed in the direction from which they had been taken. Heracles was completely fooled by this detraction, but he heard the mooing and bellowing of the stolen beasts and came running to the cave where Cacus had hidden them. Heracles tore open the cave and crushed Cacus to death in a wrestling hold. As he drove the cattle onward, Hera sent a gadfly to annoy them, and they scattered across Greece. It took Heracles months to gather the cattle together again.

Above **Heracles' journey.** Over the centuries, many historians have put forward their own versions of the labors, and their own maps of the route they believe Heracles followed. This version was compiled by Apollodorus in the third century B.C.

Left *The Giant Antaeus* by **Gustave Dore (1832–1883).** The giant Antaeus derived his amazing strength from contact with the earth. By breaking that contact, Heracles was able to overpower him. Some say he did this by breaking Antaeus's neck, others that he crushed Antaeus's bones until he suffocated.

Then, as he was driving them toward Mycenae, he met another giant, Alcyoneus of Corinth. This giant happened to be a stronger opponent than either Cacus or Antaeus, and he hurled an enormous rock at Heracles, completely decimating 12 chariots that were clustered round, full of startled onlookers. Then the giant picked up the rock again and threw it at Heracles, who thumped it back toward him with his club, crushing Alcyoneus to death. This was the last obstacle that Hera put in Heracles' way during this labor. He was able to bring the cattle to Mycenae with no more trouble, and there they were promptly sacrificed to Hera by Eurystheus.

Below *Heracles and Atlas* by Walter Crane (1845–1915). Heracles used the sun god's huge golden cup to see him safely across the ocean. Helius provided him with the cup after Heracles, overcome by the immense heat, threatened the sun with his arrows. Helius gave him the cup, either to appease him, or in admiration of his boldness.

The Eleventh Labor

The king next came up with a labor that he considered totally impossible to achieve. Eurystheus told Heracles to fetch him the golden apples of the Hesperides. No one knew where the Hesperides might be—that is, no one mortal. But Heracles was a favored son of Zeus, and perhaps his half-sister Athene whispered to him the idea that he should ask for directions from the Fates. These three ancient goddesses are usually busy spinning and weaving the threads of human lives, but they set aside their tasks for a moment to speak to the hero. "We have been here almost since the beginning," they said, "but even we do not know where the island of the Hesperides might be. Only a sea god would be sure to know where such an island might lie. Find Nereus, the old man of the sea," they advised Heracles, "and hold him tightly until he gives you directions."

Nereus was a shape-shifter, and he did not want to talk to Heracles. First he shifted shape to a fire that burned, then to a sea serpent that tried to slide through his fingers, then to water that almost slipped away into the sea. But Heracles held fast, and Nereus eventually took on his own form as a sea god, and told him which way to journey, first on land and then by sea. It was on this journey that Heracles came to Mount Caucasus and heard the sorrowful story of Prometheus. For once, the hero could make life better rather than spread violent death. When he heard that Prometheus could only be freed if some immortal would agree to die in his place, he remembered the wound he had given the Centaur Cheiron, and that is how Prometheus became unbound.

Heracles now had to travel by ship, or rather by cup, for the sun god Helius (Sol) provided him with a huge golden cup, the one in which the sun traveled across the ocean each night from farthest west to farthest east, ready to rise the next dawn. Heracles sailed the cup from east to farthest west, getting ever closer to the remote island of the Hesperides with its tree of golden apples guarded by serpents. This tree was a wedding gift from Gaia, the earth goddess, to Hera, and so Heracles risked enraging an already angry goddess by taking her apples. He looked around for help, and found it in the giant Atlas, a Titan from the time before Zeus ruled the gods. Atlas had been one of those who rebelled against the new king of the gods, and Zeus had punished him by forcing him to carry the weight of the heavens on his shoulders. When Heracles came asking for help, Atlas could not believe his luck. At last someone else might be tricked into holding up the skies. "You have to take the weight for only an hour or two," he assured Heracles. "As soon as I have brought back the apples for you, of course I will take up my burden again." Atlas did steal the apples from Hera's tree, and he did bring them back to Heracles, but then he refused to bend his back and take up the weight of the heavens again. "My shoulders are hurting," Heracles complained, "and I need a cushion. Take the heavens back for just a moment, while I make myself comfortable." When the Titan agreed, Heracles eased himself out from under the sky and walked off, leaving Atlas trapped under his burden. So he remained, until the day that Perseus flew by and turned the giant to stone.

The Twelfth Labor

Heracles had survived even this task. Eurystheus had been confident that Hera would be so angry with him that he would not survive. What worse labor could he devise, that would certainly mean the death of Heracles? "The death of Heracles…" thought the king. "A visit to the place of death would be just what I am looking for." And so he told his cousin to bring up from the underworld the three-headed dog, Cerberus. Only Persephone (Proserpina) had so far come back from Hades' kingdom to the world of the living, and only with difficulty, even though she was a goddess. What chance did Heracles have?

It turned out that he had all the skills needed to force his way down to the underworld and back to the world of life. He had no coin to buy his passage across the Styx, but Charon was too terrified of his mortal strength to refuse to ferry him over. Cerberus saw him coming, and fled to the side of his master, Hades. Heracles found Theseus and Peirithous stuck fast to thrones that their own folly had brought them to, and pulled Theseus free by force. He met the ghost of Meleager, who begged Heracles to marry his sister Deianeira. He even met the ghost of Medusa and

Cerberus, monster cruel and uncouth,
With his three gullets like a dog is barking
Over the people that are there submerged.

DANTE ALIGHIERI (1265–1321), *THE DIVINE COMEDY,*
"INFERNO," CANTO VI

somehow outfaced her stony stare. Then Heracles arrived at the throne room of Hades and Persephone, daughter of Zeus and Demeter (Ceres). Like Athene, Persephone was Heracles' half-sister, and she wanted both to please her father by helping the hero, and also to rid the underworld of its invincible visitor as soon as possible. Persephone told Heracles that he could take Cerberus up to the world of the living, if he could do so with his bare hands. No sword or spear or club had any power in the underworld; Heracles would have to try his wrestling tricks on the three-headed dog.

Despite his three heads, Cerberus was no match for Heracles, and soon he was dragged up into the light. He growled and snarled his way to Mycenae, where Eurystheus fled into his bronze jar once more, cursing himself for ever asking for death's dog. Cerberus did not stay long in the upper world. Once Eurystheus had seen him, and acknowledged that the 12 labors had been properly accomplished, Heracles freed him, and he raced back to his customary darkness.

After the Labors

Heracles conducted his own Trojan war, a generation before the war over Helen. The king of Troy at that time was Laomedon, and when Apollo and Poseidon had worked for him for a whole year for wages, the foolish king cheated them of their pay, a team of horses that Zeus had given him. Perhaps he was emboldened by seeing the immortal gods reduced to serving as mere shepherd and laborer, but he failed to consider how they would behave once their term of service was completed. As soon as their contract had ended, Apollo proceeded to fire plague arrows into Troy, and the sea god sent a sea monster to torment the coast. The oracle told Laomedon that the only way to appease the angry gods was to allow the terrifying sea serpent to take his daughter, Hesione.

Below *Heracles in the Garden of the Hesperides* by William Hunt (1827–1910). Some say there were not only serpents guarding the apple grove, but also three sweetly singing nymphs as well—Aegle, Erytheia, and Hespera—the Hesperides, whom it is said were the daughters of Atlas.

Left *Heracles Bringing Cerberus to Eurystheus,* Greek School (sixth century B.C.). Heracles again showed his amazing strength by subduing the monster-dog Cerberus. It is said that when Cerberus faced the light of the living world for the first time, foam fell from his jaws onto the ground. From his spittle sprang wolfsbane, a poisonous plant, which, it was claimed, flourished ever after in that region.

Hearing of the king's promise that he would give his horses to anyone who rescued his daughter, Heracles went out onto the beach to fight the monster. It came at him with a gaping mouth and swallowed him. Heracles stayed in its stomach for three days, but then he cut his way free, killing the monster. Laomedon promptly refused to give him the reward, and Heracles rampaged through the city of Troy, killing at will. Laomedon died at the hands of Heracles, and so did all his sons except the youngest, Priam, who became the next king of Troy. Heracles married Hesione to his comrade, Telamon, and she became queen of Salamis.

Heracles had not seen much of his wife, Megara, during his labors, but they had managed to have three sons (some accounts say eight). While he was away in the underworld, taming Cerberus, many people assumed that he was dead and would never return. Lycus, the son of Poseidon, killed Creon and became tyrant of Thebes. The tyrant Lycus was so confident of Heracles' death that he began to persecute Megara and old Amphitryon, Heracles' stepfather, who had been living in the Theban palace for years. Heracles' family believed that they would all be killed, but he hurried back to them just in time. He found Lycus and his supporters in the palace, and instantly began to shoot his poison-tipped arrows at them. Those who were not shot dead, he clubbed to death. Then Hera struck madness into him. He hallucinated that the children clinging to him were the sons of his enemy, Eurystheus, and he killed his wife and all his children before falling into a stuporous sleep.

Above *Heracles and Omphale* by Santi di Tito (1536–1603). While in Queen Omphale's servitude, Heracles performed many deeds and defeated many of her enemies. Some historians say that before she freed Heracles, they married and had a son called Lamus.

When he woke, he had forgotten everything that he had done in the palace. As soon as Heracles remembered what had happened, all Thebes rang with his cries of grief, guilt, and horror.

What he had done to his wife and children was dreadful, but it was an act of madness sent by the goddess. The next dreadful thing that he did had no such excuse. He went to Oichalia to compete in an archery contest. The winner's prize was to be the daughter of King Eurytus, Iole, but when Heracles won the competition, the king withheld the prize. Heracles lashed out and killed two of King Eurytus's sons, and he forced the king to give Iole to him in marriage. So far, the gods considered Heracles to be in the right, but when King Eurytus's son Iphitus came to Heracles' city of Tiryns, the hero welcomed him as a guest, then threw him to his death from a tower. Such a betrayal of hospitality called out for punishment from the gods; it

THE OLYMPIC GAMES

Heracles (Hercules) was believed to be the founder of the Olympic Games, at the city of Olympia. Previously there had been a festival at Olympia in honor of Zeus (Jupiter), but Heracles organized an athletics competition and a truce, which all the Greek cities agreed to honor while the games were in progress. Like the modern Olympic Games, these games were held once every four years. At their peak, they included running, chariot racing, boxing, wrestling, and the pentathlon (running, jumping, discus, javelin, and wrestling). Heracles competed in the first games, and won every contest.

Right **Heracles.** Before the Olympic Games were founded by Heracles, a festival of games held in honor of Hera, called the Heraean Games, had been founded by Pelops, the husband of Hippodameia.

Left *Struggle for the Delphic Tripod* by Roulez (1854). Some believe that Heracles went to the oracle at Delphi for help. He was consumed with guilt and remorse over his actions, and he was desperate to be purified. However, when the priestess refused to speak to him, Heracles became angry and seized the tripod.

was as though Heracles was somehow seeking to be punished for his tragic fit of madness before.

Then he directly offended one of the gods, going to Apollo's shrine at Delphi and stealing the tripod on which the Pythia used to sit to give her oracles. Heracles was helped by his half-sister Athene, and the two of them got a long way down the road before Apollo caught up with them, accompanied by his sister Artemis. The four children of Zeus confronted one another, and were just about to start fighting when Zeus himself intervened, sending down a thunderbolt to force them apart. The tripod went back to Delphi, and Heracles was punished for all his previous wild behavior by going back into service, this time as a slave. Hermes sold Heracles in the common market, and he became the property of Queen Omphale.

Omphale was the queen of Lydia, and the Greeks liked to imagine her court as the height of decadence. There women played the men and men played the women. Omphale entertained herself by dressing her new slave in women's clothing, while she draped herself in the lion skin and tried to lift his club. As a slave, Heracles was assigned women's work and he promptly set to the task of spinning.

Blood and Death

Once his term of slavery was over, Heracles went in search of a new wife. He remembered that Meleager had spoken of his sister Deianeira in the underworld, asking Heracles to marry her, and now he wanted to find out why Meleager had said that Heracles was

HALCYON DAYS

King Ceyx and Queen Alcyone of Trachis had a very happy marriage, but the queen unfortunately had an inordinate fear of storms that the winds blew up at sea. When her husband decided to consult the oracle at Delphi, she knew that he would be forced to go by sea, because the land road was completely blocked by their enemies. Alcyone prayed to Hera (Juno) for his safe return, but all that the goddess could grant was that he would always love and cherish Alcyone best of all women. Ceyx died in a storm at sea, and poor Alcyone discovered his body, washed up on the coast of Trachis. The gods transformed this faithful husband and wife into a pair of halcyon birds, kingfishers that build their nest in the ocean during seven days of calm in the stormy winter. Such days of calm in a stormy winter season are still called halcyon days.

THE MILKY WAY

Though Hera (Juno) is always described as hating Heracles (Hercules), she was once deceived into nurturing him like a mother. While she was asleep, the trickster god Hermes (Mercury) carried the baby Heracles to Olympus and put his mouth near her breast. The goddess instinctively began to suckle him, until he bit her breast so hard that she woke and threw him off. Heracles was not harmed at all by this, but Hera's milk continued to spurt out, jetting far into the sky to form the Milky Way.

Right *The Birth of the Milky Way* by Peter Paul Rubens (1577–1640). In another version, Athene deceived Hera into nursing the baby Heracles.

the only man in the world who was suitable to be her husband. Heracles made the long journey to Calydon, where Deianeira lived in the palace of her father, Oeneus, and discovered that she was being courted by the river god Achelous, a deity who enjoyed shifting his shape to that of bull and snake. Deianeira did not want a husband such as this, and welcomed Heracles as a rescuer. As so often before, Heracles used his skills as a wrestler to overcome the river god. He snapped off Achelous's horn when the river god turned into a bull, and that was the end of the fight. The horn became the miraculous horn of plenty, the cornucopia, that always spills over with food.

Heracles had won both the horn of plenty and Deianeira as his wife, but as usual, he attracted trouble on the way home. He was about to cross the River Lycormus when the Centaur Nessus came up to him, saying that he was the ferryman, and that it was his responsibility to carry them across the river

Right **Detail from a crater showing Heracles fighting Achelous.** Some claim that Achelous begged Heracles to give him back his horn, and in its place gave him the horn of Amaltheia. Amaltheia was, depending on the myth, either a nymph or a goat who had been Zeus's nurse.

on his back. "First," he said to Heracles, "let the bride sit on my back, and when she is safely across, I will come back for you." Heracles lifted Deianeira onto the Centaur's back, and off they went into the surging river. When they were nearly at the other side, Nessus started to pull Deianeira toward him, threatening to rape her, and she screamed to her husband for help. Heracles took up his bow and shot the Centaur. Nessus took a few moments to die, and with his last breath, he kept trying to injure Heracles, "Deianeira," he whispered, "my blood is worth keeping. It has the power to restore your husband's love if he ever loses interest in you." Deianeira collected his blood, keeping it hidden from her husband, and on they went to the city of Trachis.

Heracles now went on another campaign, fighting yet another war, and he brought back a captive, Iole the daughter of Eurytus. Deianeira became overwhelmingly jealous of Iole and decided to make use of Nessus's magic blood to win back her husband. She gave him a magnificent robe, smeared on the inside with the Centaur's blood. But instead of restoring love, the blood burned flesh to the bone, for the arrow that had killed Nessus had been tipped with the caustic poison of the Hydra. Heracles was

not able take off his robe, because the blood stuck to his body, and he immediately knew that he would soon die. At this moment, he remembered an oracle, which had told him that he would never be killed by anyone living. Now the oracle had been fulfilled. Heracles ordered a pyre to be built on Mount Oeta, and was transported there to die. No one would step forward to light the pyre, as he was still alive, and he was forced to wait until a stranger, a man called Philoctetes, came by and agreed to help relieve him from his agony. As a reward for lighting the pyre,

Heracles gave this man his great bow, and Philoctetes took it with him to the Trojan war.

Heracles did not die in the funeral pyre. He became a god in the flames, and Athene came down for him in her chariot, to take him to Olympus. Now, at last, Hera forgave him, and he took his place with Apollo and Artemis, Hermes and Athene, all children of Zeus. Deianeira killed herself when she found out that the robe was killing her husband, and in Olympus Heracles made his third and final marriage, to the goddess Hebe, daughter of Zeus and Hera.

Above *The Apotheosis of Heracles* by Francois Lemoyne (1688–1737), showing a detail of the gods on Mount Olympus. At last Heracles achieved the immortality he had won with his 12 labors. Reconciled with Hera, the goddess permitted Heracles to marry her daughter Hebe.

JASON AND THE ARGONAUTS

The story of Jason begins with Ixion, the prince of the Lapiths, who wanted to seduce the queen of the gods. Zeus (Jupiter) was well aware of his intentions and shaped a phantom Hera (Juno) out of a cloud, naming her Nephele. Ixion seduced Nephele, believing that he was sharing a bed with the great goddess, and Zeus punished him for his presumption by first whipping him, and then binding him to a wheel of fire that whirled forever through the sky without a pause. Hera was grateful to Nephele, and married her to King Athamas of Boeotia. They had two sons, Phrixus and Leucon, and a daughter, Helle.

After some years of marriage, Athamas's attentions strayed to Ino, the daughter of Cadmus, and she became his lover; some say that he abandoned the goddess and married the mortal woman in her place. Athamas and Ino had two children, Learchus and Melicertes. Nephele turned to Hera for recourse, and the goddess swore eternal enmity to Athamas and his family. Ino was well aware of what was going on, and plotted to take revenge on Nephele's children. She did not dare to injure Nephele directly, because she knew that the cloud-woman was Hera's favorite. In the spring, Ino persuaded the women of Boeotia to cook the seeds of grain before planting them. No grains sprouted and there was no harvest. Then, as Ino had hoped, the king sent messengers to the oracle at Delphi to find out how to bring fertility back to the land. Ino bribed Athamas's messengers to suppress the oracle's answer, and to tell the king instead that he must sacrifice his and Nephele's son, Phrixus. Athamas took Phrixus to a mountaintop and reluctantly prepared to slit his throat. Just in time, Heracles (Hercules) came by, and he was appalled to see a father getting ready to kill his own son. "The gods abhor human sacrifice," said Heracles, and took the knife out of Athamas's hand. Then Zeus sent a miraculous ram flying down from Olympus, a creature with wings and a golden fleece. Phrixus

leaped onto its woolly back, and his sister Helle climbed on behind him. The ram flew for Colchis, but its journey was long and Helle grew weary. She fell into the straits now called the Dardanelles, which the Greeks named the Hellespont after Helle. Phrixus clung to the ram's fleece and arrived safely at Colchis, a land far to the east, where the sun rose each morning. He sacrificed the ram, and its golden fleece was placed in the sacred grove of Ares, god of war. This ram was commemorated by the gods in the heavens in the form of the constellation Aries.

Ino's deceitfulness became clear when the messengers confessed that she had bribed them to give a false report of what the oracle had said. Nephele was furious, and appealed to Hera for revenge. The goddess drove Athamas mad, so that he shot his son Learchus, one of Ino's children, believing that he was shooting a stag. Then Athamas tore apart the boy's body while it was still warm and bleeding. He looked around for Ino and her remaining son, Melicertes, but madness clouded his vision. He grabbed hold of a goat and started to whip it, believing that he was punishing Ino. She jumped into the sea with her son and drowned. Ino and Melicertes were turned into deities by Zeus, as usual going against his wife's wishes. The family of Athamas was almost obliterated in a single day, and his remaining son, Leucon, died shortly afterward.

Athamas lost the kingship of Boeotia and was exiled because of the horror of what he had done. He asked the oracle at Delphi where he should live, and the Pythia told him to settle down in the place

where his dinner was provided by wild beasts. He wandered through Greece until he came to wild countryside in Thessaly where he noticed a pack of wolves attacking a flock of sheep. The wolves ran off, leaving the dead sheep for Athamas to cook and eat. Athamas obeyed the oracle and founded a city there, marrying again and starting another family.

Jason

Aeson, king of Iolcus in Thessaly, was the grandson of Athamas's brother, and Aeson's son was Jason. When Jason was a child, Aeson was dethroned by his half-brother, Pelias, and at once he sent his son away in secret to keep him safe. On Mount Pelion, Jason was educated by the Centaur Cheiron, wisest of his kind, and he was favored by the goddess Hera. One day he was out hunting, and he met an old woman by a river in flood. Without hesitating, he offered to carry the woman over the river on his back. The weight on Jason's back was far more than that of a human body, and he staggered as he waded

across the current, but he managed to get both of them safely across. Once across the river, she revealed that she was the goddess Hera, and from that moment he was her particular favorite. Jason lost a sandal in the water while carrying Hera across, but he kept walking downriver until he reached the coast, dusty and footsore.

On the beach, Pelias was making a sacrifice to the sea god Poseidon (Neptune), and he was horrified to see this man with one sandal limping past, because he had been given a prophecy that a man with one sandal would bring about his death. He ordered Jason to come closer and asked him, "If an oracle had named someone as the man who would kill you, what would you do?" Jason replied, "I would send him to fetch the Golden Fleece, knowing that it is guarded by a serpent and that he will probably die in the attempt." Pelias nodded his head and was about to tell Jason that he had passed sentence upon himself, but first he asked the stranger's name. When the king discovered that

Still what a royal aspect he retains! That Jason is, who by his heart and cunning The Colchians of the Ram made destitute.

DANTE ALIGHIERI (1265–1321), *THE DIVINE COMEDY*, "INFERNO," CANTO XVIII

Above **Detail from a vase showing Phrixus escaping on a ram (c. 460 B.C.).** Once in Colchis, Phrixus married Chalciope, the daughter of King Aietes. When he eventually died, Phrixus was denied a proper burial, so his ghost haunted Pelias (who had dethroned King Aeson), demanding proper burial rites as well as the return of the Golden Fleece.

THE ARGO AS A SHIP OF WAR

Like the fighting ships of Greek history, the 50-oared pentecolours, the great ship Argo was built long and narrow so that it could ram enemy ships, either directly attacking to sink another ship or sailing alongside and breaking off the enemy ship's oars. The Argo's fighters also served as oarsmen; Heracles (Hercules) rowed so long and hard that he broke one of the oars. Orpheus the musician played the flute to help the oarsmen keep time. The Argo was a ship of shallow draft, so that the Argonauts could carry it overland. Ships like this were not built to withstand savage storms out at sea, and it is for this reason that voyagers in Greek myth rarely ventured too far from a coastline.

Right *The Argonauts' Ship Argo* by **Lorenzo Costa (1459–1535)**. When the Argonauts made a sacrifice to Apollo before they left, Idmon, the seer, predicted from the coils of smoke that he was fated to die on the voyage.

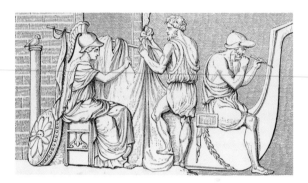

Above **Building the Argo.** Athene and Apollo were said to be protectors of both the Argo and the Argonauts. On their departure, the crew made sacrifices to Apollo, who was known as the god of embarkations.

the man with one sandal was the only son of his half-brother Aeson, he congratulated himself doubly on getting rid of a man who would probably have tried to kill him and regain the kingdom for his ousted father. "Jason," he said, "it will serve the kingdom well if you go in quest of the Golden Fleece, for the ghost of Phrixus is calling to me in my dreams, asking to be brought home along with the fleece. If you succeed in this quest, I shall renounce my kingship in your favor."

Jason knew that he could not achieve the quest for the Golden Fleece without some help. The forth-coming journey would be arduous, going up into the Black Sea and beyond, and then he would have to confront or outwit King Aietes, who was the son of the sun god Helius (Sol) and likely to enjoy the god's protection. Jason decided to assemble a band of

heroes to go with him, and they were known as the Argonauts (meaning "those who sailed in the Argo") after the name of his ship, the Argo (meaning "swift"). The goddess Athene (Minerva) helped with the building of the ship, and because its prow was made of oak wood from Zeus's sacred grove at Dodona, the great ship Argo could prophesy in human words. The Argo was built for sailing, and it could also be rowed when the winds were not favorable. It had

The Voyage of the Argo

The Argonauts experienced many adventures on their way to Colchis. First they visited Lemnos, an island where the women did not enjoy the company of men. The Lemnian men brought women from beyond the island to provide them with children, and the Lemnian women did not tolerate this arrangement either. They killed all the men on the island, all the foreign women, and all the male children, including the newborn babies. The sole survivor of this terrible massacre was the Lemnian king, Thoas, whose daughter Hypsipyle enclosed him in a chest and then sent it out to sea. She subsequently became queen of this nation of women. The Argonauts were forced to land here because of a storm and the Lemnian women tried to prevent them from setting foot on the island. Jason was already skilled at charming women, and he managed to charm Queen Hypsipyle into letting the Argonauts disembark. She did not tell Jason the truth about the absence of men on the island; instead, she talked vaguely about the women forcing the men to leave. The Argonauts intended to stay for just a few days, but days stretched to years, while Jason and Hypsipyle delighted in one another's company. She became pregnant, and gave birth to twin sons, Euneus and Thoas, and the other women

Above *Heracles and the Argonauts* attributed to the Niobid Painter (475 B.C.–450 B.C.). As well as Heracles, among the men who joined the Argonauts was Acastus, the only son of Pelias. It is not clear whether he defied his father out of sympathy for Jason, or for the love of adventure and glory.

seats for 50 rowers, and Jason sent heralds through all of Greece inviting heroes to join his crew.

All the famous men of Greece answered his call, including Heracles and Orpheus the musician. Castor and Polydeuces (Pollux) also became Argonauts, and so did Augeias of the filthy stables that were cleansed by Heracles. Zetes and Calais, sons of the wind, joined the voyage, as did Meleager and Atalanta, Theseus and Peirithous, and a host of many others.

Above *Hylas and the Nymphs* by John Waterhouse (1849–1917). It is said that Heracles was wild with grief at the loss of his beloved companion Hylas. Heracles searched everywhere, and made the local people promise to keep looking for the boy. For centuries after, it became an annual tradition to wander the countryside calling out Hylas's name.

of Lemnos also took the opportunity to replenish the island's population. The Argonauts might have stayed there for the rest of their lives, forgetting their quest, but Heracles, who had remained on the shore guarding the Argo, stormed into the royal palace one day demanding that they leave. The Argonauts sailed on in their ship to the next adventure of the journey, leaving behind a new generation of male babies, and from that time on, Lemnos was no longer an island solely populated by man-hating women.

It is young Hylas, that false runaway
Who with a Naiad now would make his bed
Forgetting Herakles

OSCAR WILDE (1854–1900), "CHARMIDES"

KING CYZICUS

Before traveling out of the Mediterranean and into the Black Sea, the Argonauts visited the Arcton Peninsula, a region dominated by Mount Dindymon. The king of this region, Cyzicus, welcomed the visitors, and warned them not to climb the mountain, a warning that made the Argonauts all the more eager to explore. Six-armed giants, children of the earth goddess Gaia, lived on this mountain, and began attacking the Argonauts when they went

THERE'S MANY A SLIP...

Anchaeus was the helmsman of the Argonauts. He was the king of Tegea, and a seer told him that he would not live long enough to drink the juice of his own vines. Anchaeus hoped to prove the oracle wrong, and when he returned from the quest for the Golden Fleece, as soon as the first crop was harvested, he squeezed the juice of the grapes into a cup, and put it to his lips. The seer warned him again: "There's many a slip 'twixt the cup and the lip." Anchaeus was about to drink when suddenly someone called out that a wild boar was ravaging his vineyard. Out he ran, grabbing his spear and shield, but the boar was too strong for him. In a moment, he lay dead. The seer had spoken the truth.

earth-giants, and now she sent bad weather that kept the Argo in the harbor for many days. Eventually the Argonauts' soothsayer, Mopsus, learned from a bird's song that they would be able to leave only if they propitiated the goddess. Argus, the man who built the Argo, carved a fine statue of Rhea, and then the winds blew fair and they sailed on.

THE LOSS OF HYLAS

At the next stop, Hylas became lost. He was Heracles' friend and lover, a beautiful young man. When he went to collect water, the naiads of the pool saw how handsome he was and longed to kiss and fondle him. They stretched out their arms and pulled him down into the water, drowning him. None of the Argonauts could find any trace of him, except for a water jug lying beside the pool. Heracles searched again and again for Hylas, until eventually Jason and the Argonauts sailed on without him. Some say that the Argo's speaking oak told Jason to leave Heracles behind, because he was too heavy for the ship. In the end, Heracles went back to Thebes to continue with his labors.

POLYDEUCES THE BOXER

The next hero to find an adventure was Polydeuces, the great boxer. On the island of Bebrycus lived King Amycus, a man who believed that he was the greatest of boxers. He used to force all visiting men

to box with him and had so far killed every opponent, not only because he was a huge, heavily muscled man, but also because his boxing gloves had steel spikes concealed in them. This time he challenged the Argonauts, who sent Polydeuces out as their champion. Polydeuces did not flinch when he saw the spiky boxing gloves, because he knew that he would be much faster on his feet than the rather too solid king. Amycus never even had a chance to land

Above **Mopsus the sooth-sayer.** Mopsus was a warrior seer from Thessaly, although he won more fame for his prophetic powers than his combat abilities. Mopsus could read the future in the flight of birds, an art he learned from Apollo.

climbing, but Heracles and the other heroes had no trouble in killing them all. Then the Argonauts went back to their ship and set sail, but the winds were against them, and in the night they were driven back toward the island. King Cyzicus thought that he was under attack from enemies, and took his soldiers to the coast to fight off the invaders. The Argonauts fought back, and by morning the king was dead along with many of his soldiers. The ancient mother goddess Rhea (Cybele) had been angered when Cyzicus killed a lion sacred to her, and the unfavorable winds that led to Cyzicus's death were sent by her. She was also angered by the Argonauts' killing of the

as soon as they were sure that no god would be offended by what they planned to do, they soared into the air and plummeted down on the Harpies. Many of the creatures died, and the rest retreated far to the south, never to trouble Phineus again.

Phineus was most grateful for all the help that the Argonauts had given him, and in return he told Jason the secret of safe passage through the Symplegades, clashing rocks that had always previously exacted the toll of a life when anyone tried to pass through them. The rocks took a toll even on the doves of Zeus when they carried ambrosia to Olympus; out of a flock, one always died. Although the Argo was the fastest of ships, the rocks would still close in on her if the gods did not favor Jason's voyage. Phineus gave Jason a caged dove, and told him to set the bird free when he drew close to the rocks. If the bird flew through and lived, it would be a good omen, and the Argo should be able to get through safely as well, but if the bird died, Jason should give up the quest. The ship set sail for the huge, sheer-sided rocks, and the Argonauts could see them lean toward each other and then surge apart. The dove scudded through, and the rocks clashed shut as it passed, catching only a few tail feathers. Then the Argo scudded through, and the rocks caught just the tip of her wooden stern. Some say that Athene lent a hand to hold the rocks apart for the ship that she had helped to build. From that moment, the Symplegades no longer had the power to clash together. The Argonauts were now on the last stage of their journey, up the Black Sea to Mount Caucasus, and then up the River Phasis.

Above *Phineus Is Delivered from the Harpies by Calais and Zetes* by Bernard Picart (1673–1733). Some say Phineus was blinded not by Zeus, but by Poseidon. The soothsayer was apparently being too helpful when he assisted Phrixus in finding his way to Colchis.

Above right *The Argonauts Pass the Symplegades,* French School (nineteenth century). The Symplegades were also known as "The Clashing Rocks," as they were said to clash together when driven by the wind.

a blow with his gloves. In less than a minute after the start of the match, Polydeuces knocked King Amycus down, fracturing his skull and killing him.

PHINEUS AND THE ARGONAUTS

Then the Argo went on into the Bosphorus, where they landed in Thrace and met a blind seer called Phineus. He had been so successful as a soothsayer that Zeus had punished him with blindness, and a band of Harpies arrived to harass him whenever he tried to eat, squabbling, shrieking, and befouling his food. These Harpies had the bodies and heads of women, but the wings and claws of carrion-eating birds. Phineus was starving to death in the middle of a prosperous country, his tables laden with food. He appealed to the Argonauts for help, and Calais and Zetes, sons of Boreas, offered to drive the Harpies away. As sons of the North Wind, they could fly, and

JASON AND MEDEA

Once the Argo was through the clashing rocks, the Argonauts found themselves in a world of more marvels. First, they saw bright Apollo, the sun god, walking toward the east just before sunrise, and turned their eyes away in dread. Then they sailed by the land of the Amazons and came to the island of Ares, which had recently been populated by the birds that Heracles had expelled from Lake Stymphalus in one of his labors. The Argonauts had been forewarned about their feathers that were sharp enough to cut like knives, and as the Argo drew closer to the island, half the rowers stayed at their oars while the others held up their shields as a wall against the birds. They hit their spears on the underneath of the shields, making such a din that the birds were afraid to attack.

Further Travels of the Argo

Farther into the Black Sea went the ship, and now the Argonauts could see Mount Caucasus in the distance, and they heard the cries of Prometheus, tortured daily by beak and claw. Heracles would soon arrive to end his centuries of pain, but the Argonauts did not want to offend Zeus (Jupiter) by interfering, and sailed past, up the River Phasis. At last they arrived in the harbor of Aia, and went to the palace of King Aietes. The king was not welcoming, intent that his visitors should not gain the Golden Fleece. Phrixus had died childless after marrying Aietes' daughter, and Aietes would not give the fleece back to anyone akin to Athamas's family. After all, the last thing that Athamas had done to his son Phrixus was to try to cut his throat. If the fleece belonged to anyone, Aietes believed, it was to the king who had taken Phrixus into his family.

THE THREE TESTS

"You can have the fleece," Aietes mocked Jason, "if you can pass three tests. First, equal me at the task of plowing. Then take the fleece from its guardian serpent, and finally sow the teeth of a dragon and kill the warriors who will spring up from your sowing." Phrixus had placed the fleece in the sacred grove of Ares where it was guarded by a gigantic serpent, and the king was confident that anyone who tried to retrieve it would die either by venom or asphyxiation, so that the other two tasks were little more than ornamental flourishes. He did not realize that his daughter Medea was falling in love with Jason as he spoke. Hera (Juno) had asked Aphrodite (Venus) to inspire Medea with an irresistible passion for Jason, so that he could win the Golden Fleece, and Eros (Cupid) flew unseen into the palace, drew his bow, and pierced Medea's heart. As her father named the three tasks, Medea was already planning how to help Jason achieve them.

First came the plowing match. Poseidon (Neptune) had given King Aietes two fire-breathing bulls made of bronze, and an iron plow that never rusted. Aietes plowed a deep furrow, and then dared Jason to take hold of the plow. While the king was busy in the field, his daughter Medea secretly gave Jason some magical ointment that would protect his skin from the heat of the bulls' bodies and breath. With her help, he was easily able to plow his own deep furrow, and so he passed the first test.

Jason requested that King Aietes let him complete his second task unobserved, because Medea had whispered to him that she would help him if no one was watching. At midnight he walked quietly toward

Above *Jason Taming the Bulls of Aietes* by Jean Francois de Troy (1679–1752). Jason was well able to accomplish the first task, having enlisted the help of Medea. Some say that the magic drug she gave him was from a plant that had grown out of the blood of Prometheus as it dripped from the eagle's talons.

Above **The Argo.** The Argo was built by Argus, the son of Arestor, and was subsequently named after him. With the help of Athene, Argus built the largest and most elaborate ship of his time.

Above **Engagement of Jason and Medea.** It is said that Aphrodite was concerned that Medea would be torn between filial duty and her love for Jason. The goddess appeared to her in the form of Circe to persuade her to follow her heart, even if it meant betraying her father.

Opposite page **Medea and the Fleece.** Medea, meaning "cunning" or "knowing," was a priestess of the underworld goddess Hecate. Lulling the serpent to sleep was an easy task for Medea, who was well acquainted with magical herbs and potions, and could work miracles for both good and evil.

the sacred grove of Ares, and, as he had hoped, there was the princess waiting for him. She asked him to swear to take her to Greece with him, marry her, and always remain faithful to her. Once he had murmured his vows, she crept over to where the serpent was coiled around one of Ares' sacred trees, with the fleece hanging beside its head. As she moved closer, she began to sing and hum a magical charm of sleep, and the serpent's head drooped. She dripped a sleep potion into its eyes and it fell deeply asleep. Jason took the fleece and left without disturbing the serpent's sleep. Now he owed his life twice over to the magic-maker Medea.

Medea was a priestess of the goddess Hecate, who was a triple goddess, manifesting as maiden, mother, and crone. In some accounts of Hecate, the triple goddess was made up of Persephone (Proserpina) as maiden, Demeter (Ceres) as mother, and Hecate as crone. In these accounts Hecate was a fearsome goddess of witchcraft and death, but when she was understood as the full triple goddess, she had powers over life as well as death. Hecate was the goddess of the crossroads, the place where decisions must be made and where one can look back into the past and forward into the future. The coming of Jason was a crossroads in Medea's life, and it was Hecate's magic that Medea used to betray her father's treasure into the hands of her new lover.

For Jason's final task, he needed no help from Medea. He took the dragon's teeth and sowed them in the field where he and the king had plowed their furrows. Jason knew exactly what to do with the warriors who had erupted from the ground, as Cadmus had previously faced a very similar problem in Thebes. He hurled a rock right into the middle of the crowd of armed men, and at once they all started pushing each other around, each one blaming the next for trying to attack him with the rock. Very soon they were all dead.

Right *Jason and the Golden Fleece* by Erasmus Quellinus (1607–1678). Jason was finally able to take possession of the Golden Fleece. The famous ram who saved Phrixus was said to have been an offspring of Poseidon and Theophane. It was blessed with intelligence and reason, and was able to speak, as well as fly.

THE SACRED OAK

Erysichthon was a foolish man who continued to cut down an oak tree after he saw blood oozing from his first cut. His servants gave him fair warning that the oak was sacred to Demeter (Ceres), but he did not pay any attention. Demeter sent a fearful punishment, instructing Famine to stay close to him, day and night, so that he could never fill his stomach. He gorged himself until he had spent all his wealth on food, yet still he was starving. Then he sold his daughter as a slave to buy food. Poseidon (Neptune) took pity on her and changed her into a fisherman, and so she escaped. Time and time again Erysichthon sold her and then retrieved her, but the food that he bought could never satisfy his stomach's demands. In the end he started consuming his own body, and so he died. That is how the goddess of all growing things took her revenge.

Above *Erysichthon Punished* by I Matheus (c. 1610). The blood from the oak tree is said to be that of the Dryad or tree nymph.

Above right *Medea and Pelias* by I. Briot (c. 1610). In another version of this story, Jason returned home to find that King Pelias, who thought that Jason had perished, had killed Jason's father and younger brother. Jason's mother, as a result, had committed suicide.

Right *Medea's Flight to Corinth with Jason* by the Policoro Painter (fifth century). Some say that Medea's half-brother Apsyrtus was not a child, but a grown man. When Medea learned of his deal with Jason to leave her behind in return for being allowed to keep the Golden Fleece, she convinced Jason to kill him.

FLIGHT FROM COLCHIS

Now Jason and the Argonauts fled from Colchis, with the Golden Fleece and Princess Medea, who snatched up her baby half-brother Apsyrtus from his cradle as she ran. The king of Colchis and his navy followed them, ready for a sea battle, and Medea could see that the Argo would be attacked and sunk if she did not act. She sacrificed her brother to the goddess Hecate, slicing up his small body and throwing the pieces into the sea. Jason joined in the murder, desperate to delay the enemy. Aietes yelled for his men to stop, to jump into the water, and retrieve the body of his son. By the time all the pieces had been recovered, the Argo was safely away.

Jason and Medea had committed a crime that only Hecate as crone goddess would countenance. Their existence was now an offense to all the other gods, polluted as they were by murder. The

Argo's oracular oak wood prophesied that they would reach home again only if Jason and Medea went to the island of Hecate's daughter Circe, who had the power to cleanse them of their crime. Circe performed the ritual of purification, but she did not welcome Medea into her house, because the princess was still guilty of betraying her father.

Onward the Argo sailed, past the rocks where the Sirens sang their lethal song, as they would sing two generations later to Odysseus (Ulysses) and his men. The Argonauts sailed safely past, because the musician Orpheus sang one of his lovely songs so loudly that the Sirens could not be heard. They went past the islands that Odysseus would visit on his way home from Troy, and Jason married Medea on the island of the Phaeacians. Orpheus sang the wedding song, and the Golden Fleece was the blanket for their bed.

A storm drove them to the country of Libya, and a huge wave carried the Argo a long way inland, leaving the ship aground in the desert. Here Jason had a prophetic vision of the three daughters of Libya, who told him that he and his men must carry the Argo across the desert, as their mother had carried them in the womb. After 12 days of trudging across the sandy, rocky desert, the Argonauts came to the site of another of Heracles' labors, where the apples of the Hesperides—Aegle, Erytheia, and Hespera— had grown. Heracles had been there only the day before their arrival, and the most keen-sighted of the Argonauts, Lynceus, swore that he could just make out the figure of Heracles walking away, slowly receding into the distance.

The Argonauts found their way to a salt lake, but they could find no outlet to the sea. Then Jason remembered that the

Pythian oracle had advised him to take two tripods on the voyage. He offered one of them to the local god, not knowing what name to invoke. Poseidon's son, the half-man, half-dolphin Triton, rose from the lake in response, gave a lump of earth to one of the Argonauts, a man called Euphemus, and then helped them pull the ship to the open sea.

The Argo then traveled across the Mediterranean to Crete. The island was guarded by a metal creature called Talus, made by Hephaestus, which sleeplessly walked around the shores, circling the island three times a day. Talus's only weakness was a vein that ran the length of his body, and Medea bewitched him so that he tripped and fell, tearing open this vein. Ichor, the fluid that runs in the veins of the gods, spurted out of his body, and so he died. Onward sailed the Argo, calling in at many other islands on the way. The gods sent a dream to Euphemus, reminding him of the clod of earth that the Triton had given him. In his dream, he held it close to his heart, where it changed into the form of a nymph. "I am the daughter of the Triton and the goddess Libya," she told him, "and I want to live in the sea." When he woke, Euphemus threw the clod of earth into the sea, and up rose a new island, the volcanic isle of Thera.

Medea among the Greeks

Jason returned with his new bride to Iolcus, where he found his father, Aeson, close to death. Medea was glad to use her magical powers for life rather than death. She ordered servants to cut up the body of Aeson and boil the pieces in her magic cauldron. Soon the body took shape again, as a young man. Pelias, the king who had sent Jason on the quest for the Golden Fleece, was also ageing, and eager to be transformed back into a young man by Medea. She ordered his daughters to cut up his body and boil it in a cauldron, but without her magic, he remained dead. So the oracle was fulfilled, that his death would come about through the man with one sandal.

Jason knew that it was for the love of him that Medea had organized the killing of Pelias, and so he went willingly into exile with her to Corinth. There he beached the ship Argo, dedicating it to Poseidon in gratitude for a safe voyage. For a while Medea and Jason lived together happily, but Jason became restless, stirred up by ambition and perhaps by love. He decided to set aside his marriage with Medea on the pretext that she was a foreigner, and wed instead

When the first Ship sailed for the Golden Fleece— ARGO—exalted for that daring feat To fix in heaven her shape distinct with stars.

WILLIAM WORDSWORTH (1770–1850), *MEMORIALS OF A TOUR ON THE CONTINENT*

Princess Glauce, daughter of King Creon of Corinth. On Creon's death, Jason could become king. When Medea found out what he had planned, she was overcome with anguish. For this man she had betrayed her father, killed her brother, caused the death of a king, and gained a reputation as an evil witch, and now he was proposing to send her into fresh exile from the exile she already endured for his sake. First she wept, then she argued the injustice of what he was doing, and then she spoke sweetly to him. "Let me give a bridal gift to Glauce," she said, "and rather than showing my unwelcome face to her,

Below *Orpheus Plays Harp* by T.H. Robinson.

Orpheus played his harp and sang loudly so the Argonauts would not hear the deadly songs of the Sirens. Some say the Sirens were originally the nymph companions of Persephone. When the goddess was snatched away by Hades, the nymphs prayed for wings so that they could search the seas for her. Their wish was granted, and they became half-maiden and half-bird.

Above *Jason and Medea* by Carle van Loo (1705–1765). Some say that it was the vengeful Medea herself who murdered her children, others assert that her children had taken refuge at Hera's altar and were stoned to death by the people of Corinth, who were enraged by Medea's actions.

let me send my children with the gifts." Jason agreed, and Medea piled their arms full of finely woven cloth. It was a wedding robe, enchanted so that it would burn its wearer, and with it came a golden diadem, which would sear the forehead of its wearer to the bone. Glauce and her father died in torment, and in the outcry and confusion, Medea also killed her children. She did all of these things to put Jason through as much misery as she suffered through him, and the cost of her children's lives did not seem such a high price to pay.

Any other woman behaving like this might expect the wrath of the gods to fall upon her, but for Medea, granddaughter of Helius (Sol) and priestess of Hecate, the gods sent a chariot drawn by dragons so that she could escape. She fled to Athens and married Aegeus, and remained living there until Theseus arrived and cast her out when she tried to have him poisoned. Next she traveled to the country of Persia,

becoming the goddess of the Medes, a people named after her. Jason lived on in wretched obscurity, hated by the gods because he had broken his oath to Medea. Years later, when he was sitting on the shore in the shadow of his beloved ship, the Argo, a piece of its oracular oak wood fell on his head and killed him. The great ship was not guilty of murder, and to commemorate its amazing voyage, the constellation Argo was placed in the night sky.

Of all the heroes of Greek myth, Jason was the one who owed most to a woman. It was Medea who provided the magic ointment that saved him from being burned alive by the bulls. It was Medea who enchanted the serpent into sleeping, so that he could steal the Golden Fleece. It was Medea who slaughtered her own brother to delay the pursuing navy, and it was also she who brought about the catastrophe that ended Jason's hopes of starting a new life, with a new bride. Jason was never a hero in his own quest.

MELEAGER AND ATALANTA

Meleager was the son of Queen Althaia of Calydon, but his father was Ares, the god of war, and not Althaia's husband, King Oineus. At Meleager's birth, the three Fates appeared in Althaia's bedroom. The youngest, Clotho, who spins the thread of mortal life, prophesied that the baby boy would become a man of courage and noble deeds. The grown woman, Lachesis, who weaves the cloth of human life, prophesied that he would be a hero of great renown. The oldest of the Fates, Atropos, who cuts off the thread of life, looked at the fire, where a log was burning, and prophesied that he would live until the log was totally burned. Althaia jumped out of bed and pulled the log out of the fire. Then she hid it in the palace, hoping that it would never be found again.

Meleager grew up to be devoted to the hunt. When he was a young man, a wild boar came to Calydon. It was sent by Artemis (Diana), the goddess of the hunt, angry because King Oineus had forgotten to honor her with sacrifice. No one could catch or kill the boar, and Meleager decided to summon all the hunters of Greece to the Calydonian hunt. Many heroes joined the quest for the boar. Heracles (Hercules) did not come, because he was busy with his labors, but Jason joined in, along with Theseus and some of the Argonauts. The huntress Atalanta also came to Calydon, and caused much disagreement among the huntsmen, who did not want any women on this quest. Meleager insisted that Atalanta should be allowed to hunt, for the arrow of the love god had pierced his heart as soon as he first saw her.

When Atalanta was born, her father was disappointed that she was not a boy, and ordered her to be exposed on the nearest mountain. She was saved from death by a mother bear that suckled her, and then she was found by hunters and reared among them. Atalanta grew up to be a magnificent runner, and she vowed that she would marry only the man who could outrun her in a race. The conditions of the race were difficult, for she gave herself the right to kill any man who failed. Many men were tempted by her beauty, and they all died with her arrow in their heart.

There was no time for Meleager to challenge her to a footrace, but he made sure that he was close to her for the six days of the hunt. At last the two of them killed the boar together, Atalanta shooting it with an arrow and Meleager slitting its throat. Then it was time for the banquet, along with the presentation of the boar's head and skin to the victor. Meleager should by rights have kept these prizes, as he struck the blow that actually killed the boar, but he offered them to Atalanta. Feasting turned to furious debate among the hunters, then to fighting,

Left **Hunting the Calydon boar.** Meleager joined the Argonauts in the search for the Golden Fleece. When he set sail, his uncle, Lacoon, had to accompany the celebrated warrior because he was too young to be on his own.

Below *The Three Fates* by Sebastiano Mazzoni (1611– 1678). In some stories, the Fates appear to carry out the will of the gods, while in others, it is the gods who bow to the will of the Fates.

GEMINI

The twin brothers Castor and Polydeuces (Pollux) were sons of Leda. Polydeuces was the child of Zeus (Jupiter) and Castor the child of the mortal king, Tyndareus of Sparta. When Castor died, Polydeuces prayed to his father, Zeus, begging that he might also die, even though he had been born immortal. He had no wish to outlive his mortal brother. Zeus offered Polydeuces eternal life among the Olympians, but Polydeuces would not accept this gift unless Castor could share it. In the end, Zeus decreed that the twins should share both immortality and death, alternating their places in the underworld and among the gods on Olympus. He marked their brotherly love for one another with the two brightest stars in the constellation of Gemini, the Twins.

Left **Dioscuri (Castor and Polydeuces).** The heavenly twins were known as Dioscuri, which means "sons of Zeus." When they became stars, they also became the guardian of seafarers.

Below *Atalanta and Melanion* by John Batten (1860–1932). Filled with delight in his prize, Melanion forgot to pay Aphrodite suitable honors. When the newlyweds consummated their union in a sacred temple, Aphrodite punished them for their sacrilege by turning them into lions, which, it was believed, did not mate with one another, but only with leopards.

and Meleager ended by killing his uncles, who were also Althaia's brothers.

The palace was full of turmoil. Althaia crouched down on the floor in grief and anger, praying to Hades (Pluto) and Persephone (Proserpina) that her son might join them in the underworld as soon as possible. Then she went to her bedroom, where she had hidden the log from her fire in a chest of finely woven clothes. Althaia took out the charred log and thrust it into the flames. Meleager felt the fire attack his limbs, then climb up toward his heart, and then he died, killed by his distraught mother.

Atalanta and the Apples

After the disastrous end to the Calydonian hunt, more suitors challenged Atalanta to a footrace and died as a result. No man alive could run as fast as this favorite of the goddess Artemis. Her cousin Melanion fell in love with her, and thought carefully

about the race that he would have to run in order to claim her. She could be won only through trickery, he concluded, and he prayed to the goddess of sexual desire, Aphrodite (Venus), for help. The goddess was very impatient with Atalanta's attitude toward her admirers, and came down from Mount Olympus to give Melanion three golden apples, irresistibly beautiful fruit that she had begged from Dionysus (Bacchus). "Use them wisely," she told Melanion, "and Atalanta will be yours."

The day of the footrace came, and Melanion made ready at the starting line, carrying the apples in his hands. Atalanta was about to mock him, to ask if he thought that holding weights in his hands would make him run faster, but then she saw the apples more closely, and their golden sheen captivated her. Once the race was over and Melanion dead, she thought, the beautiful fruit would be hers, and she promised herself that she would run her fastest for the sake of these golden marvels.

The race began, and Atalanta was already ahead of Melanion, when he threw one of the apples past her, away from the racetrack. She left the track, unable to help herself, chasing the apple and scooping it up into her hand. Then she hurtled back in pursuit of Melanion, and quickly overtook him again. He threw the second apple, and despite herself, she followed it away from the racetrack until she had it safely in her hand. Now Melanion was ahead once more, and the race was nearly over, but even so, she was fast enough to catch and kill him—but there went the third apple, and Atalanta's feet followed it off the track as though she were running for her life. Now she was back again, running faster than she had ever run before, but Melanion was already at the finishing line—the race was over and the bride had been won.

THESEUS BECOMES A HERO

There are two stories about the birth of Theseus. In one, he was the son of the sea god Poseidon (Neptune); in the other, he was the son of a mortal man, King Aegeus. In the first version, Athene (Minerva) sent a dream to the unmarried princess of Troezen, Aethra. Athene said that Aethra must visit her temple and make a sacrifice there to the ghost of a charioteer buried close by. Aethra went to the temple the next day and there she met Poseidon, waiting to take her virginity by force. Nine months later, she gave birth to his son, Theseus, who grew up in Troezen as heir to the kingdom. It was most unusual for the virgin goddess Athene to approve of anyone, even another Olympian, engaging in sexual activity within her temple, yet this time she not only approved, but even sent the girl to her attacker. It was more important to her for Theseus to be born than for her temple to keep its virginal purity.

In the other version, Aethra gave her virginity to King Aegeus of Athens, with the encouragement of her father. After two childless marriages, Aegeus longed for a son, and asked the oracle at Delphi how he could become a father. The oracle told him, "Do not open your wine skin until you get

back to Athens." Aegeus did not understand the veiled meaning of these words and, rather than returning to Athens by the direct road, he visited the king of Troezen, Pittheus, who was an expert at deciphering the meaning of oracles. Pittheus understood at once that the oracle had been telling Aegeus to stay chaste until he was back in Athens, because the first time he had sexual relations with a woman, he would father a son. The king of Troezen did not explain this, because he wanted his daughter Aethra to be the mother of Aegeus's son who would become Aegeus's heir as king of Athens. That night, he persuaded his daughter to share her bed with the guest, and in the morning, before leaving for home, Aegeus asked her

MEDEA'S MAGIC

Medea was expert at the use of magical herbs. When she prepared the poisoned cup for Theseus, she put some wolfsbane into it. This noxious plant came into being when Heracles dragged the three-headed dog, Cerberus, up from the realm of the dead. Cerberus was foaming at the mouth as he tried to escape, and drops of this foam fell to the ground, becoming the poisonous wolfsbane. Much earlier in her story, the ointment that she gave to Jason, to protect him from being burned to death, was made from the Caucasian crocus, sprung from the blood that flowed from Prometheus's liver as Zeus's (Jupiter's) bird ripped at it daily.

Right *Jason and Medea* by John Waterhouse (1849–1917). Some say that as well as using her magic to help Jason, the sorceress Medea also cured Heracles of the madness that caused him to murder his children.

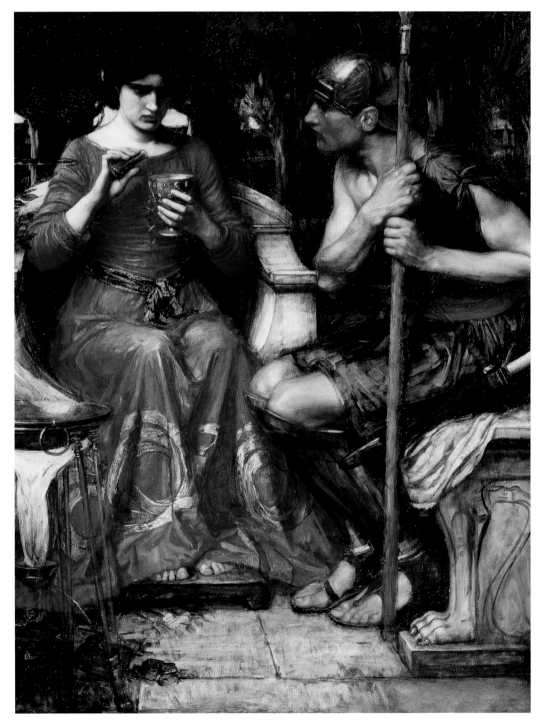

Below *Theseus Finding His Father's Sword* by Giovanni Ghisolfi (1632–1683). When Theseus grew to manhood, he traveled to Delphi to offer, as was the custom, the first clippings of his hair to Apollo. It was on his return home that his mother told him the story of Aegeus and took him to the rock under which the sword and sandals were hidden.

to ride a little way out of the city in his chariot. He found a place where there was a deep hollow in the road, and there he put his sandals and sword. Then he rolled a huge rock over them with a great effort, until it sat snugly in the hollow. "Aethra," he said, "only a hero will be able to shift this rock and find my sword and sandals. I doubt that you are pregnant with my child, but if you do give birth to a son of mine, take him here and let him try his strength against the rock. If he can move it away, let him come to Athens carrying the sword and wearing the sandals so that I can recognize him and make him heir to the kingdom. It would not be safe for him to come to Athens before then, in case one of my unpleasant nephews tried to assassinate him." Then Aegeus left, standing barefoot in his chariot.

Nine months later, Aethra gave birth to Theseus, and he grew up at the court of King Pittheus. When he was seven years old, Heracles (Hercules) came visiting, in the course of his 12 labors, and threw off his fearsome lion skin so that he could be

> *From Themistocles began the saying, "He is a second Hercules."*
>
> PLUTARCH (C.46–C.120), *LIFE OF THESEUS*

more comfortable at the welcoming banquet. All the other children at court panicked at the sight of the lion skin on the floor, looking just like a live lion; but Theseus seized an ax and ran up to the creature, ready to kill it, before he realized that it was only an empty skin. This was his first heroic deed, but he was not yet strong enough to lift the rock and take his father's sword.

Dangers on the Road

When Theseus was no longer a child, his mother took him to the place where Aegeus had buried the sandals and sword under the rock. The young man effortlessly pushed the rock out of the hollow and uncovered his father's tokens of recognition. He put on the sandals and, with sword in hand, started the long walk to Athens. The road was beset with murderers, as he knew, and he could have chosen a safer route by sea, but he wanted to prove himself a hero. Theseus admired Heracles and wanted to win the same kind of glory; as well as this, he wanted to meet his father in Athens, not as an unknown young man but as an established hero.

Above *Theseus's Adventures* by the Dinos Painter (c. 425 B.C.). Theseus wanted to be known as a great hero like Hercules, so he traveled to Athens along a road haunted by scoundrels, murderers, and savage animals. Among the many villains and beasts he met along the way was the Crommyonian Sow, a fierce creature that had killed many travelers.

THESEUS AND PERIPHETES

Soon after he set out, he met Periphetes, the crippled son of the lame god Hephaestus (Vulcan), who used to lurk in the undergrowth beside the road and assault passersby with a large bronze club. Because he took people by surprise, Periphetes had killed and robbed many travelers, but Theseus was on the lookout for trouble. When Periphetes jumped out onto the road behind him, Theseus turned, took hold of him, and threw him to the ground. Then the murderer was battered to death with his own club. Theseus took this massive club with him, perhaps in deliberate imitation of Heracles, and it was to kill many more men on his travels.

SINIS THE PINE-BENDER

Farther along the road to Athens was a pine forest, the haunt of a murderer called Sinis, the son of Poseidon. Whenever Sinis captured a traveler, he used to bend two pine trees together and tie his victim to both of them; he even forced the poor wretch to help bend the trees. Then Sinis would release the pine trees and the victim would be torn apart. Theseus allowed Sinis to take him into the forest, and even helped him choose two sturdy pine trees and bend them together, but then it was Theseus who tied Sinis to the trees, paying no attention to his screams for mercy, and let them spring apart again. So died the pine-bender, torn apart as he had torn apart so many others.

SCIRON THE MURDERER

The road then passed along the very steep slope of a mountain with a cliff to one side and, on the other side, a precipitous drop to the sea. Any travelers who fell from the path or tried to wade around the foot of the mountain, were eaten by a turtle one of the servants of Hades (Pluto). A rascal called Sciron took full advantage of the narrow mountain path. He used to sit on a rock in the middle of the road and demand that every traveler wash his feet, as a toll. As soon as his victims knelt down, Sciron would kick them over the mountainside and into the sea, where the turtle was waiting to devour them. Theseus came up to Sciron's rock and gave it a mighty kick, so that it toppled into the sea. Sciron tumbled with it, straight into the mouth of the waiting turtle, and did not even have time to scream as he fell.

> *I know, indeed, the evil of that I purpose; but my inclination gets the better of my judgment.*
>
> EURIPIDES (484 B.C.–406 B.C.), *MEDEA*

CERCYON AND PROCRUSTES

Closer to Athens, near Eleusis, there lived a wrestler called Cercyon. He forced all passersby to wrestle with him, and all of them lost both the competition and their lives. Theseus was far more skilled as a wrestler, and he killed Cercyon by hurling him against the ground and smashing his bones. A little way down the road lived Sinis's father Procrustes, another murderer, who used to offer travelers a bed for the night. He had two beds, one was a very long one and the other was very short. He measured tall people on the short bed, and sliced off the overhanging parts. Similarly, he measured short people on the long bed and then stretched them to fit. All who suffered this kind of rough measurement died.

Theseus forced Procrustes onto his short bed and measured and pruned him until he died.

By the time Theseus reached Athens, every Athenian had heard about the new hero who had made the road safe for travelers, but no one knew that he was the son of Aegeus and heir to the throne—no one except the king's wife, Medea. This was the same Medea who had helped Jason win the Golden Fleece. Now, as queen of Athens, she wanted her son, Medus, to be the heir to the ageing king's throne. Using her magic, she persuaded Aegeus to poison the new champion with wine at his welcoming banquet. All that Theseus could think about was the moment when his father would recognize him. He took the wine cup from Aegeus and offered him the sword in return. The king suddenly recognized the weapon that he had hidden so long ago in Troezen. He knocked the cup out of Theseus's hand and cried out, "Seize that wicked woman, my wife!" Medea could not hide her guilt, and was banished from Athens with her son Medus, while Theseus was welcomed afresh with honor as the king's son and heir.

Theseus, the New Heir

Not everyone welcomed the new heir. Aegeus had a brother, Pallas, who had 50 sons. For years they had expected to rule the kingdom between them when Aegeus died, and now they planned to ambush Theseus and kill him. Luck ran Theseus's way, for he discovered this plan and killed most of the 50 sons of Pallas. After this, Aegeus wanted his newfound son to stay in Athens and not risk his life on any more adventures. After all, he told Theseus, the killing of so many rogues while he was on his way to Athens had established his reputation as a hero. He had no need at all to prove himself any further. But Theseus fretted at court, as though he were in a gilded prison. At the first chance, he crept out of the royal palace to seek another adventure.

Heracles had brought a firebreathing bull to Marathon, as part of his labors, and it was

Below **Detail from a calyx-crater showing Theseus and Procrustes by the Dinos Painter (c. 425 B.C.).** The scoundrel Procrustes was also known as either Damastas or Polypemon. He was quickly given the nickname of "Procrustes," which means "the stretcher."

The Rape of Helen

Theseus had a friend, Peirithous, the king of the Lapiths, who was a son of Zeus (Jupiter). Each of the friends was a bad influence on the other. They told each other that sons of gods deserved the very finest of women in their beds, and that they would settle for no less than daughters of Zeus. They had heard of a daughter of Zeus, Helen of Sparta, who was rumored to be the most beautiful of girls, and they planned to abduct her and force her into marriage, casting lots to decide who was to be the lucky man. It did not bother them that she was still a child. Theseus won, and with Peirithous's help, he abducted Helen, offending the gods by seizing her in the temple of the virgin goddess Artemis (Diana). He took her to his mother, Aethra, for safe keeping after marrying her by force. Helen's brothers, Castor and Polydeuces (Pollux), came to free her, and took Aethra back to Sparta as a slave. When Helen was stolen away again, years later, by Paris of Troy, Theseus's mother went to Troy with her, still as a slave. Theseus did himself no credit by this adventure, and brought years of suffering and humiliation upon his mother. Peirithous and Theseus learned nothing from this, because their next unsuccessful plan was to carry off another daughter of Zeus, Persephone (Proserpina), from the underworld. This attempt ended with the two men stuck to thrones in the underworld, from which Heracles rescued Theseus, but Peirithous was left there forever. Theseus had longed to equal Heracles' feats, and so far he had proved himself a hero in his dealings with wicked men, but in his dealings with women, he was proving himself to be a scoundrel.

now rampaging in the plain and terrorizing the villagers. As soon as Theseus heard of this problem, he found his way secretly out of Athens and went to Marathon. Long before he could see the bull, he heard its roars, but they did not frighten him at all. What Heracles had achieved before him, he promised himself, he would be able to equal. Theseus walked fearlessly up to the bull, knowing exactly what to do. With one hand, he grabbed hold of one of its horns, and with the other, he grasped its nostrils; then he pulled its head sideways and down, so that the bull fell to its knees. Then he tied a rope around its neck, and the bull did not dare to give any more trouble as it walked behind him all the way to Athens.

Left *Helen of Troy* by Dante Gabriel Rossetti (1828–1882). It is believed that Theseus sent the beautiful Helen to be with his mother because he was so worried about the consequences of his marriage. The Athenians were displeased with his actions, afraid that they would be attacked by Sparta in retaliation for the abduction.

Below **Detail showing Heracles and Greek heroes by the Niobid Painter (c. 475 B.C.– 450 B.C.).** When Theseus and Peirithous ventured into the underworld, they accepted the offer to be seated. Unbeknown to them, they sat down on the Chairs of Forgetfulness. At once their bodies became one with the chairs and the men lost all memory of who they were and why they were there. Heracles eventually rescued Theseus, but could not help Peirithous.

THE MYTHS OF CRETE

The Greek myths of Crete speak
of a kingdom contemporary
with the royal families of
Thebes and Athens, superior
in might to any realm on
the mainland of Greece.
Archaeological evidence
suggests that these myths
of Crete look back to a
realm that existed well
before Thebes, Mycenae,
or Athens became powerful
cities. The civilization of
Crete, called Minoan after the
mythic King Minos, lasted for
about 1,500 years but went into
decline after the volcanic eruption
of Thera in about 1450 B.C. The
Cretans worshipped a mother goddess,
and surviving pottery shows young men performing
a gymnastic dance with a bull, perhaps in celebration
of the goddess. Memories of this bull dance, distorted
over generations, may have contributed to the story
of the Cretan Minotaur.

Minos and the Minotaur

Minos was one of the three sons of Zeus (Jupiter) and
Europa. He became the king of Crete, after a struggle
for power with his brothers. "Send me a bull from
the sea," Minos prayed to Poseidon
(Neptune), "to confirm that the
kingship is rightfully mine."
A magnificent white bull swam
to the Cretan shore, and there
Minos should have sacrificed it in
honor of the sea god, but he admired the
bull so much that he could not bear to have it killed.
Instead, he kept it among his herds, sacrificing an
inferior animal in its place and hoping that Poseidon
would not notice the difference.

Poseidon was not fooled, and he swiftly took
revenge. Minos's queen Pasiphae
also noticed the magnificence of
the white bull. Now Poseidon
asked Aphrodite (Venus),
the goddess of desire, to
inflame Pasiphae with
lust for the animal, and
she became obsessed
with the idea of having
sexual intercourse
with it. She ran the

*Sing to me of
the Labyrinth in which the twi-
formed bull was stalled!*

OSCAR WILDE (1854–1900),
"THE SPHINX"

risk of being trampled to death
if she approached the bull
unprotected, and she turned
to the great Greek inventor
Daedalus for a solution. He
built her a wooden cow in
which she could conceal
herself, something like
a miniature version of
the Trojan horse, and
the bull was deceived
by this. Pasiphae became
pregnant with the bull's
offspring, and nine months
later she gave birth to a
child, Asterius. His name in
Greek means "starry," but he
was born with the head and
upper torso of a bull and the lower
body of a man, and he was most
commonly known by his nickname, the
Minotaur (meaning in Greek, "the bull of Minos").
Minos felt ashamed and disgraced by the monstrous
birth, and wanted to hide the Minotaur from view.
He asked Daedalus to build a labyrinth at Knossos,
a huge underground maze with a locked door as its
sole entrance and exit. There, he hoped, the Minotaur
would live out his days in secrecy. In the meantime,
Pasiphae recovered from the mad longing with which
Aphrodite had afflicted her, and she became her
husband's faithful wife once more. Pasiphae and
Minos went on to have many children,
including two daughters, Ariadne
and Phaedra, and a son, called
Androgeus. Androgeus visited
Athens to take part in athletic
games, all of which he won, but
the Athenian king, Aegeus, started to
suspect that this Cretan champion was not only an
athlete but a supporter of the rebels who were
causing trouble in his kingdom. On the way home,
Androgeus was ambushed and killed by Aegeus's
men. That crime was the starting point for a war
between Athens and Crete, which ended in the
defeat of the Athenians. Their punishment was to
provide a tribute once every nine years, made up
of seven young men and seven young women. Everyone knew that these young Athenians were doomed
to be eaten by the Minotaur.

Daedalus and Icarus

After Daedalus had built the intricate maze of the
Cretan labyrinth, Minos imprisoned him together
with his son, Icarus, in a tower. He wanted the

Minotaur's existence to be kept secret, even though he was aware that everyone was gossiping about it, but his most compelling reason to keep the secret was to stop the spread of scandal about his wife, Pasiphae, and the bull. The tower was high and Minos had Daedalus and his son imprisoned at the top, with the stair under heavy guard. He was confident that neither of them could escape, and so he did not bother with shackles.

Daedalus looked around the room for something to work with, to devise a way to escape. He had some wax tablets with him, and the corners of the room were littered with leaves and feathers blown in through the window. No one had cleaned the tower since it had been built. Daedalus collected the feathers and made two pairs of wings from them, sticking them together with wax. He put on the larger pair and gave the others to Icarus. "Be careful," he urged his son. "You must follow me closely. Do not fly too close to the sea, because you will drown if your feathers become wet; do not fly too close to the sun, because you will fall to your death if the wax gets too hot and melts."

Father and son flew out of the tower window, and the Cretans who saw them thought that they were immortal gods. They flew on past many of the Greek islands, and Icarus grew bored with the slow, steady pace that his father was setting, and the unvarying height at which they were flying. Surely, he told himself, his father would not notice if he tried just a

Above **Daedalus and Pasiphae.** Pasiphae, like her sister Circe, was skilled in the use of herbs, charms, and spells. A lesser known version of the myth of Daedalus is that it was Pasiphae who freed the father and son from their prison. Daedalus escaped with Icarus in a boat propelled by a sail that he had just invented.

little maneuvering with those splendid wings. Soon Icarus was swooping and somersaulting through the sky, always gaining height until he flew too close to the sun. The wax very quickly melted and he fell into the sea and drowned. When his father looked back, all that he could see was a collection of feathers floating on the surface of the sea. That is how the greatest of inventors, Daedalus, helped his son Icarus to both freedom and death.

Years later, Minos tried to force Daedalus back to Crete. He did not know where the inventor might have gone, and devised a plan to find him that was worthy of Daedalus himself. Minos offered a reward to anyone who could pass a thread through a spiraling conch shell, from opening to tip. He believed that only Daedalus would be clever enough to work out this puzzle, and so it turned out. Daedalus bored a hole at the tip of the shell and smeared it with honey. Then he tied a thread to a large ant, which he stood at the shell's opening. The ant found its way to the honey, pulling the thread along behind it. The king of Sicily took the reward, and soon revealed to Minos that the problem had, in fact, been solved by his guest, the great inventor. Minos came in search of Daedalus, but the Sicilian king's daughters did not want to lose their beloved guest, and so they lured Minos into a bath where they murdered him. Daedalus's final invention for Minos was a pipe that came out of the roof just above the bath where Minos was, down which the princesses poured scalding water until the Cretan king died.

Above **Detail from an oil flask showing Ariadne and Theseus (c. 460 B.C.).** The piety of Theseus was certainly rewarded. Before leaving for Crete, Theseus made vows and a sacrifice, and was told by a priestess to pay particular homage to Aphrodite. By keeping in favor with the goddess of love, he secured a wife, Ariadne, and his safety.

Theseus and Ariadne

When he entered Athens as a hero, Theseus knew nothing of the hostages that were sent to Crete to die, but soon he noticed that everyone in the city was more anxious than usual, and saw the palace being readied for some sorrowful ritual. When he learned the story, he was determined to help, if only by volunteering to be one of the hostages this time. Aegeus was desperate to convince him not to go, but

Theseus announced his decision in the market-place, and once it became public, the king was forced to send him to Crete. "Trouble yourself no more," said Theseus. "I promise to bring all these hostages back in triumph, along with the head of the Minotaur." So convincing did he sound that Aegeus gave him some white sails for the ship's return voyage. Previously, the ship traveling between Athens and Crete with its death-bound cargo carried black sails to signify death and sorrow. Now, Aegeus dared to hope that he would see the ship return with white sails of happiness.

On the voyage, Theseus told the ship's captain to make sure that he and his men stayed in Crete over-night, ready to spread sail at any time. The ship arrived at the Cretan harbor, and King Minos came down to inspect the hostages, along with his wife and his daughter Ariadne. The princess fell in love with Theseus as soon as she saw him, and as they went in slow procession back toward the palace, she snatched her chance to whisper to him, "The Minotaur is my half-brother, but if you will marry me, I will help you to kill him." Theseus nodded in satisfaction; luck, as usual, was running his way, or was this the work of golden Aphrodite, the goddess of desire, to whom he had made a sacrifice just before leaving Athens?

THROUGH THE LABYRINTH

Ariadne devised a way for Theseus to track his path through the black maze of the labyrinth, so that he could find his way out again if he managed to kill the Minotaur. She gave him a ball of thread, telling him to tie the end to the door. The thread would unwind as he walked into the maze, and to find his

Below **Theseus slaying the Minotaur.** According to most authors, the Minotaur devoured the victims who were offered up to it in the maze. Others maintain, however, that the poor wretches simply wandered about the labyrinth until they eventually starved to death.

way out, all that he needed to do was to follow the thread and let it lead him back again. In the evening, the hostages were taken to the doorway, and thrust, one after another, into the darkness that smelt of slaughter. Theseus managed to tie Ariadne's thread to the door as soon as it clanged shut. He told the Athenians to stay there, without wandering away and losing themselves, while he went into the maze to find the monster and kill it. He was weaponless, of course, and groped forward in the dark, pausing to listen at every turn of the maze. Eventually he heard the Minotaur, who was waiting patiently for the first victim to start panicking and screaming. Theseus fought his hardest fight there in the darkness, with his bare hands, against an enemy

with lethally sharp horns, but the Minotaur had grown complacent on his limited diet of terrified Athenians and misjudged his opponent. In the end Theseus threw him to the ground, then twisted his head by the horns until his neck was broken.

Ariadne stole the key to the labyrinth and was waiting at its open door with the Athenian hostages when Theseus returned, clutching at her thread. They ran to the harbor and jumped into the ship, which set sail at once for Athens. The captain and crew had not wasted their time

to be changed from black to white. Aegeus was looking out from the Acropolis, the high rock with precipitous sides, for the first glimpse of Theseus's ship. Seeing the black sails, he believed that his son was dead, and threw himself from the Acropolis to his death. It is from the death of Aegeus that the Aegean Sea derived its name.

KING OF ATHENS

Theseus then became king of Athens and ruled long and, for the most part, wisely. One of his less wise decisions was to marry the Amazon Hippolyta, the same woman whose girdle Heracles (Hercules) took as one of his labors; other versions of the story speak not of Hippolyta but of her sister, Antiope. Whoever the Amazon was, Theseus abducted her and brought her to Athens where she later gave birth to his son, Hippolytus. Hippolyta's sisters traveled to Athens and attacked the city, but with no success. They had the misfortune to kill Antiope (or was it Hippolyta?) with an arrow during the fighting.

Theseus's next wife was an equally reckless choice. Phaedra was the daughter of Minos and Pasiphae and the sister of Ariadne, whom Theseus had abandoned on Naxos. When Theseus brought her to Athens, she became infatuated with Hippolytus, who was not at all infatuated with her. Aphrodite brought this love-madness on Phaedra because she was offended by Hippolytus, who had vowed himself to chastity as a devotee of the virgin goddess Artemis (Diana), and scorned the goddess of sexual desire. Phaedra fell ill with longing. Eventually her nurse found out her secret desire and approached Hippolytus, who was

Left *Theseus Leaves Ariadne* by Innes Fripp. After abandoning Ariadne on the island of Naxos, Theseus sailed on to Delos where he dedicated a statue of the goddess Aphrodite to the temple of Apollo. While on Delos, he and his companions celebrated his slaying of the Minotaur in Crete, by taking part in dancing and festivities.

while waiting in the harbor. They had punched holes into most of the Cretan ships in the darkness, and there were few left that were seaworthy. Someone sounded the alarm, and the Cretans rushed to their ships to prevent Theseus from leaving, but in the confusion, only a couple of the Cretan ships got close to the Athenian ship, and they could not prevent it from slipping away.

The voyage home was leisurely, and after a few days, Theseus and Ariadne arrived at the island of Naxos. Ariadne soon fell asleep on the shore, and Theseus crept back on board and sailed on. No one knows why he deserted her. Was he already regretting his promise to marry her? Was he instructed by Dionysus (Bacchus), who was planning to wed Ariadne himself? Or was he tired of her after a couple of nights' pleasure, and already pursuing some other woman? Whatever the reason, Ariadne's alarm and misery when she awoke did not last long. She prayed to the gods for help, and at once Dionysus appeared with his wild companions, ready to marry her on the spot. The crown that Ariadne wore for this marriage was later placed in the skies as the Corona Borealis.

Theseus sailed on to Athens without her. Somehow, in the tumult of their adventures, he forgot to order the sails

Below *Phaedra and Hippolytus* by Baron Pierre-Narcisse Guerin (1774–1833). Phaedra bore Theseus two sons, Demophon and Acamas, and then fell passionately in love with Hippolytus, her stepson. It is said that she went to great lengths to be near him. She even built a great temple to Aphrodite, which over-looked the gymnasium where the young man exercised each day.

Opposite page *Dionysus and Ariadne* by Nicola Carta (nineteenth century). Why Theseus abandoned Ariadne is uncertain. Whatever the reason was, Ariadne found happiness afterward with Dionysus .

THE WATERS OF LETHE

Lethe was one of the rivers of the under-world along with Styx (across which the dead were ferried by Charon), Acheron, Cocytus, and Phlegethon, the river of fire. The waters of Lethe gave their drinker the gift of forgetfulness, and apart from those tormented for their crimes, all the dead drank from Lethe. They could regain their memories only temporarily when some hero descended to the underworld and gave them blood to drink. The philosopher Plato speculates that souls are reborn after

death, and that rather than drinking Lethe waters soon after death, they are given Lethe's gift of oblivion just before their next birth. This is why people have no memories of their past lives.

Above *The Waters of Lethe by the Plains of Elysium* by John Stanhope (1829–1908). The souls of the dead drank from the River Lethe not only to forget their former life, but also to forget the horrific images of death and the underworld.

Right *The Death of Hippolytus* by Peter Paul Rubens (1577–1640). According to some tales, Hippolytus was revived by Asclepius. However, since it was against the law to return to life, Artemis changed Hippolytus's appearance and took him with her to Italy, where he was honored as the minor deity, Virbius.

with any woman, but most especially his father's wife. Phaedra was now terrified that Hippolytus would tell Theseus about her guilty desire for him, and in desperation she hanged herself, leaving behind a wax tablet containing an accusation against Hippolytus, claiming that he had tried to rape her. Theseus believed his wife and sentenced his son to exile. Poseidon had long ago given Theseus the gift of three wishes, and now Theseus wished for his son to die. As Hippolytus drove his chariot along the coast, away from Athens, Poseidon shook the earth and sent a bull from the sea. Completely out of control, the horses galloped along the beach, and dragged Hippolytus along until he died. Some say that the constellation of the Charioteer represents Hippolytus. The goddess Artemis appeared to Theseus, revealing the truth, that Hippolytus was innocent. If gods had been allowed to weep, she would have wept for her beloved friend's death. Theseus performed no further deeds of note before his death. With his accomplishments, he had freed the world from many wicked men, but his life had been filled with troubles that were largely of his making, especially his rash and foolish dealings with women.

THE HOUSE OF TANTALUS

The Trojan War, the last great assembly of heroes in Greek myth, had many causes. There were the present grievances that brought the Greek fleet to Troy; there were causes going back a generation; and there were causes going back to humankind's earliest days, when gods and men mingled more freely. The causes of the Trojan War can be traced back as far as Tantalus, a son of the Titans from before the wars that left Zeus (Jupiter) as the new king of the gods. Tantalus was king of Paphlagonia and had three children, Pelops, Niobe, and Broteas, all of whom offended the gods. Niobe was the woman who considered herself superior to a goddess in her wealth of children, and ended up turned to stone. Broteas came to an even worse fate, and Pelops's behavior redoubled the offense that Tantalus gave to the gods.

The troubles began when Tantalus abused the trust that Zeus had shown him. He was a frequent guest at banquets on Mount Olympus, and enjoyed the sweet taste of ambrosia a little too much. He stole some of the food of the gods and took it back to share with his human friends. This was an unwise act, which Zeus might have ignored out of friendship, but when Tantalus invited the gods to a feast at his palace and cooked up the body of his son Pelops for them, he committed a crime against the laws of gods and men alike, and his monstrous act could not be ignored. No one knows for certain whether he made this monstrous feast in the hope of pleasing the immortal gods, or whether he was testing the limits of Zeus's knowledge. The strange meat appalled the gods, who instantly recognized it as human flesh and refused to eat it—all except Demeter (Ceres) who was still grieving for her lost daughter, Persephone (Prosperpina) and, as a consequence, absentmindedly ate Pelops's left shoulder.

Zeus struck Tantalus down with his thunderbolt, and punished him after his death by hanging his body in a fruit tree that dipped over a stream. Tantalus thirsted for the water, which flowed almost within his grasp, but when he bent down to drink, it would recede out of hands' reach. He hungered for the fruit, which was bountiful, but when he reached out for it, the branches always swayed out of his grasp. Tantalus was forever frustrated, and his fate is still commemorated in the English language in the word "tantalize."

> *Immersed in the fountain,*
> *Tantalus tastes not*
> *The water that wastes not!*
>
> HENRY WADSWORTH LONGFELLOW (1807–1882),
> *BIRDS OF PASSAGE*

Above *Tantalus's Torment* by Bernard Picart (1673–1733). Some say that Tantalus was tormented even further by having a huge stone perched over his head, ready to fall.

Below **Detail from a cup showing a banquet scene (c. 500 B.C.).** Banquets at Mount Olympus offered nectar and ambrosia. These were said to possess life-giving properties.

Right **Artemis with bow and arrow**. Artemis was usually represented in art as tall, noble, and extremely beautiful. The stories tell, however, that beneath this attractive exterior she was a quick-tempered and jealous woman, known for her harsh and sudden punishments.

Below **Pelops and Hippodameia**. Another explanation given as to why Oenomaus was so determined Hippodameia should never marry is that the king had been warned by an oracle that he would die by the hand of his daughter's husband.

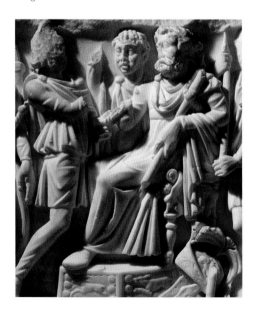

hunter, and he followed his father's example in defying the gods. He refused to honor Artemis (Diana), the goddess of the hunt, and as punishment she drove him mad. He came to believe that he was invincible against fire, and jumped onto a burning pyre to prove it. The flames consumed him, reinforcing the fearful lesson of Tantalus's death, that the gods will destroy those who offend them. Yet even with these two examples before him, and his own death and remaking to reinforce the message, Pelops did no better than either his father or his brother.

A Curse on the House of Pelops

Pelops lost his kingdom to barbarians, and looked for a new kingdom to conquer in Greece. He also looked for a wife, and chose Princess Hippodameia, the daughter of King Oenomaus of Arcadia. Oenomaus was reluctant for his daughter to marry, perhaps because he himself secretly lusted after her, and he set up a chariot race in which every suitor must compete against the king. The prize would be Hippodameia, and the cost of failure would be death. The king was prepared to give these suitors a generous start, and even allowed his daughter to ride in their chariots, but he was confident of victory, because his horses were the gift of Ares (Mars) and ran swifter than the wind.

Oenomaus had already killed at least 12 suitors, nailing their heads above his palace gates, and he was hoping to pile up enough skulls to build a temple in mockery of the immortal gods. Pelops prayed to Poseidon for help, and the god provided him with winged horses and a winged chariot that could ride over the ocean without breaking the surface of the water. Pelops should have trusted the god's gifts, but when he arrived at Oenomaus's palace and saw the rotting heads above the gates, he began to doubt. He spoke to the king's chariot driver,

Zeus ordered Hermes (Mercury) to collect all the pieces of the murdered child's body and cook them again in the cauldron. Then the king of the gods used his divine powers to restore Pelops, but his shoulder was missing. Demeter fashioned a new shoulder for him out of ivory, and he became the next king of Paphlagonia. His restored body was so beautiful that Poseidon (Neptune) fell in love with him, taking him to Olympus as his cupbearer. Tantalus's other son, Broteas, was a great sea. As he sank to his death, the wretched Myrtilus cursed Pelops and every member of his house.

Pelops conquered most of the southern part of Greece, renaming it the Peloponnese. He built a great kingdom and for the most part ruled wisely, but he also cut up the body of a rival king, Stymphalus of Arcadia, and scattered the pieces so that no one, not even a god, could reassemble them. Pelops and Hippodameia had numerous children, including Pittheus of Troezen, the twins Atreus and Thyestes, and Sciron the murderer whom Theseus slew. Pelops had another son, Chrysippus, whose mother was the nymph Astyoche. King Laius of Thebes visited Pelops and became besotted with Chrysippus, abducting him in his chariot and taking him back to Thebes by force. Hippodameia had long been jealous of Pelops's affection for Chrysippus, fearing that the illegitimate son would be named heir to the kingdom in preference to her own children. She was so intensely jealous that she pursued Chrysippus to Thebes, where she found him in Laius's bed and stabbed him to death. Chrysippus just managed to name his murderess before he died, and Hippodameia fled from Thebes and then killed herself. This was the first unfortunate consequence of Myrtilus's curse on the house of Pelops.

Myrtilus the son of Hermes, promising him anything he wished if the man would betray his master. Myrtilus asked for half the kingdom, and the privilege of sharing Hippodameia's bed on the marriage night, and Pelops hastily agreed.

Myrtilus took out the lynch pins that held the wheels to the axles of Oenomaus's chariot, and replaced them with pins made of wax. The king gave Pelops the usual start, and then ordered Myrtilus to drive his chariot faster than the wind, while he readied his spear to kill Pelops. But as the chariot raced faster and faster, the wax melted and the wheels suddenly fell away from the chariot. The chariot crashed, and Oenomaus was killed in the wreckage. Then Pelops married Hippodameia, and as part of the marriage celebration, he drove their winged chariot over the sea, in the company of the traitor Myrtilus. Hippodameia became thirsty, and so Pelops landed his horses on an island and went in search of water. When he returned, Hippodameia was in tears, and recounted to him how the driver had tried to rape her. "That is not true," interrupted Myrtilus. "You yourself promised that I could enjoy your bride on her wedding night, and I was only taking what was mine." Pelops said nothing, and on they drove until they neared Euboea. Suddenly Pelops kicked Myrtilus out of the chariot into the

Left Pelops and Hippodameia by Burney. Myrtilus paid dearly for betraying his king. It is thought that as Oenomaus lay dying, he cursed the charioteer for his treachery and prayed that Pelops, too, would die a painful death.

EUREKA!

Archimedes was a figure in Greek history rather than myth, a brilliant mathematician who invented machinery still in use today. One of his discoveries was the law of displacement. The king of Syracuse thought that someone might have made his new crown out of alloy, rather than pure gold,

and ordered Archimedes to find out without damaging the crown. The story goes that Archimedes got into his bathtub to think about it, and noticed water overflowing onto the floor. "Eureka! (I have found it!)" he cried, bursting out of the bathroom and running down the street naked. He realized that the volume of water displaced by his body equaled the volume of his body. Now he could work out the volume of the crown by putting it into a full basin of water, and then weigh it against a pure gold ingot of the same volume. If they matched, the crown was pure gold too. The "Eureka!" story is only doubtfully historical, but it has become one of the inspiring myths of Western science.

Above Archimedes by Giuseppe Nogari (1699–1763). The Greek mathematician, physicist, and inventor was thought to have lived between 287 B.C. and 212 B.C. He was credited with discovering the principles of the lever and specific gravity.

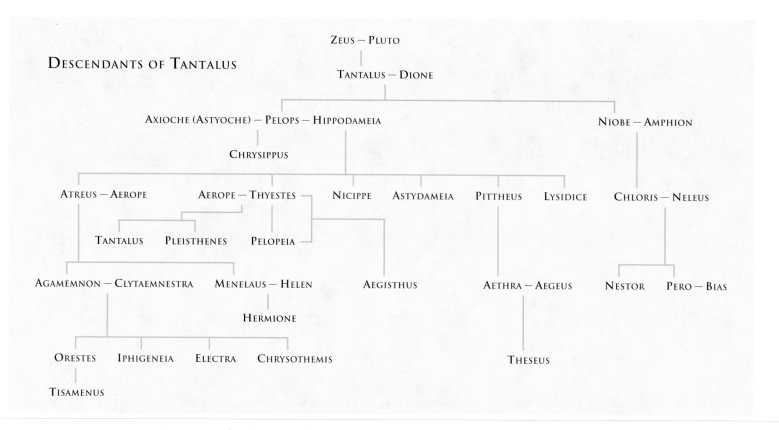

DESCENDANTS OF TANTALUS

ZEUS — PLUTO

TANTALUS — DIONE

AXIOCHE (ASTYOCHE) — PELOPS — HIPPODAMEIA   NIOBE — AMPHION

CHRYSIPPUS

ATREUS — AEROPE   AEROPE — THYESTES   NICIPPE   ASTYDAMEIA   PITTHEUS   LYSIDICE   CHLORIS — NELEUS

TANTALUS   PLEISTHENES   PELOPEIA

AGAMEMNON — CLYTAEMNESTRA   MENELAUS — HELEN   AEGISTHUS   AETHRA — AEGEUS   NESTOR   PERO — BIAS

HERMIONE

ORESTES   IPHIGENEIA   ELECTRA   CHRYSOTHEMIS   THESEUS

TISAMENUS

A Curse on the House of Atreus

Pelops gave a flock of fine sheep to his sons, Atreus and Thyestes, anticipating that joint ownership of the flock would teach them how to live together peacefully, but they soon quarreled over it. The fault lay with Hermes, who wanted to avenge the death of his son Myrtilus and sent a lamb with a golden fleece to join the flock. Atreus had promised to sacrifice the best of his sheep to the goddess Artemis, but he could not bear to give up this new treasure. He killed the lamb but kept its golden fleece, having it stuffed to resemble a living lamb. His brother Thyestes became extremely envious, coveting the golden lamb. When Atreus's wife, Aerope, made a sexual advance toward him, Thyestes said to her, "I will do anything you want, if only you will give me back the golden lamb. After all, it really belongs to me, because it belonged to my half of the flock in the first place."

Aerope opened the chest in which the golden lamb was stored, and secretly gave it to her new lover.

The king of Mycenae died, leaving no heir, and the people of Mycenae sent a herald to the oracle to ask who should be their next king. "The one with the golden lamb," the oracle replied, and as soon as the herald returned, Atreus claimed the throne. "Do you agree that the man with the golden lamb should be king?" Thyestes asked his brother, and when Atreus agreed, he produced

Below **Hermes.** Hermes was heartbroken over the death of his son Myrtilus. He placed him in the sky as the constellation Auriga, the Charioteer. At Olympia, charioteers made sacrifices to Myrtilus (whose ghost haunted the stadium) so he would not frighten the horses or harm the drivers.

the golden lamb and claimed the throne for himself. Now it was Zeus's turn to interfere with the brothers' lives. He wanted Atreus, not Thyestes, to rule over Mycenae, and he sent Hermes down to the city to ask Thyestes whether he would be prepared to give up his claim to the throne if the sun started to move backward in the sky. Thyestes thought that this was utterly impossible, and blithely agreed. Zeus then turned the horses of the sun back in their tracks, and Thyestes was forced to renounce the kingship of Mycenae, going into exile.

ATREUS'S REVENGE

Atreus now knew that his wife had been his brother's lover, but he pretended to forgive them both, even when Aerope gave birth to Thyestes' twin sons, Pleisthenes and Tantalus. Aerope and Atreus had two sons, Agamemnon and Menelaus, and a daughter, and Atreus also had a son, Pleisthenes, by a previous marriage. The curse against the house of Pelops came into play once more when Atreus sent murderers to kill Pleisthenes the son of Thyestes, and they killed Pleisthenes the son of Atreus by mistake. Then Atreus again offered Thyestes his forgiveness, and half the kingdom along with it, and Thyestes was foolish enough to believe him. He came back to Mycenae

Opposite page **Detail from a tapestry showing Hector, Menelaus, Agamemnon, and Achilles.** For the most part, Agamemnon and Menelaus were known as the Atreidae, "the sons of Atreus." However, some say they were sons of Atreus's son Pleisthenes.

with Aerope's baby sons, Pleisthenes and Tantalus, and three more, older children whose mother was a nymph. Atreus invited him to a feast of reconciliation, and made elaborate preparations for the banquet. He killed the three older sons of Thyestes, cutting them into small pieces, and then he added the flesh of the two babies and cooked it all up in a huge pie. The pie was served to the guest of honor, Thyestes, who ate his fill. At that point, Atreus signaled for a servant to carry in a dish piled with the children's severed hands, feet, and heads. Horrified and grief-stricken, Thyestes vomited up what he had eaten, and then laid a curse on his brother's house.

Say what meant the woes By Tantalus entailed upon his race, And the dark sorrows of the line of Thebes?

WILLIAM WORDSWORTH (1770–1850), *THE EXCURSION*

Thyestes consulted the oracle at Delphi to find out how best to take his revenge on Atreus, and was told that he must father a child by his own daughter. He felt so much hatred toward Atreus that he did not hesitate to seek out his daughter Pelopeia, a priestess of Athene, and rape her, hiding behind a mask so that she would not recognize him. He dropped his sword as he fled, and Pelopeia kept it as the only clue to his identity. She was already pregnant when Atreus came courting her, having had his first wife, Aerope, thrown

into the sea to her death. Pelopeia married Atreus but the child that she gave birth to, eight months after the wedding, was Thyestes' son. She named the baby Aegisthus and then tried to kill him by leaving him exposed on a mountainside, but Atreus believed that Pelopeia was suffering the aftereffects of giving birth, and sent servants to the mountain to rescue the child. Aegisthus was treated as Atreus's true son, and was proclaimed the rightful heir to Mycenae.

So far so bad, but this was not the worst. Atreus's true sons, Agamemnon and Menelaus, captured Thyestes and brought him back to Mycenae. Atreus ordered his so-called son, Aegisthus, to kill Thyestes in his dungeon, even though he was only seven years old. Thyestes easily overpowered the boy, wrenching his sword from his hand, and was about to kill him when he suddenly recognized the weapon. It was the same sword that Thyestes himself had lost when he raped his daughter. "I will spare your life if you swear to do three things that I command," he told the boy. "First, bring your father's wife here in secret." Aegisthus kept his word, and brought Pelopeia into the dungeon. She was overjoyed to see her father again—that is, until Thyestes revealed that he was the owner of Aegisthus's sword, and the man who had raped her. Pelopeia was so horrified that she thrust the sword into her heart, dying in front of her rapist-father and son-brother. Then Thyestes ordered his son Aegisthus to show Atreus the bloody sword and tell him that Thyestes was dead, as ordered. Once this was done, Thyestes finally explained to Aegisthus who he was, and told the boy to kill King Atreus for him. Aegisthus took Atreus by surprise as he sat celebrating his brother's murder. On the death of King Atreus, Thyestes once more became king of Mycenae, with Aegisthus as his heir. And still the curses on the house of Pelops and the house of Atreus had not been completely fulfilled.

Below **The Delphic Oracle.** The Delphic Oracle featured in countless myths and legends. While it had a reputation of being reliable, this was perhaps because of the ambiguous wording used by the priests. Sometimes the advice was cryptic, sometimes clear but misleading, and sometimes clear but seemingly unreasonable.

of Troy. Their mother was the beautiful Leda, queen of Sparta, one of the many mortal women that Zeus (Jupiter) found desirable. While Leda was walking by the river Eurotas, Zeus transformed himself into a magnificent swan and raped her in that form. She gave birth to four children: Helen, Clytaemnestra, Castor, and Polydeuces (Pollux). Some say that Helen and the two boys were hatched from a single egg, as children of Zeus; others say that Helen and Polydeuces were children of Zeus, and Clytaemnestra and Castor were children of King Tyndareus of Sparta. Clytaemnestra, all agree, was entirely of mortal birth.

Clytaemnestra's twin brothers, Castor and Polydeuces (also known as the Dioscuri, meaning the sons of Zeus) marched to the rescue of Clytaemnestra when they learned that Agamemnon had taken her by force, but Agamemnon appealed to her father Tyndareus and gained his consent to the marriage. Then Menelaus asked Tyndareus for the hand of Leda's other daughter, Helen. When she was a child, she had already been abducted and forcibly married by Theseus, and when she was of an age to be properly married, she was so beautiful that her many suitors seemed likely to start a war over her. Tyndareus wanted to marry Helen to Menelaus and hand over the kingship of Sparta to him, but he did not know how to prevent violence from the other suitors. He asked the wise Odysseus (Ulysses), king of Ithaca, who had come to Sparta with all the other suitors, though well aware that as a poor king of a rocky island, he had few prospects. Odysseus said, "I will help you, if you will help me in turn. I wish to marry Penelope, daughter of Icarius, and

Left **Leda and the swan.** According to some writers, Leda was completely overcome with shame when she learned that her daughter Helen had eloped with Paris. She was so distressed that she eventually hanged herself.

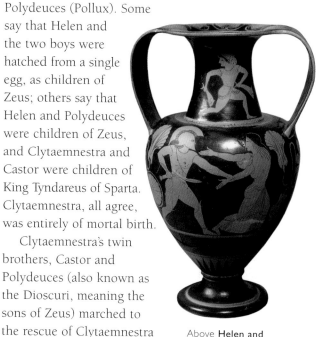

Above **Helen and Menelaus.** It is not really known whether Helen chose Menelaus herself. Regardless of her wishes, the gods had devised their own plan for Helen and Menelaus's future.

THE START OF THE TROJAN WAR

When Thyestes murdered his brother Atreus and claimed the kingship of Mycenae, Atreus's sons Agamemnon and Menelaus fled for their lives to Sparta. King Tyndareus of Sparta eventually helped them to overthrow Thyestes, and the kingship passed to Atreus's older son, Agamemnon. Thyestes and Aegisthus were now the ones that had to flee for their lives. Agamemnon proved to be a great general and leader of men, and soon the kings of many Greek kingdoms paid him tribute.

He killed his cousin, the second Tantalus, and married his widow, Clytaemnestra, as a spoil of war. Clytaemnestra was the twin sister of Helen, soon to be called Helen

Left **Agamemnon and Clytaemnestra.** The brothers of Clytaemnestra were alarmed to find that she and Agamemnon were together. Not only had Agamemnon killed her husband, but he had snatched Clytaemnestra's child from her breast and murdered it.

Above *The Feast of Peleus* by Sir Edward Burne-Jones (1833–1898). Eris, who attended the feast of Peleus, was the goddess of discord. She was known to stir up strife by inciting jealousy and creating hatred. She is said to have given birth to abstract divinities such as Hunger, Pain, and Oblivion.

need someone powerful to speak for me." When Tyndareus agreed to this, Odysseus advised him to make all of Helen's suitors swear an oath that they would accept her chosen husband and aid him against anyone who tried to injure their marriage. That is why so many Greek rulers came to Menelaus's aid when Helen was lost to him.

Agamemnon and Clytaemnestra had four children, a son Orestes, and three daughters, Electra, Chrysothemis, and Iphigeneia; Menelaus and Helen had four children, three sons and a daughter, Hermione. Both married couples seemed to be settling into prosperous, happy lives, but the curse against the house of Atreus had not died, and the goddess Aphrodite (Venus) was also angry with Tyndareus for neglecting to worship her. She made up her mind to punish Clytaemnestra and Helen for their father's offense. With trouble brewing, neither the royal family of Mycenae nor their kin in Sparta had any chance of a strife-free marriage.

The Apple of Discord
It was the goddess of Strife, Eris, who had started the chain of events that led to the abduction of Helen and Clytaemnestra's murder of her husband. Many years earlier and far away from Mycenae or Sparta,

Was this the face that launch'd a thousand ships, And burnt the topless towers of Ilium? Sweet Helen, make me immortal with a kiss!

CHRISTOPHER MARLOWE (1564–1593), *FAUSTUS*

Eris had attended the wedding between Peleus and the sea goddess Thetis, the same goddess whom Zeus had longed for, and whose son was destined to surpass his father. Zeus arranged the marriage of Peleus and Thetis to avert war in the heavens, but Eris slyly set in motion the trouble that would lead to the greatest war among men in Greek myth, the Trojan War. She threw down on the banquet table a golden apple that was inscribed with the words, "For the fairest," and laughed spitefully as the goddesses wrangled over it. Hera (Juno), Athene (Minerva), and Aphrodite were each convinced it belonged to her, and when none of the gods could stop the quarrel, Zeus sent them to a human judge, Prince Paris of Troy.

Paris was the son of King Priam and Queen Hecabe (Hecuba) of Troy. Before his birth, Hecabe dreamed that she gave birth to a firebrand that set fire to the whole of Troy. The seer Aesacus interpreted the dream as saying that the son in her womb would destroy the kingdom, and told her to expose the child on the mountainside, to stop the dream from coming true. The baby Paris was exposed on Mount Ida, but a she-bear suckled him and then he was adopted by shepherds. Only the chief herdsman of Troy, Agelaus, knew the truth of his parentage. Paris

Aphrodite's victory would mean the destruction of Troy.

Paris went from Mount Ida to Troy to compete in some athletic games, and he won every event that he entered. The princes of Troy, Priam's other sons, became angry and talked of killing this fellow who put them all to shame. Then Agelaus cried out, "This is your brother, Paris." Hecabe and Priam were delighted, even when an oracle warned them that they must kill him at once, or else Troy would be destroyed. When Priam had agreed, years ago, to expose his baby son on the mountainside, that decision had aged him and given him years of regret. Now, whatever message of doom the oracle spoke, he refused to kill his son a second time. "I would rather see Troy burn," he said, prophesying his city's doom as accurately as any oracle.

Preparing for War

Paris forgot about Oenone entirely and became obsessed with the idea of winning the most beautiful woman in the world—and who could this be but

fell in love with the naiad Oenone, famous for her healing skills, and lived the carefree life of a shepherd on Ida. Perhaps Zeus chose him to act as judge because he was such a simple, carefree young man, or perhaps the king of the gods had already decided upon a war that would consume the youth of Greece and Troy for the next 10 years. It would be easy for Zeus to use the contest among the goddesses to induce Paris to abduct Helen, and so cause the Trojan War.

The three goddesses came down to Mount Ida, with Hermes (Mercury), who was the messenger of the gods, to tell Paris what Zeus wanted him to do. Paris did not know which way to turn. Whichever one of the goddesses he chose, he would make two powerful enemies. He begged them to accept his decision without taking offense, and then requested that the goddesses stand in front of him, naked. As he hesitated, Hera said, "Choose me, shepherd, and I will make you ruler of all Asia, and give you all the wealth that you desire." Athene of the flashing eyes quickly added, "Choose me, and I will give you wisdom and prudence, and you will win every battle." Aphrodite waited until last, and murmured, "Choose me, and I will give you the most beautiful woman in the world." Paris was intoxicated with this promise, and gave the apple to Aphrodite, goddess of sexual desire. Hera and Athene had promised Paris that they would not take offense, but inwardly they seethed with fury, and promised themselves that

Below *The Judgment of Paris* by Jacques David (1748–1825). Paris could not resist the thought of having the love of the most beautiful woman in the world. Aphrodite honored her promise by protecting him and enabling the prince to abduct the lovely Helen.

Right **Agamemnon preparing to leave for Troy.** With the Greek fleet assembled ready to sail, it is said that Agamemnon himself caused the delay in departure. He boasted of having slain a stag with skill greater than that of the goddess Artemis (Diana).

Below *Odysseus Trying to Tempt Achilles, Disguised as a Girl, Away from the Court of Lycomedes* by Alessandro Tiarini (1577–1668). Once discovered, Achilles was eager for battle. He was a strong and swift fighter who instilled terror into the hearts of the enemy. He was made admiral of the fleet when he was only 15 years old.

Helen, the daughter of Zeus and Leda and the wife of King Menelaus of Sparta? He told his family that he was going in search of Hesione, the woman taken by Heracles a generation earlier, but he was really planning to visit Sparta and somehow entice Helen onto his ship. He sailed to Greece and visited Menelaus's palace, where he was treated with the hospitality appropriate for a prince of Troy. After a few days, Menelaus sailed away to Crete, leaving his wife to accommodate their guest. Aphrodite took all of Helen's powers of reason and self-restraint away and in their place put an overwhelming passion for Paris, so that by the time that Menelaus returned, guest and wife had succumbed to temptation and gone off together to Troy.

When Menelaus learned that his wife had gone off with Paris, willingly or under duress, he turned to his brother for help. Agamemnon first asked the king of Troy to return Helen, and when Priam refused, he

full well that his career at Troy would be violent, glorious, and short.

The Greek fleet assembled at Aulis. Then the curse on the house of Atreus manifested again, with unfavorable winds that trapped the fleet in the harbor. The men began to talk of abandoning the war, for the gods were clearly against them. The seer Calchas told the king that the only way to placate the gods was for him to sacrifice his daughter Iphigeneia to the goddess Artemis (Diana). Agamemnon sent for Clytaemnestra and Iphigeneia, saying that he wanted to marry his daughter to the young hero Achilles. He offended Achilles with this fabrication, and did worse than this when he carried out the sacrifice of his own daughter, slitting her throat. Some say that as his knife started to bite, Artemis replaced the girl with a young deer, but in most versions of the myth, Agamemnon actually killed his daughter. His wife Clytaemnestra returned to Mycenae, planning to take vengeance when he came home from Troy. The winds blew fair, the fleet set sail, and the war was about to begin.

Left **The sacrifice of Iphigeneia.** Accounts disagree as to what actually happened to Iphigeneia. One version recounts that, having been rescued by Artemis at the last moment, she was then transported to Tauris. Iphigeneia's duty as a priestess in the temple was to prepare all strangers who inadvertently came to Tauris so they could be human sacrifices for Artemis.

sent messengers to all the kingdoms of Greece to remind Helen's suitors of their oath. He summoned them to gather their soldiers and provide ships for an expedition to Troy to fetch Helen home. Almost everyone obeyed, but at least two people were opposed to this expedition. The young prince of Ithaca, Odysseus, wanted to stay at home like a sensible man with his wife Penelope and his newborn son Telemachus. When Agamemnon and Menelaus came to Ithaca to summon him and his men to war, Odysseus pretended to be mad, yoking a donkey and an ox to the plow and then sowing the land with salt instead of seed. The kings knew of Odysseus's reputation for craftiness, and tested just how mad he was by putting the baby Telemachus on the ground in front of the plow blade. Odysseus stopped his plowing, and admitted that he was sane enough to go to Troy with the rest.

The young Achilles, the son of Pelias and Thetis, would gladly have gone to the war, but his mother wanted to keep him safely at home, and dressed him in girl's clothes to fool the messenger, Odysseus. He was aware of her trick, and played a trick of his own in return, piling up in the palace such presents as girls tend to like, fine garments and jewels, and among them a spear and a shield. He had already ordered his men to clash their spears on their shields and sound the war trumpet outside the palace; as soon as Achilles heard the noise, he grasped the spear and shield and ran outside. Thetis wept bitterly, because an oracle had told her that Achilles would enjoy a long life only if he stayed at home. She knew

GREEK BURIAL RITES

It was very important in classical Greek belief for correct funeral rites to be held for the dead. This meant either cremation or burial, with a coin placed in the dead person's mouth to pay the ferryman Charon to ferry the dead soul over the River Styx to the underworld. Those left unburied, or without a coin, were forever stranded on this side of the River Styx and came back to haunt the living. Similarly, those who died by drowning, and whose bodies were never recovered, stayed on this side of the Styx as uneasy ghosts. The fate of those who were given a proper funeral was not much more cheerful, as they became gray, twittering shades in the realm of Hades, but at least they were where they properly belonged.

Above *Charon's Boat* by James Gillray (1757–1815). Charon, the immortal son of Erebus (Darkness) and Nyx (Night), was usually portrayed as a squalid, bad-tempered old man.

169

Above **Fighting in the Trojan War.** It did not take the Greeks long to work out that the wealthy and strong-walled city of Troy would never fall as long as it could count on aid and supplies from nearby cities. As a result, the Greeks set about destroying the surrounding allies one by one.

THE TROJAN WAR

The war lasted 10 years, as all the seers had predicted. The Greek ships were hauled ashore, close enough to Troy for the Greek troops to drive their chariots for a day's fighting in front of the walls of the city, and for the Trojan troops to drive their chariots over to threaten the ships with fire. Many of the warriors fought heroically, many men died of wounds and many of disease, but for over nine years the Greeks could not storm the gates of Troy and the Trojans could not drive them away. The gods of Olympus took an interest in the war, for some of the warriors were their children or grandchildren. Ares (Mars) and Apollo took the side of the Trojans, along with Aphrodite (Venus), who did not prove to be much of a fighter in battle, while Athene (Minerva) favored the Greeks, especially the crafty Odysseus (Ulysses). Hera (Juno) and Poseidon (Neptune) also favored the Greeks over the Trojans, and Zeus (Jupiter) kept the war going evenly for the 10 years that it was destined to endure.

The day shall come,
that great avenging day
Which Troy's proud glories
in the dust shall lay

ALEXANDER POPE (1688–1744),
THE ILIAD OF HOMER

In the tenth year, the soothsayer Calchas, who had been a Trojan and had left the city of Troy when he foresaw its fall, wanted his daughter Briseis to join him in the army of the Greeks. He asked King Agamemnon to send envoys to King Priam of Troy, to ask for Briseis to be sent to her father. With Priam's consent, Briseis came to the Greeks, and soon she shared the bed of Achilles. Then Chryses, a priest of Apollo, came to ask for his daughter back from Agamemnon, who had captured her and kept her as a concubine. When the king refused his request, Apollo sent disease upon the Greeks until she was finally surrendered. Then Agamemnon demanded Briseis from Achilles as her replacement in his bed. Achilles was obliged to obey his leader, but he nursed his resentment and refused to keep fighting.

With their best warrior unwilling to fight, the Greeks proposed a general truce for the two armies while Helen's lover, Paris, and her injured husband, Menelaus, fought for her in single combat. Paris was an expert archer but not so skilled at fighting hand-to-hand, and Menelaus was winning the fight when Aphrodite wrapped Paris in a mist, so that Menelaus could not see him to strike at him. The goddess whisked him back to the city, to the arms of Helen. Then the champion of the Trojans, Prince Hector, challenged Achilles to single combat, but Achilles still refused to fight. The Greeks chose Aias (Ajax) as their next best champion and he fought Hector for hours, without either gaining the advantage. They left off their fight when it was too dark to see one another. The Trojans agreed to observe a truce while the Greeks went onto the battlefield to bury their dead, but as soon as this was over, the Trojans came forward to attack again and drove the Greeks almost to their ships. Another day's fighting like this, and the Trojans would win the war.

The Greeks were on the verge of mass panic. Achilles was now threatening to take his soldiers and sail home with them. Then the resourceful King Odysseus came up with a crafty plan. He and his friend Diomedes crept out from the Greek tents and raided the tents where the allies of the Trojans were

Right **Briseis being taken away.** After Agamemnon ordered Briseis to be taken away from him, Achilles and his troops could not be persuaded to fight again. Only after the death of Achilles' friend Patroclus did the hero take up arms again, and Agamemnon restored Briseis to him once more.

sleeping. They killed one of Troy's allies, King Rhesus, and stole his horses. An oracle had prophesied that Troy would never fall if these horses ate Trojan food and drank from the River Scamander that flows close by the city of Troy. They had still not done so, and when the Trojans found them gone, they lost heart and retreated from all the territory that they had gained the day before.

To and fro the battle surged the next day, with Hera favoring the Greeks, then Zeus helping the Trojans until they reached the Greek ships and began to set them on fire. Then Achilles relented. He still would not fight, but he sent his friend and lover Patroclus out to battle in his place. Patroclus wore Achilles' armor and drove Achilles' chariot onto the battleground. The Trojans retreated, fooled into thinking that Achilles had returned. The ships were saved, and Patroclus led a charge against

the walls of Troy. Apollo intervened, striking Patroclus and bewildering his brains, and then Hector of Troy had no trouble in killing him. Achilles forgot his hurt pride and resentment in grief for his beloved friend, and solemnly promised that he would avenge Patroclus on Hector's dead body.

Above *Achilles Contemplating the Body of Patroclus* by **Giulio Romano (1492–1546).** Achilles refused to bury the body of Patroclus, or even to eat until he had exacted his revenge.

THE ORIGIN OF DEW

Memnon, son of the dawn goddess Eos (Aurora) and Tithonus, was killed by Achilles at Troy. Eos sent Memnon's brothers, the four winds, to carry his body away. In her grief, she wept all night for her dead son, and her tears can still be seen every new morning in the form of dewdrops. There is an enormous statue in Egypt that the ancient Greeks (but not the Egyptians) called the statue of Memnon. The Greeks claimed that every morning the enormous statue uttered a musical sound as Memnon greeted his immortal mother, the dawn. The statue still stands, but it no longer sings at dawn.

Left **Eos carrying the body of Memnon.** Drops of blood are said to have fallen from Memnon's body, becoming a river known as the Paphlagonia, whose waters flowed each year on the anniversary of Memnon's death.

Above *Thetis Giving Achilles His Arms* by Giulio Romano (1492–1546). Hephaestus fashioned a new set of arms for Achilles as a favor for his mother, Thetis. When Hephaestus was just a child, he was thrown out of heaven by Hera, and it was Thetis and her sister nereids who found and cared for him.

Right **Battle between Achilles and Hector.** Hector was a noble character in Greek literature—honorable, compassionate, and courageous. Although he did not approve of the war and he knew he was destined to die if he joined it, he still fought valiantly.

The Death of Hector

Achilles was now impatient to get back to the battlefield, but his armor had been taken by Hector from Patroclus's body. Achilles' mother, Thetis, brought him a new set of arms forged by Hephaestus (Vulcan). Wearing his new arms and carrying his splendid new shield, Achilles drove the Trojans to the River Scamander, and beyond it to the walls of Troy. All the Trojans were afraid to face Achilles in his wrath—all, that is, except Hector. He adequately prepared himself to fight Achilles in single combat, as he had long wished to do. Hector's father, King Priam, and his mother, Queen Hecabe (Hecuba) wept with fear that their beloved son might die. Hector's wife Andromache wept too, holding out his small son Astyanax to say goodbye to his father. As a last goodbye, Priam, Hecabe, Andromache, and the

baby boy watched from the top of the wall as Hector marched on through the great gate of Troy.

Hector—wearing Achilles' own armor that he had taken from Patroclus—at first stood his ground, until Achilles came close, and then he shuddered with fear and ran away. He ran three times around the city, trying to retreat through one of its gates, but Achilles was too close on his heels. In the end Hector turned to face his enemy and Achilles stabbed him through the neck. Hector begged that the Trojans might ransom his body so that it could receive a proper burial, but Achilles refused. He pierced Hector's ankles behind the anklebone and threaded leather thongs through each foot, then tied these straps to his chariot and drove three times around Troy before dragging the body back to his tent. All Troy feared that the death of Hector meant the city's imminent fall.

Achilles inflicted further violence on Hector's body, dragging it three times around Patroclus's tomb every day. The gods abhorred this outrageous behavior and took pity on Hector, whose shade could not find its way to the underworld without a proper burial. Apollo kept the body from decay and Zeus sent his messenger, Hermes (Mercury) to help King Priam visit Achilles' tent secretly by night and ransom his beloved son. Achilles agreed to exchange the body for its weight in gold, and the Trojans piled up all the gold that they could find on one side of a huge pair of scales, while the body rested on the other scale. Princess Polyxena, one of the daughters of Priam and Hecabe, came forward with her golden bracelets to add to the pile, and Achilles fell in love with her on sight; but he did not love her enough to abandon the war for her sake.

Even though Hector was dead, there were still many warriors in Troy, and new allies came to help the Trojans. Among these was Penthesileia, the Amazon. She was the warrior who killed Theseus's wife, Antiope, so that she could not have been young at the time of the Trojan war, a generation later. She arrived during the funeral of Hector and went

out to battle after the 11 days of mourning. Achilles killed her during that battle, a deed that he regretted when he saw, too late, that his enemy was, in fact, a beautiful woman. Shortly after came another ally from far away, Memnon of Ethiopia. Zeus weighed the fates of Achilles and Memnon in his scales, and the fate of Memnon proved the heavier. Soon he lay dead, pierced by Achilles' spear.

The Death of Achilles

Achilles seemed to be invincible in his wrath at the killing of his friend Patroclus. Now he drove the Trojans into the city and followed them through the Scaian gate. It seemed as though the Trojan war would be over by the end of the day, with the Greeks ready to pour through the gate after him. But Achilles was struck on the heel with an arrow that Prince Paris shot at him, helped by Apollo. It seemed not much of a wound, but it proved deadly, for his heel was the only vulnerable part of his body. His mother, Thetis, knew from an oracle that her son would surpass his father, and she wanted to protect Achilles, as a baby, from the dangers in battle that she guessed he would face as a man. She dipped the baby in the River Styx, holding him by the heel, and the waters rendered his whole body invulnerable, all but the heel (this story is the origin of the name "Achilles tendon" given to a tendon at the back of the ankle, which athletes are prone to injure).

It was this one weak spot that Paris struck, and then the rest of Achilles' body lost its god-given

Left **Detail from a shield showing Achilles and Penthesileia fighting.** The Amazon queen was no match for Achilles. It is said that the god Ares was so enraged by the death of his daughter that he was about to kill Achilles when Zeus intervened.

Below *Thetis Immerses Son Achilles in Water of River Styx* by Antoine Borel (1743–1810). It is said that Thetis had tried to save Achilles from his fate by placing him in flames when he was a baby (to burn away his mortality) and then rubbing him with ambrosia. She was unable to perform the entire rite and so it was unsuccessful.

Above *The Death of Achilles* by Peter Paul Rubens (1577–1640). It is said that the mournful wailing of Achilles' mother Thetis, the nereids, and the Muses was so frightful that the Greeks fled to their ships in terror.

protection. Paris shot a second arrow and Achilles fell dead, struck to the heart. It was now the Greeks' turn to retreat, carrying Achilles' corpse back to his tent. The goddess Thetis came to the tent to mourn for her son, along with the nine Muses and the nereids, sea-nymph daughters of Nereus. Achilles went down to the underworld where Odysseus met him years later, while journeying home from Troy.

There the great Achilles told Odysseus that he would rather be the least of living men, a poor slave, than the greatest of the shades of the dead, a king in the underworld. He was the greatest of Greek warriors of his generation, yet his final judgment on himself was that he had wasted his life on war and its glories.

Achilles' death led to another death among the Greeks, as Odysseus and Aias (Ajax) competed for the armor that Hephaestus had given Achilles. Odysseus was judged the braver warrior and was awarded the armor. Aias planned murderous revenge on all the Greeks. That night, Athene maddened Aias, so that he mistook cattle and sheep for Greek warriors, tying them up, taunting them, and then killing them. In the morning he realized how ludicrous his behavior had been, and in shame and misery, he killed himself.

Bereft of Achilles, the Greeks now looked for help to prophecies, to discover if there might be some condition set by the gods that they must fulfill in order to conquer Troy. They found three prophecies: they must fetch Achilles' son Neoptolemus to the war, Philoctetes must use his bow in the fighting, and the Palladium must be stolen from Troy. To fulfill these prophecies, the Greeks turned to the crafty Odysseus, who had a well-deserved fame for eloquence and was much favored by Athene.

It was easy enough for Odysseus to sail to Scyros and fetch Neoptolemus, but Philoctetes was much more difficult to persuade. When Heracles lay dying on his funeral pyre, it was to Philoctetes that he gave his bow. Philoctetes set sail for Troy with the other Greek heroes, but he was wounded long before they came to Troy with a snake bite that did not heal. It discharged pus and gave off such an intolerable stench that the other warriors abandoned him on the island of Lemnos. Now Odysseus had to try to win him over to the Greek cause again. Odysseus tried all his tools of flattery and cajolery, but Philoctetes was not moved. It was not until Heracles appeared and told him to go to Troy that he agreed to leave Lemnos. The doctors among the Greek army healed his wound, and he bent Heracles' bow against Paris and shot him dead.

The Fall of Troy

Odysseus then turned his mind to stealing the Palladium. This was a statue of Pallas, Athene's friend whom she had killed as a child, and it was said to have fallen from heaven. Athene favored the Greeks in the Trojan War, but the presence of the Palladium in Troy, with all its implied personal meaning, held her back from destroying the city. It would not be easy to steal the statue; not only did Odysseus have to enter a city at war, but he also had to take the genuine Palladium. The Trojans had made many replicas of the statue, knowing that it was crucial to the survival of their kingdom.

Odysseus disguised himself as a beggar and found his way to Helen's bedroom in Priam's palace. Now that Paris was dead, Priam had married her to another of his sons, Deiphobus, but she was longing to leave Troy. Helen was the only person whom Odysseus could not deceive, and she saw through his beggar's disguise. She was eager to help him, explaining where the statues were kept and how to tell the real one from all the copies—it would be the smallest one. Odysseus crept out of Troy and back in again, with Diomedes. They entered the palace through its drain, and brought the Palladium out the same way. Troy had lost its protection.

Left *Diomedes stealing the Palladium* by the Diomed Painter (fifth century B.C.). The Palladium was said to have protective powers. Some say "palladia" was the name given to objects that were not made by human hands, but fell from heaven instead.

Below **Detail from an oil flask showing the dispute over the arms of Achilles** (fifth century B.C.). When Aias (Ajax) killed himself in shame, he used a sword that Hector had presented to him in admiration of his skill after their combat.

THE WOODEN HORSE

Now Athene helped Odysseus devise a brilliant stratagem—the building of the wooden horse. This was a huge creature, hollow on the inside and able to conceal 30 warriors. It towered higher than the great Scaian gate of Troy, so that the Trojans would have to destroy part of the gate if they decided to take the horse into the city. The Greeks carved an inscription on the side of the horse, saying that it was their gift to Athene in recompense for the theft of the Palladium. Then they made ostentatious preparations to leave the coast of Troy, setting fire to their tents. When the Greeks had gone, the Trojans came out cautiously at first, then running and shouting for joy because their enemies had abandoned the war and no more men need die. Only two people in the whole of Troy thought otherwise. Cassandra, the daughter of Priam and Hecabe, had been given prophetic powers by the sun god Apollo when he was wooing her, and when she refused him, he cursed her, saying "You will always foretell truly, but no one will ever believe you." Now Cassandra ran to and fro urging the Trojans not to trust the Greeks, especially when they were offering gifts. No one bothered to listen.

Laocoon, who was the priest of both Apollo and Poseidon, urged the same caution as Cassandra. Sensing that the horse contained many armed men, Laocoon tried to probe it with his spear. Two huge snakes suddenly appeared and came out of the sea, coiling their heavy weight around Laocoon and his two sons, pulling them into deep water and then drowning them, before slithering toward a statue of Athene in the Trojan citadel. The Trojans should have been appalled at these omens, and alerted to the ensuing danger. Athene no

Right Men pulling the Trojan Horse by a rope. The wooden horse was too large to fit through the city gates, so the Trojans broke them down. Building the horse so large was a deliberate act by the Greeks to lend more support to their story that the horse was to stay outside the walls as a sacrifice to Athene.

plan. She called out in different voices to the warriors inside the horse, sounding like each of their wives in turn. She fooled everyone except Odysseus, who recognized Helen's strategy, and Neoptolemus, who did not yet have a wife. Odysseus held the trapdoor shut, whispering to his friends that their wives could not all suddenly be in Troy, and they felt ashamed of themselves for succumbing to Helen's trick. She kept calling out seductively, but no one was now tempted to jump down into her arms. Why she did this, no one can be sure. Was it a last attempt by Aphrodite to save the Trojans, whose cause she favored? Or was Helen a woman of moods, fickle as the wind, first betraying her husband, then her new home, then trying to betray the Greeks again?

THE END OF THE HOUSE OF TROY

Helen left and very soon the Trojans were all asleep. Odysseus opened the trapdoor and the Greek warriors leaped out of the wooden horse into the city, ready to slaughter their defenseless Trojan enemies. They proceeded to set fire to houses and herd women together to take home as slaves. The fires sent a signal to the Greek ships, which hurried back to shore. Agamemnon and the rest of the army ran to the Scaian gate and joined in the killing. Achilles' son Neoptolemus turned his sword against old King Priam who had taken refuge at the altar of Zeus. He also killed Hector's baby son Astyanax, to make sure that the boy would not grow up to kill him in turn. Andromache was taken captive, as she had foreseen on that fateful day when she watched her husband die outside the walls of Troy. Old Hecabe did her best to strike back against the Greeks until she died. Then her shade

Left *The Construction of the Wooden Horse of Troy* by Giulio Romano (1492–1546). According to the poet Tryphidorus (fifth century A.D.), the wooden horse was white, with a purple-colored mane and a gold fringe. Its eyes were green beryl and purple amethyst, and it even had ivory teeth. The harness was inlaid with bronze and ivory, and was also purple.

longer favored them at all, and neither Apollo nor Poseidon protected their priest. Some god drove the Trojans to their doom, so that they paid no attention to these warnings. They pulled the wooden horse into the city, breaking down the great gate to let it in, and then they feasted late into the night.

Inside the horse, Odysseus waited with the best of the Greek warriors. While the Trojans were still feasting, Helen approached the horse with her new husband Deiphobus, and she nearly ruined Odysseus's

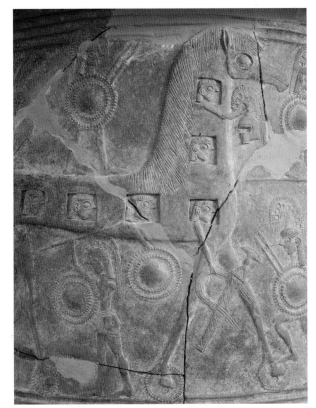

ORIGIN OF THE TROJAN HORSE

The Greeks and Trojans did not ride warhorses into battle; prolonged hand-to-hand combat from horseback depended on the invention of the stirrup, which would be introduced into Greece centuries after the classical period. The poor fought on foot, while the rich and powerful had horse-drawn chariots. Each chariot would house a warrior and a driver, and on the battle-field the warrior would either fight from the chariot or jump down to fight hand-to-hand. The Trojan Horse was not, then, a gigantic representation of a warhorse such as the knights of King Arthur might have used. It probably derives from siege engines such as the ancient Greeks used, movable towers full of armed men.

Right **Detail from an amphora showing the Trojan Horse (seventh century B.C.).** As the Trojan Horse was described as towering over the city walls, some people believe that the story could be a representation of the use of scaling ladders.

Right *Menelaus Spares Helen* by H. J. Ford. When Menelaus charged forth to confront his wife, it is said that he had every intention of killing her. First he killed her husband, Deiphobus, but once his eyes rested on Helen, he forgot his anger and embraced her.

Below *The Sacrifice of Polyxena* by Giovanni Pittoni (1687–1767). The sacrifice of Polyxena on Achilles' grave was no coincidence. The ghost of Achilles appeared to his son Neoptolemus and demanded that she be slain on his tomb so that they might be united after death.

became a dog-spirit, a follower of Hecate. Polyxena, whom Achilles had loved, was sacrificed on his tomb. Cassandra was taken by Agamemnon as spoils of war. The royal house of Troy was destroyed.

Menelaus ran to find Helen. Some say that she melted away in front of his eyes, for this was only a phantom Helen, and that he regained his true and loyal Helen in Egypt, where she had taken refuge for the 10 years of the Trojan war. Others say that the true Helen had lived in Troy, married first to Paris, then to Deiphobus, and now she expected Menelaus to kill her. She said nothing in her defense. The only thing that she did was to uncover her breasts. Menelaus remembered his passionate love for his beautiful wife, and it was as though the war had never happened. Aphrodite smiled to see the husband and wife in each other's arms. For this couple, there were no more trials to come. However, for the rest of the Greeks, with the exception of the wise and prudent Nestor, returning to Greece proved difficult and sometimes deadly.

Left *Sacrifice of Iphigeneia* by Giambattista Tiepolo (1696–1770). Clytaemnestra had to endure the death of two of her children by the hand of her second husband, Agamemnon. The first daughter—the child of her first husband Tantalus—was murdered when Agamemnon took Clytaemnestra as his wife, and now Clytaemnestra had been tricked into sending Iphigeneia to her death.

THE HOUSE OF AGAMEMNON

One of the spoils of war for Agamemnon as leader of the Greeks was his pick of the women of Troy. He chose Cassandra, the daughter of Priam and Hecabe (Hecuba), even though she kept prophesying doom to him and all his house. He took this as the ravings of a woman demented by the deaths of all her family, and paid it little attention. At home in Mycenae, his wife, Clytaemnestra, was waiting with their children, Orestes, Electra, and Chrysothemis. Another daughter, Iphigeneia, had been sacrificed by Agamemnon to gain a fair wind for his fleet to reach Troy. During the 10 years of the Trojan War, Clytaemnestra had taken her husband's half-brother Aegisthus as her lover. Both of them brooded over past injuries, Clytaemnestra over her innocent daughter's death, Aegisthus over wrongs going back to the time of Tantalus.

There was a prophecy that Agamemnon could be killed neither on land nor in water, neither naked nor clothed, neither inside nor outside the house, a prophecy which seemed to promise him immunity from violent death. Clytaemnestra and Aegisthus had 10 years to work out just how the prophecy could be fulfilled. When Agamemnon returned, the queen had a purple carpet ready for him to walk upon, when he

dismounted from his chariot. This act would displease the gods, as the privilege of purple cloth belonged only to them. Agamemnon arrived, with Cassandra beside him in his chariot, and demurred only for a moment when he saw the carpet. Then Clytaemnestra ushered him to the bathhouse to take a bath before his welcome feast. Cassandra was left in the courtyard, prophesying her own death and his, but her listeners had nothing to offer her except pity.

From inside the bathhouse came shouting, then silence. Agamemnon had been killed in accordance with the prophecy. The bathhouse was built onto the side of the palace, so that it was neither inside nor outside. Clytaemnestra waited until Agamemnon had one foot in the bath water and the other on the ground, then she threw a net over him. After he was captured in the net, Aegisthus ran in with an ax and they both hacked at him until he died. Clytaemnestra announced that she and Aegisthus were now joint rulers of Mycenae, and no one ventured to say otherwise. The unfortunate Cassandra was led away to her death, since Clytaemnestra blamed her for

Below **The death of Agamemnon.** Clytaemnestra, whether considered strong and fearless or a monster, felt she was completely justified in killing her husband. In fact, she claimed the day as a monthly festival.

HERO AND LEANDER

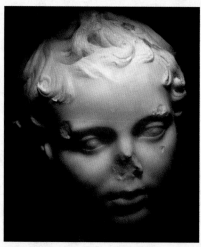

goddess of desire, yet her parents wanted her to stay chaste. She lived in a tower on the sea coast, and every night she lit a lamp in a high window to guide Leander to her tower. He swam the Hellespont to spend the night with his beloved Hero, enjoying the rituals of Aphrodite's worship, then swam back again before daybreak. They kept their passion secret, knowing that Hero's parents would disapprove. One stormy winter night, the wind blew out Hero's lamp. Leander lost his way and drowned. The next morning his body was washed up beside Hero's tower, and she threw herself down to die beside her lover.

Hero was a beautiful young woman who lived in Sestus, and Leander was a handsome young man who lived in Abydus. These cities faced one another across the straits of the Hellespont (now called the Dardanelles). Hero was a priestess of Aphrodite (Venus),

Above **The head of Hero.** As with many tragic love stories, Hero could not face the world without her lover, Leander. Their story was told by Musaeus, who was said to have been either one of the sons or one of the teachers of Orpheus.

becoming Agamemnon's partner in bed, without any regard for the fact that she had been taken by force.

Vengeance Comes to Clytaemnestra and Aegisthus

Orestes grew up a long way from Mycenae, with King Strophius of Crisa. His older sister, Electra, made sure that he left the city immediately after Agamemnon's murder, so that he would be safe from Clytaemnestra and Aegisthus, who were bound to fear that he might avenge his father's death upon them. At Crisa, Orestes found a faithful friend in the king's son, Pylades. Electra stayed at the court in Mycenae, hating her mother and her mother's consort, Aegisthus. Chrysothemis also stayed at court. She had been too young at the time of Agamemnon's murder to remember anything about it, and like Oedipus's daughter Ismene, she was a peacemaker, always trying to reconcile her angry sister Electra to their mother.

Clytaemnestra and Aegisthus expected Orestes to come back for his revenge when he was old enough. Aegisthus was a fearful man, and he even feared that Electra might marry someone who would try to avenge Agamemnon's death. He and Clytaemnestra therefore forced her to marry a peasant who could never raise an army against Mycenae. It would have been simpler to kill the daughter as they had already killed the father, but they kept her alive, not wishing to offend the gods any more than they had already

Death is not the worst evil, but rather when we wish to die and cannot.

SOPHOCLES (C.496 B.C.–406 B.C.), *ELECTRA*

done. Electra kept denouncing her mother and Aegisthus, and secretly corresponded with Orestes in Crisa. The desperate longing that he would return was all that kept her alive.

ORESTES' DILEMMA

When Orestes was old enough to take his revenge, he went to the oracle at Delphi to ask if he should perpetuate the troubles of his family by killing his mother and Aegisthus. He was in mental anguish, facing a terrible prospect as either the man who refused to avenge his father's murder or the man who murdered his own mother. The oracle told him that unless he took revenge, he would be afflicted with leprosy and barred from all the temples of the gods. He was instructed not to raise an army but to take revenge by guile. He should cut off a lock of his hair and place it on Agamemnon's tomb as soon as he arrived in Mycenae. The oracle warned him, however, that the Erinyes, the Furies who torment the minds of criminals, would set upon him if he murdered his mother. Apollo gave Orestes a bow, to drive the Erinyes away temporarily at least, and promised his protection if Orestes returned to Delphi after heeding his advice. In the end, he decided to follow the advice of the Pythian oracle and kill Clytaemnestra.

Pylades accompanied Orestes to the tomb of Agamemnon, and joined him in prayer to Hermes (Mercury), the god of cunning lies. Then Orestes cut off a lock of his hair and put it on the tomb. In a little while, some slaves came to the tomb to pour libations to the ghost of Agamemnon. Clytaemnestra had sent them after suffering a nightmare in which she gave birth to a snake that she put to her breast. As she was suckling it, the snake bit her nipple and drew blood. The soothsayers interpreted this dream not with its true meaning, that her son Orestes had come back with the intention of killing her, but as an omen that the ghost of Agamemnon needed placating. Clytaemnestra sent the slave women to ask Agamemnon's shade to pardon her, but Electra went with them, and her prayers were for vengeance, not forgiveness.

Electra saw the lock of hair on the tomb and recognized it as Orestes' offering to his father, but she was afraid to hope. Soon he came out of hiding and put his arms around his beloved sister, proving that he was really her brother by showing her the garment in which he had been wrapped when he escaped from Mycenae as a child. Electra and Orestes prayed to Zeus (Jupiter) that their revenge might not end with their own deaths, and then Electra went back to the palace, trying to act as if nothing unusual had occurred. Orestes stayed behind for a short while and then walked over to the palace in order to seek an audience with the queen.

Clytaemnestra came out to talk to the stranger. Orestes made up an elaborate lie, saying that he had heard from someone else of the death of Orestes. Clytaemnestra was delighted to hear this news and invited Orestes inside, sending for Aegisthus so that he could rejoice with her. As Aegisthus entered the palace, so too did Pylades, holding an urn that, he said, held the ashes of the dead Orestes. Aegisthus came closer to look at this evidence of his enemy's death, and Orestes slit his throat from behind. Then Clytaemnestra at last recognized her son, and begged for mercy as his mother. She opened her robe and showed him her breast, but he would neither look nor listen. He lifted up an ax and cut off her head.

Vengeance Comes to Orestes

On the same day that he killed his mother, Orestes was tracked down by the Erinyes—Alecto, Megaera, and Tisiphone. These three females with the heads of dogs and serpents for hair, with bat wings and blood-red eyes, were immortal inhabitants of the underworld, existing long before the Olympian gods. They avenged wrongs done by child to parent or host to guest, bad treatment of suppliants or murder, with ceaseless mental torments. Their victims soon died under this savage and constant punishment. These incarnations of a guilty conscience were much dreaded, and when people spoke of them, they were named not the Erinyes (Furies), but the Eumenides (the kindly ones). Changing their names, however, did nothing to change their nature.

Orestes fell sick, under constant attack from the Erinyes whom he alone could see and hear. He lay on his bed, slowly starving himself to death. Then Clytaemnestra's father, Tyndareus, arrived from Sparta, to charge Orestes before the nobles of Mycenae with the crime of killing his mother. Menelaus and Helen arrived for a remarkably ill-timed visit, and they were not welcomed either by Electra or by Tyndareus. "Why," Tyndareus asked, "did Orestes not simply banish his mother? Since he killed her, he must be punished as befits a matricide, by stoning to death. Electra deserves that death too, because she urged her brother on."

The trial finished with the judges' decision that Orestes and Electra should not be stoned to death, but should be allowed the dignity of killing themselves. Pylades now took action. He had fallen in love with Electra and hoped to marry her, and could not bear to lose both her and his beloved friend, Orestes. He planned to kill himself along with them, but first he decided to kill Helen, as the origin of all the troubles that had befallen the house of Agamemnon from the killing of Iphigeneia onward. Orestes and Pylades attacked Helen and could easily have killed her, but Zeus raised his daughter to Olympus, finally freeing her from all the perplexities and assaults of mortal life.

Above **A mask of Agamemnon.** According to the great poet Homer (c. 750 B.C.), Agamemnon was known not only for his dignity and majesty, but for his eyes and head that closely resembled those of the god Zeus.

Left **Orestes and Electra.** Orestes was deeply troubled by the knowledge that, as a good son, he should avenge the death of his father. There was no such doubt, however, from Electra, who was convinced it was his filial duty.

Left **Orestes and Pylades in Tauris.** Apollo, who had advised Orestes to kill his mother in the first place, now offered him peace of mind. The god told the young man that he would regain his sanity if he traveled to Tauris to retrieve the wooden statue of Artemis and bring it back to Attica.

While Orestes and Pylades were assaulting Helen, Electra was abducting Helen's daughter Hermione as hostage. Menelaus stormed into the room, and death was imminent for Orestes at the hands of Menelaus and for Hermione at the hands of Electra. Suddenly Apollo appeared, halting the violence. He told Menelaus that Helen had gone to Olympus and that he should now return to Sparta and marry again. He told the king to wed Hermione to Orestes, while not promising that Orestes would ever recover his peace of mind. When Apollo spoke, humans obeyed. The people of Mycenae buried their dead, and Orestes married Hermione. Still the Erinyes tormented his mind. Apollo's intervention had prevented slaughter, but it did not to cure the voices that berated Orestes.

THE SECOND TRIAL

Orestes wandered across Greece, tormented by the Erinyes, moving in and out of sanity. He finally came to Athens, pursued by Tyndareus, who still wanted him to die as a punishment for killing Clytaemnestra. Athene (Minerva) called together the Athenian judges, and a second trial began, with Apollo defending Orestes and the Erinyes prosecuting him. Nobody disputed the facts of what happened, and the trial arguments centered on whether it was more important to honor one's father or one's mother, or whether, in this case, Orestes had been correct in killing his mother to avenge his father. The judges were deadlocked, equal numbers voting both ways. Athene used her casting vote in favor of Orestes.

The Erinyes were furious with the outcome of Orestes' trial, and threatened to blight Athens. Athene offered them a shrine, on condition that they dealt kindly with her people, and the Erinyes consented to be worshipped at the side of the citadel of Athens, the Areopagus. Orestes was now legally free from blood-guilt, and one version of his story ends here, with Pylades marrying Electra. In another version, the Erinyes still tormented him. He finally found peace of mind when he followed Apollo's instructions and sailed to Tauris, where his sister Iphigeneia was still alive. In this version of her story, she had been miraculously rescued from Agamemnon's knife by Artemis (Diana), and lived on through the Trojan War, Agamemnon's return, and Orestes' revenge, far away on the island of Tauris. She helped Orestes and Pylades escape from Tauris, with the help of Poseidon, and eventually married Pylades. With this happy ending, Orestes' sanity was forever restored, and he lived long with his wife Hermione, ruling both Mycenae and Sparta. For other accursed families in Greek myth, the curse ended only with the death of the whole family. For the house of Tantalus, after generations of bloodshed, Athene and Apollo found a way to appease the pangs of conscience, to honor the law, and to counter the curse. Orestes' trial marks a crucial change in ideas of civilization from the rule of vengeance to the rule of law.

Above **Iphigeneia.** According to some stories, Iphigeneia, having been reunited with her brother and sister, ended her days serving as a priestess in a temple in Brauron, where the wooden statue of Artemis that Orestes retrieved from the island of Tauris was then kept.

Opposite page **Orestes and Iphigeneia.** Some say Iphigeneia, Orestes, and Pylades escaped from the island in Orestes' ship.

ODYSSEUS AND OTHER TRICKSTERS

Like most other myth systems, Greek myth abounded
in trickster figures. Inuit, Norse, Native American,
and African myth, for example, were equally full
of trickster figures, but their tricksters were
usually from the supernatural world.
In Greek myth, both gods and
humans played the trickster
role. Among the gods, Hermes
(Mercury) was the preeminent
trickster, always playing tricks
on Apollo almost from birth. From
the stories of the fathers of the gods,
with Rhea tricking her husband into
swallowing a stone, to the stories of the
Titans Prometheus and Epimetheus, Greek
myth valued cleverness rather more than
brute strength. Among humans, Odysseus
(Ulysses) was the master trickster of Greek myth,
with his wife Penelope playing the trickster at home
as he did on his long voyage to return home to her,
but many other heroes—even the powerful Heracles
(Hercules), who was not renowned for his intelligence—displayed trickster elements in times of need.

Autolycus and Sisyphus

Odysseus was the most resourceful, wily, and
ingenious of men, and it is not surprising that
he was a descendant of Hermes. Odysseus's
mother, Anticleia, was the daughter of
the king of thieves, Autolycus, who
was the son of Hermes. His father gave
Autolycus the talent of altering the
appearance of any animal, and this
helped him to acquire a very fine herd
of cattle from his neighbors. He kept
stealing cows from King Sisyphus of
Ephyra, changing them from brown to
white, from horned to hornless, from old to
young, from female to male. Sisyphus knew
that someone was taking his cows, and he noticed
that Autolycus's herd kept increasing at the same rate
as his own herd was decreasing, yet the cows were

clearly different. Sisyphus believed that Autolycus was the thief responsible, but saw no way to prove this.

One day Sisyphus had an inspiration. He decided to carve the letters SIS on the hooves of all his cows, and the next morning, he found these hoofprints going from his herd to Autolycus's fields. Autolycus vigorously denied that he had stolen the cows. "It is all your doing," he accused Sisyphus. "Your men took my cows to your fields and carved letters on their hooves, so that you could steal them from me."

Sisyphus won this battle of wits, but he was the loser in his clash with Zeus (Jupiter). It happened when Zeus fell in love with Aegina, who was the daughter of the river god Asopus. The river god looked everywhere for his missing daughter, and Sisyphus was impetuous enough to betray Zeus's secret. Asopus rushed out to rescue Aegina and found Zeus in her arms, with his thunderbolts hanging from a tree. Zeus could think of nothing better than to turn himself into a rock until Asopus had run past. Then he took back his Olympian shape, retrieved his weapons and threw a thunderbolt at the river god. Asopus walked with a limp after that attack.

Sisyphus was condemned to eternal punishment in the underworld as a result of this indiscretion. Zeus asked Hades (Pluto) to deliver the king to his realm, but when Hades came for him, Sisyphus refused to go. First he said that it was the task of Hermes, not Hades, to lead souls to the underworld, and then he said that it was not his time to die. Finally Sisyphus asked Hades how he planned to drag him down to the underworld. "With these new inventions of Hephaestus (Vulcan)— handcuffs," answered Hades. "Show me how they work," asked Sisyphus, and very soon Hades was handcuffed to the wall.

For a whole month Sisyphus kept Hades captive. No one could die, and Ares (Mars) lost all patience with the man who was taking all the fun out of his battles. He threatened to dismember Sisyphus, and in the end, reluctantly, the king released Hades and accompanied him on the dismal road to the underworld. Next he tried his golden words on Persephone (Proserpina), who allowed him to go home because he had not yet been buried. But this was his last escape. Hermes came for him the next day, and this time he died and was buried, and Charon ferried his shade over the River Styx. Sisyphus was punished by

being forced to push a large rock uphill—a rock just like the one into which Zeus had transformed himself. He kept pushing the rock to the top of the hill, and then it would roll back over his body and down to the bottom again. Then he had to roll the stone up again, and again, and again, forever.

Autolycus's daughter Anticleia married King Laertes of Ithaca, a small rocky island. Their son, Odysseus, grew up as clever as his grandfather, but not quite clever enough to slip out of his duty to fight in the Trojan War. It would be 10 years before the war ended, and 20 years before his wife Penelope and son Telemachus saw him again.

Odysseus and the Cyclops

Odysseus set sail from Troy at the same time as all the other surviving Greek warriors, but none of them took as long to return home as he did. The winds and seas were against him from the start. In stormy weather, his ships struggled across the sea to the land of the Lotus-Eaters. These people led a blissful life, doing nothing at all except eating, drinking, and sleeping. The lotus fruit gave them forgetfulness, so that they neither grieved nor worried, giving no thought to either their future or their past. Odysseus sent some of his men inland to find water, and the Lotus-Eaters offered these sailors their fruit. When the men did not return, Odysseus himself went to

Above **Sisyphus.** It is thought that Sisyphus was given eternal punishment for two reasons. One, because of the crimes he committed, and the other, to safeguard others. By keeping him busy, the gods were confident that he would have neither the time nor the opportunity to cause more trouble.

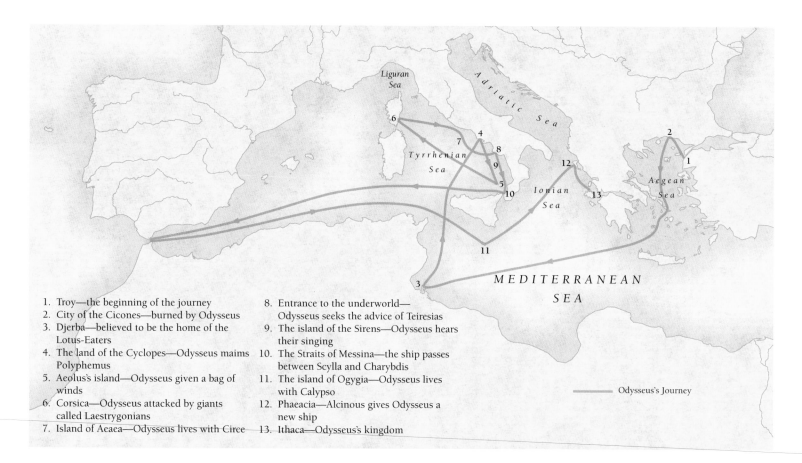

Liguran Sea

Adriatic Sea

Tyrrhenian Sea

Ionian Sea

Aegean Sea

MEDITERRANEAN SEA

1. Troy—the beginning of the journey
2. City of the Cicones—burned by Odysseus
3. Djerba—believed to be the home of the Lotus-Eaters
4. The land of the Cyclopes—Odysseus maims Polyphemus
5. Aeolus's island—Odysseus given a bag of winds
6. Corsica—Odysseus attacked by giants called Laestrygonians
7. Island of Aeaea—Odysseus lives with Circe
8. Entrance to the underworld—Odysseus seeks the advice of Teiresias
9. The island of the Sirens—Odysseus hears their singing
10. The Straits of Messina—the ship passes between Scylla and Charybdis
11. The island of Ogygia—Odysseus lives with Calypso
12. Phaeacia—Alcinous gives Odysseus a new ship
13. Ithaca—Odysseus's kingdom

—— Odysseus's Journey

Above **The journey of Odysseus.** Historians put forward many differing accounts of where the adventures of Odysseus really took place. Many locations exist only in myth. This map is just one of the possible reconstructions of his journey.

find them. They were sitting on the ground, munching on lotus, smiling and thinking of nothing. Odysseus had to send more sailors to carry them back to the ships, and then he sailed away at once, before anyone else could be tempted.

The next land that they sighted was a fertile island, full of freshwater streams, and here they caught and killed a few goats to add to their provisions. Odysseus and his men went to explore the neighboring mainland, where they came upon a large

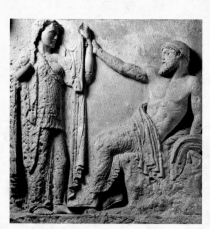

Hera (Juno) and Zeus (Jupiter) were a quarrelsome pair, but their quarrels were usually acted out below Olympus in their dealings with human beings. There was a

HERA'S PUNISHMENT

time, however, when Hera and the other Olympians became so vexed with Zeus that they bound him with leather thongs while he slept, so that he could not move. The goddess Thetis freed Zeus, and he was so annoyed with his wife as leader of the rebels that he hung her from the heights of Olympus, chaining her hands to the roof beam of their palace and hanging anvils as weights on her ankles. He only released her when all the gods promised never again to attack him.

Left **Zeus and Hera.** The ancient peoples attributed the storms in the skies to the many quarrels of Zeus and his queen. Hera allowed Aeolus, the keeper of the winds, to release them at her command.

cave with a huge stone beside its opening. The cave was clearly someone's home, with a fireplace and sections fenced off to keep goats and sheep. There were lambs and kids at the back of the cave, but the owner of the cave was not there. Odysseus and his men helped themselves to some cheese that they found in the cave. They could find no wine, but Odysseus had brought plenty of wine for their expedition, and he planned to share it with the cave owner in exchange for his hospitality.

The ground shook with the weight of the cave owner as he came home. He was a Cyclops, a descendant of the giants with one eye in the center of their foreheads who had fought alongside Zeus against the Titans. The whole island was inhabited by Cyclopes, most of whom were quite sociable, but this Cyclops, Polyphemus, had become something of a hermit after his unsuccessful wooing of Galatea. He ate raw meat, while the other Cyclopes ate cooked meat, as civilized people do. Polyphemus drove his flock of sheep into the cave and closed its entrance with the stone. Then he caught sight of Odysseus and the sailors. The giant wasted little time on conversation. He grabbed hold of a sailor and tore him apart, stuffing the pieces down his throat. Then he reached for a second man, to complete his meal. The others could do nothing but cower against the cave wall, watching the Cyclops fall asleep after his meal, and waiting for more death in the morning.

TRICKING THE CYCLOPS

In the morning, the Cyclops consumed more men and drove his flock out, shutting the cave again with its stone. By that time Odysseus had thought of a plan. He took the Cyclop's huge staff and sharpened one end with his sword, then hardened it in the fire. That night, after Polyphemus had returned and killed two more men, Odysseus said to him, "Cyclops, what good is meat without wine? We have plenty of good wine that we would like to share with you. If you would like to know my name, I am called 'No One'." The Cyclops appeared somewhat surprised that his captives were proving such well-behaved guests, but he could see no good reason to refuse their kind offer of wine. Odysseus poured him a giant bowlful of wine that was unmixed with water, then another and another, until Polyphemus was so drunk that he collapsed into unconsciousness.

Above **Odysseus and Polyphemus the Cyclops.** Polyphemus, the chief of the Cyclopes, had been warned about Odysseus. Telemus, a seer, had told Polyphemus that one day a man named Odysseus would pierce his eye with a stick.

Odysseus heated the end of the staff in the fire, then he and his men carried it over to the snoring Cyclops and rammed it into his eye. Polyphemus clutched at his charred eye socket and screamed with shock and pain. The other Cyclopes came along to find out what was causing all this noise. "Who is hurting you?" they shouted through the stone door, and all that Polyphemus could reply was, "No One," until they went away again. He groped for his enemies to kill them, but they easily slipped away. They were still trapped, though. Sooner or later, he promised himself, he would catch them and eat them all.

Polyphemus now rolled the stone sideways, making a small opening to let his sheep out. As each sheep went through, the Cyclops felt along its back to make sure that no man was trying to escape that way. Odysseus whispered to his men to hang on the underside of the fleeces, so that the giant would not notice them as the sheep carried them outside. Odysseus himself clung onto a massive ram that was the last to leave, and then, safely outside, they ran for their ship.

Odysseus ordered his men to row the ship out to sea, and as soon as he thought he was far enough away, he could not resist taunting Polyphemus, who came running to and fro on the beach, trying to catch them. "I am Odysseus, sacker of cities," he boasted. Polyphemus picked up a huge stone and hurled it in the direction of the sound. It splashed short of the ship, but the sailors rowed their hardest to get away before the next rock hit them. Polyphemus prayed to his father Poseidon (Neptune) for revenge, and for the remainder of his journey home, Odysseus was hindered by all the bad weather that Poseidon could manage to throw his way.

The Sirens

On one of the islands that Odysseus had to pass by, lived the Sirens. They were women down to the waist, and had huge wings, feathered legs, and claws. Their song promised fulfillment of each man's innermost desire, tempting sailors to their deaths. The island was littered with the bones of eaten men. Odysseus had been forewarned of the danger, and he gave all his sailors pieces of wax to put in their ears, so that they could not hear the Sirens singing. But Odysseus was insatiably curious, and he wanted to hear this irresistible song. He ordered his men to bind him to the ship's mast and not release him while they were within earshot of the island, however much he commanded and begged. Other men might have been tempted with songs of love, but for Odysseus, the Sirens sang of knowledge and wisdom. He strained at his bonds and tried to persuade the crew to release him, but they kept him tied up until they were safely past the island. That is how Odysseus became the only man to hear the Sirens' song and survive.

Our Sirens,
in those dulcet clarions,
As primal splendour that
which is reflected.

DANTE ALIGHIERI (1265–1321),
THE DIVINE COMEDY, "PARADISO,"
CANTO XII

Below **Odysseus and the Sirens.** According to some classical writers, the Sirens were doomed to die when any mortal heard their song and actually resisted them. It is said that after Odysseus had done so, the Sirens flung themselves into the sea and became rocks.

ODYSSEUS'S RETURN

One of the islands that Odysseus (Ulysses) visited was ruled by Aeolus, who had control over the winds. He gave Odysseus a leather bag that contained the winds, all except the West Wind that would blow them safely home to Ithaca. But Odysseus's men thought that Aeolus had given him some secret treasure that he would not share out with them, and while he was asleep, they cut the bag open. Out rushed the winds, and the ships were carried back to Aeolus's island. This time Aeolus refused to help, recognizing that at least one god was hindering Odysseus's return. Soon after this Odysseus lost all but one of his ships when they came to the lands of the Laestrygonians, giants and cannibals much like the Cyclops. Most of his men were now dead.

The winds blew his remaining ship to another pleasant-looking island, ruled over by Circe. Some say that she was the daughter of Helius (Sol), others that she was Hecate's child. She had the power to turn human beings into animals, and most of the animals on her island had once been human. Some of Odysseus's men came to her palace, seeking her help, and she sat them at her table, feeding them generously before waving her wand in their direction and turning them into pigs. Only one man escaped to tell the others. Odysseus set off to the rescue, and Hermes (Mercury) met him on the way, showing him an insignificant plant called moly, that would protect him against Circe's magic.

Odysseus sat at Circe's table and ate her food, hoping that he was not eating human flesh. Then Circe waved her wand and tried to transform him into an animal, but the moly protected him. She was quick to recognize that a god had helped him, and so without further ado invited him into her bed. Odysseus agreed to this, on condition that she transform all the animals back into men again. Odysseus stayed with Circe long enough to father three children.

When he started to long for home again, Circe told him what he must do next. In order to reach Ithaca, he must go down to the underworld as a living man, and ask the seer Teiresias for his advice. Circe gave him directions to the underworld and explained how to restore the voices of the dead for a few moments, by giving them the rich blood of freshly

Above **Landscape with Odysseus and the Laestrygonians.** The crew were delighted to meet the daughter of the king of the Laestrygonians when they first arrived on the island. Their delight soon turned to horror, however, when upon being presented to the king, he promptly ate one of the sailors. The men tried to escape, but most were speared like fish and eaten.

Left **Odysseus's companions being changed into pigs.** Circe was happy enough to transform the swine back into sailors when she became the lover of Odysseus. However, it is said that when she changed the crew back into human form, she made them taller and more handsome than they had been before.

189

slaughtered sheep to drink. All the shades would cluster around, eager to taste the blood, and he would have to drive off the rest to allow Teiresias to drink and speak. Odysseus found his way to the entrance to the underworld and slaughtered the sheep that Circe gave him. Among the shades that crowded close were his mother Anticleia and the great warrior Achilles. Odysseus made sure that Teiresias had room to reach the blood, and after drinking, the seer spoke. He warned Odysseus to keep his men under control when they reached the island of the Sun, or the god would become their enemy. Odysseus would have trouble in Ithaca, too, and even when safely home, he would still not have ended his travels. Eventually he would have to go voyaging again, with an oar over his shoulder, until he came to a region where oars were unknown. Only then could he finally appease the wrath of Poseidon (Neptune), and go home for good.

Losses and Gains

Odysseus passed through many more ordeals on his voyage, until he had lost all his men and his remaining ship. Six men died when the ship passed between Scylla and Charybdis. Scylla was a sea monster with

six heads, each of which devoured one of Odysseus's crew while they were avoiding the whirlpool of Charybdis. The rest of his crew died as a punishment for killing and eating the cattle of the Sun on the island of Thrinacie, while Odysseus was asleep. Zeus (Jupiter) sent a storm that swamped the ship, and only Odysseus survived, clinging to the broken mast

until he was washed ashore on the island of Ogygia, where the nymph Calypso lived. She kept Odysseus there as her lover for seven years, offering him immortality, yet every day he looked toward Ithaca and wept. Eventually Zeus sent Hermes to order Calypso to release him. Odysseus built a raft and, after this was wrecked in one more attempt on his life by Poseidon, he swam through stormy seas to an island inhabited by Phaeacians.

King Alcinous and Queen Arete ruled this island, and their daughter was Princess Nausicaa. Athene (Minerva) sent a dream to Nausicaa, suggesting that she should go to the beach to wash clothes. Here she found Odysseus, naked and in need, and brought him back to her parents' palace. The king and queen would gladly have married their daughter to the stranger, who captivated them with his stories of cleverness and bravery, but Odysseus wished only to return home. They gave him the richest of gifts and sent him on his way home in one of their ships. The ship reached the harbor of Ithaca while he was asleep, and he was left on shore with all the presents stacked beside him. Poseidon took a final revenge on the helpful sailors by turning ship and crew to stone, but not until they had brought Odysseus home at last.

Troubles in Ithaca

Odysseus was now back on his beloved island, but there were more troubles to face. Seventeen years after he had left for Troy, a host of suitors came to woo his wife Penelope, refusing to believe that he was still alive. They feasted daily at his palace, eating his provisions and drinking his wine. Penelope kept putting off making a decision, for she was certain that Odysseus would come home one day. She could not refuse them directly, for she had little support. Odysseus's father Laertes was too old to fight, and his son Telemachus was unable to dispose of the suitors on his own. But Penelope was as much of a trickster as her husband. She told the suitors that she was weaving a shroud in preparation for the burial of Laertes. Every day for three years, she would work on the shroud, and every night she would undo her day's work. Eventually one of her

serving women informed the suitors of this trick. Now she had to finish her weaving. She told the suitors that she would choose someone to marry, now that Telemachus was a man, as Odysseus had counseled her long ago.

Telemachus had grown up during his father's long absence, and Athene now inspired him to go overseas in search of his father. Telemachus was in danger from the suitors, who would not hesitate to kill the heir to Ithaca in secret. Athene thought it best to send Telemachus to visit Odysseus's old companions from the Trojan War, Menelaus and Helen in Sparta and Nestor in Pylos. He found no trace of his father on this journey, but came home loaded with presents, and with the friendship of some of the most powerful men in Greece.

ODYSSEUS THE BEGGAR

When Odysseus awoke on the Ithacan beach, Athene disguised him as an old beggar so that he could find out how matters stood in his kingdom without being recognized. He found refuge with his swineherd, one of the servants who was still loyal to him (though he did not recognize his master). Then Telemachus arrived back from his voyage, and Odysseus revealed

Below **Telemachus on Calypso's island.** Athene appeared to Telemachus in the form of Mentor, his tutor. In this disguise, she was not only able to educate him, but to inspire him with the boldness of spirit that he needed to travel the world in search of his father, Odysseus— a search that took him to Calypso's island.

insolent behavior. Later that night, Penelope decided to question the old beggar, who promised her that Odysseus was on his way home. She wept to hear news of her husband and offered him a bed for the night, ordering Eurycleia, the family's old nursemaid, to wash his feet. Eurycleia washed his feet and legs and suddenly cried out, seeing a long scar on his thigh which Odysseus had acquired as a boy while out hunting. Odysseus held her by the throat, whispering that she must keep silent.

Athene inspired Penelope with the clever idea of challenging the suitors to an archery competition. Penelope decided that she must choose one of these disagreeable men, if only to allow Telemachus to keep some of his father's rich estate, and she told them that whoever could string Odysseus's great bow and shoot an arrow through the rings of his 12 axes, could have her as reluctant bride. None of the suitors could string the bow. Telemachus ordered the bow to be given to the beggar, and he effortlessly strung it and shot an arrow through all the axes. Then he turned the arrows on the suitors. Telemachus had hidden all the weapons in the palace, and the father and son, together with their loyal swineherd and cowherd, slew these wretched men until piles of dead bodies littered the palace floor.

Then Odysseus spoke to his wife, Penelope, telling her who he was. Penelope was as subtle-minded as her husband and needed some proof, something that only Odysseus and she knew about. So she said to him, "Let me fetch the bed out of our bedroom and set it up for you in another room," knowing that her husband had fashioned one of the bedposts out of a living tree, growing in the middle of the house. Odysseus was outraged at the thought that someone had cut the bedpost so that the bed could be moved. When Penelope heard what he said, she knew that he really was her beloved husband. Her years of waiting and grieving were over at last.

The people of Ithaca discovered the next day that all the suitors, princes, and lords of the island and nearby lands had died at the hands of Odysseus, Telemachus, and their two loyal servants. Some of the Ithacans recognized that a god was helping Odysseus, and acknowledged that the suitors deserved death because of their bad behavior in Odysseus's palace. Others armed themselves to

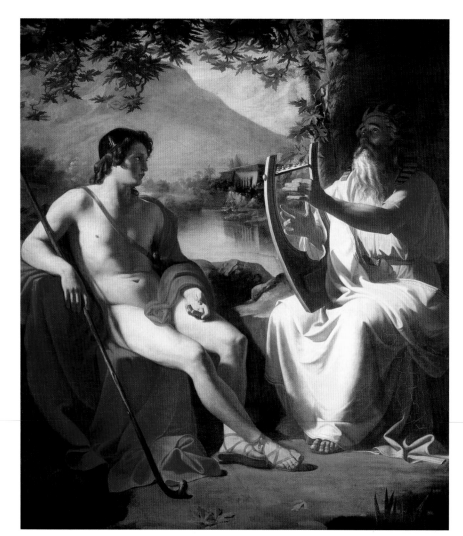

Above *Telemachus, Son of Odysseus* by Alessandro Ciccarelli. Telemachus was just an infant when Odysseus left to fight in the Trojan War. Returning home to Ithaca, Odysseus found Telemachus a mature and courageous man, ready to fight beside his father.

Right *Penelope* by J. Cavalier (1849). Penelope and Odysseus had many happy years together until the hero, by then an old man, was unintentionally killed by Telegonius, his son by Circe. The family traveled to Circe's island to bury Odysseus. Penelope eventually married her stepson.

himself to his son. They began to plot their revenge on the suitors with Athene's help. As a first step, Odysseus went to the palace as a beggar. Outside the palace, on the dung heap, lay an old dog. This was Argus, Odysseus's faithful dog that had been neglected and left to die on the dung heap. Argus immediately recognized his master and had the strength to lift his head in greeting, but he could do no more. He felt the joy of knowing that his master had returned, and then his head sank down again and he died.

In the palace, Odysseus tested the limits of the suitors' insolence, allowing them to mock him and even throw furniture at him. Penelope reproached the suitors for behaving so badly toward a guest and suppliant, an act that the gods would be sure to punish. Her prophetic words made little difference to their

take revenge, and so the goddess Athene intervened once more to bring about peace for her much-beloved hero Odysseus and his constant wife.

Dante's Odysseus

Teiresias prophesied that this was not the conclusion of Odysseus's journeyings, but this is where Homer's epic poem, *The Odyssey*, leaves him. In the millennia since Homer's poem, numerous other writers have provided sequels to this intriguing story. In the twelfth century, the Italian poet Dante wrote of Odysseus and Diomedes in his "Inferno," (part of *The Divine Comedy*) which is a visionary poem setting out his own descent into a (Christian) underworld. Dante's Odysseus burned in endless torment because of his theft of the Palladium and the deception that he practiced with the Trojan Horse. Odysseus related his final voyage to Dante, endlessly driven on by the desire for knowledge. Neither old age nor love of his wife and son could ever hold this Odysseus at home, and he died at sea, while continuing to stretch the limits of human questioning and questing.

Above *Goddess Athene Disguises Odysseus as a Beggar* by Giuseppe Bottani (1717–1784). The goddess Athene admired the ingenuity and cunning of men such as Odysseus, which is why she continued to help him. She disguised him as a beggar to keep him safe from the wrath of Penelope's suitors.

Left **Odysseus greets his faithful dog.** Odysseus was forced to take harsh action in order to assume control of his household once more. He killed not only all of the suitors, but also many of his servants who had helped the suitors in his absence.

THE TALE OF AENEAS

Aeneas was the son of Venus (Aphrodite) and Anchises, and became king of the Dardanians. After Achilles raided his cattle, he fought in the Trojan War alongside the Trojans. His mother often helped him; though she could not fight alongside him, she was quick to rescue him from trouble. Neptune (Poseidon) and Apollo also protected him, because all the gods knew that he must survive the war to found a new kingdom. Only Juno (Hera) dared to show him ill will, still brooding over the past, when Paris gave the apple to Venus, and resenting the future, when Aeneas's descendants were destined to overthrow her city of Carthage. The other gods sent omens and visions to help Aeneas survive the fall of Troy, promising that he would rule a new kingdom in Italy. As the Greeks sacked Troy, Aeneas escaped, piously rescuing his household gods and carrying his old father over his shoulder. He held the hand of his small son, Ascanius, and his wife, Creusa, followed, but she became lost and could not be found again.

Aeneas set sail with a small fleet of refugees, first for Thrace, then for Crete, and then for Italy. Along the way he visited the island where the Harpies took refuge when the Argonauts drove them away from Phineus, and like Phineus, he had his food befouled by their droppings. His people attacked the Harpies unsuccessfully, drawing down a curse from the Harpy Celaeno, who prophesied that they would eat their tables in severe hunger before building the walls of their new city, as punishment for this attack. Aeneas found Andromache living happily in Epirus with a new Trojan husband, Helenus, now that her enslaver Neoptolemus was dead. They were building a new city modeled on Troy, with a miniature Scaian gate and a little stream for Scamander. But it was not Aeneas's destiny to stay there.

Helenus advised him how to pass safely by the twin dangers of Scylla and Charybdis. The little fleet sailed past Etna in eruption, and rescued a Greek sailor left behind by Odysseus in his flight from the Cylcops's cave three months earlier. They sailed on to Sicily, where Anchises died, and then toward Italy. They would have arrived there without incident, if Juno had not intervened. She

asked Aeolus, guardian of the winds, to send out a storm. Out went the East and South Winds, then the South-West Wind, damaging Aeneas's ships. The refugees were all in danger of drowning, but Neptune ordered Aeolus to call back his winds, and the weary Trojans found shelter in a Libyan harbor.

The next day, with Venus's guidance, Aeneas found his way to the city of Carthage, still under construction. It was ruled by Queen Dido, a widow who had fled from her brother's persecution in Tyre. Dido welcomed the Trojans, offering them help with their onward journey or a new home in Carthage. That evening, at the welcoming feast, Venus's son Cupid (Eros) disguised himself as Ascanius and inspired in Dido a passionate love for Aeneas. She began to think of marrying him, and prayed to all the gods for their support, especially to Juno, the goddess of marriage. Juno was anxious that Carthage,

Below *Aeneas and Anchises* by Pietro Bernini (1562–1629). Aeneas, a good and faithful son to his father, carried Anchises for two reasons: because his father was old and because he was lame. Anchises had been crippled by a thunderbolt sent by Zeus when he revealed the name of Aeneas's mother, Venus (Aphrodite).

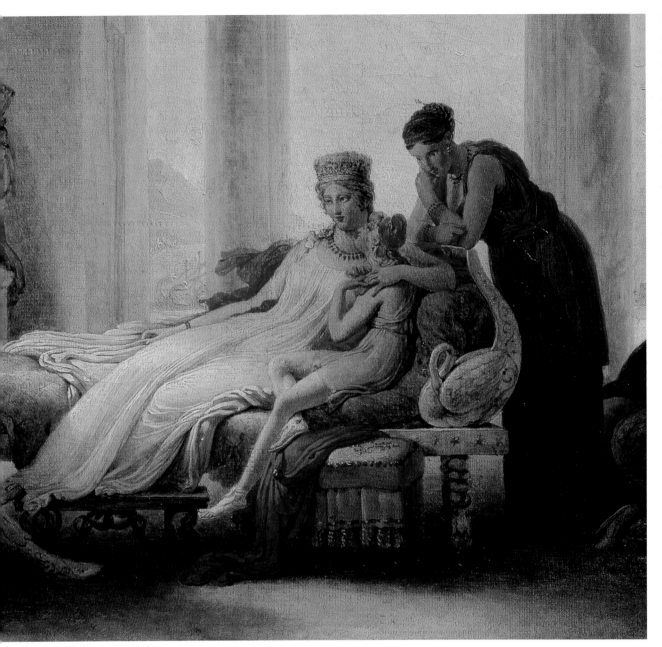

Left *Dido with Aeneas Recounting the Misfortunes of Troy* by Baron Pierre Guerin (1774–1833). Many scholars believe that Aeneas was as eagerly in love with Dido as she was with him. In fact, Aeneas was so infatuated that he forgot about his destiny in Italy. Mercury (Hermes) was twice sent to remind him, and it was with great regret that Aeneas had to leave.

not Rome, should fulfill the prophecies of a new empire, and she granted Dido's prayer. Out hunting the next day, the Tyrians and Trojans were scattered in a violent storm, and Dido and Aeneas found themselves sheltering together in a cave. Here they married with Juno as celebrant and the heavens as witness—a ceremony that Aeneas found it easy to repudiate when Jupiter (Zeus) recalled him to his destiny and ordered him to leave Dido. She wept, then reproached, then cursed him, and finally, as the Trojans rowed hastily out to sea, stabbed herself to death with the sword that he had left behind.

Descent to the Underworld

The winds did not favor a voyage to Italy, and Aeneas ordered his fleet to sail to Sicily once more, to the place where his father had died a year earlier. He held elaborate funeral games, where the men

HOUSEHOLD GODS

The Romans worshipped household gods called the Penates and Lares. The Penates were two household gods of the storeroom, where provisions were kept. The amount of stores amassed in this room told the Romans whether the Penates were favoring them. The Lares were the spirits of dead ancestors who brought good luck to the living, if properly honored, with one main Lar for each family. They were offered food every morning and on special occasions such as birthdays, sacrifices were made to them. The Romans feared the Lares' opposites, the Larvae and Lemures, malevolent ghosts of dead criminals, suicides, and the like, who appeared in terrifying shapes at night and could drive people mad.

Left **The Altar of Lares.** The Lares were sometimes worshipped as fertility spirits who brought the family prosperity. A Lar was often represented as a youth with a drinking horn and cup—both symbols of fertility.

ANCIENT ITALY

Only one man died on the short voyage to Italy, Palinurus the helmsman, who was overpowered by Somnus (Hypnus), god of sleep, and fell into the sea. The ships arrived safely at Cumae where Apollo's Sibyl lived, giving out her prophecies in a huge, dark cave. She informed the Trojans that they would arrive safely in their destined country, but then they would be afflicted with war. Aeneas asked the Sibyl to help him go down to the underworld as a living man, to revisit his beloved father. "Easy is the descent," replied the Sibyl, "for the door stands open at Avernus, but it is a hard task to return. You must go into the forest and find a golden bough, sacred to the goddess Juno. Only those chosen by fate can take the bough, and once it has been broken off, the tree grows another golden bough ready for another hero. If you can find the golden bough and break it off, this is a sign that you will be allowed both to go and return."

THE JOURNEY
Venus's doves led Aeneas into the forest, flying a short way, then stopping to feed, then flying again,

competed at rowing, running, boxing, and archery. Meanwhile the Trojan women bewailed the death of Anchises, and Juno sent Iris, the messenger of the gods, disguised as one of these women, to create fresh difficulties for Aeneas. She reminded the women of their weary years of wandering, and suggested that Sicily would be a good place to build a new city. In the end she persuaded them to set fire to the ships, to force Aeneas to stay there. Jupiter promptly sent heavy rain to douse the fires, but four ships had been destroyed, and the remaining ships could not carry all the Trojans. Anchises' shade appeared to Aeneas, advising him to leave behind all those too old to fight, too tired from the voyage, or too reluctant to go on. They could found their own city of Acesta in Sicily, while the best and strongest went on to Italy.

Right *Aeneas and the Sibyl in the Underworld* by Jan Brueghel the Elder (1568–1625). The Cumaean Sibyl was one of the most famous of all prophetesses. Remembered for her descent to the underworld to guide Aeneas, she was also known as an author. Over her thousands of years of life, she wrote down many of her riddling prophecies.

JANUS AND THE GATE OF PEACE

Janus was the Roman god of openings and thresholds of all kinds. He was represented as having two faces looking in opposite directions. In terms of place, he was the god of doorways and crossroads, and the sources of rivers and streams were sacred to him. He was also a god of travelers, those who cross boundaries by land and sea. In terms of time, he was the god of dusk and dawn, the thresholds between night and day, and of the transition from month to month and year to year. The first month of the year, January, is named after this god. In Rome the gates of his shrine were opened when war was declared, and shut in time of peace (a very rare event in Roman history).

Right **Double-headed Janus.** Janus was also the god of beginnings. The Romans believed that all beginnings were crucial to the success of any venture, regarding them as portals to the future. Janus's blessing was sought at the beginning of each day, month, and year.

but the golden bough allowed him free passage. As the living man stepped into the boat, its planks groaned under the weight and took in water.

On the other side of the River Styx, Cerberus was barking, but the Sibyl gave him a poppy cake that sent him to sleep. Aeneas went on, hearing the laments

Below *Dido's Suicide* by Liberale da Verona (c. 1445–1529). The heartbroken queen of Carthage ordered a pyre to be raised so that she could destroy everything that reminded her of Aeneas. Rather than be without him, she stabbed herself with a sword he had given her, and threw herself into the flames.

until they came to the golden bough, shining like bright-leaved mistletoe on a tree in winter. Aeneas easily broke off the bough and went into the dark gorge of Avernus with the Sibyl, after making sacrifices to Hecate, Proserpina (Persephone) and Pluto (Hades), to Nox (Nyx) and Gaia, the goddesses of Night and Earth. They passed Disease and Old Age, Famine and Fear and Penury, War and Death, Sleep and Dreams, and the Furies. They met the monsters of Greek myth, the Centaurs, the Gorgons and Harpies, the Chimaera and the Hydra, but these were only phantoms and had no power to hurt. Aeneas walked on in the constant gray dusk of the underworld to the rivers of Acheron and Cocytus, to the ferry over the Styx and its aged ferryman Charon. He saw the shades of the dead clustering around the ferry as thickly as autumn leaves, and he saw Charon taking on board the shades of those properly buried and turning away the unburied. He saw his missing helmsman, Palinurus, who said that his body could be found in the foam, just off the coast of Italy. Palinurus begged Aeneas to spread earth over his body so that he could pass over the Styx, but the gods did not permit it. Charon tried to forbid Aeneas from crossing the Styx,

of babies who died almost as soon as they were born, then the laments of those judged guilty and executed, though they were innocent. He saw the shades of suicides, longing for the life that they had thrown away, and of those who died for love. Dido wandered here, like the moon half-visible through cloud, and when she saw Aeneas, her face set in a grim glare

Above *The Vision of Aeneas in the Elysian Fields* by Sebastiano Conca (1680–1764). Even after he died, Anchises continued to help his son. His ghost told Aeneas to visit him in the underworld, where he would find out what the future held. Anchises pointed out the souls that were to later win honor in the new empire Aeneas was destined to found.

phantom body. Anchises gave his son a reassuring prophetic account of the future rulers of the Italian kingdom that was to be founded by Aeneas.

THE RETURN

Then Aeneas returned to the upper world through the gates of ivory, through which false dreams travel each night. His fleet set sail again and passed safely by Circe's island, arriving at the mouth of the River Tiber. The land here was ruled by King Latinus, whose daughter Lavinia was courted by many men. Turnus was the man that her parents wanted her to marry, but the omens were unfavorable, pointing instead to a marriage with some foreigner who would go on to establish an empire.

and then she turned away. He entreated her to stay and make peace with him, but in vain.

Then he met other famous shades of the dead from the Trojan War and before, some eager to speak with him, others shrinking away as if he might give them a second death. He saw the great wall of Dis with Phlegethon as its fiery moat and a Fury as its guardian. Since he was not a wicked man, Aeneas was not allowed to pass beyond this wall and only heard about the torments of the damned from the Sibyl. She hurried him onward to the Elysian Fields where he at last met his dead father and tried to embrace him, but his arms kept slipping through the

Aeneas and his men were now eating their first meal on land, piling fruit and vegetables on wheat cakes that they had placed on the ground. Then they ate the cakes, and in doing so fulfilled the Harpy's curse, that they would eat their own tables. Now they could begin building the walls of their new city, while negotiating for the land with King Latinus. Recognizing that this was the prophesied stranger, Latinus was happy for Aeneas to marry his daughter and establish a new city, but Turnus declared war on Aeneas. This war was short and bloody, and concluded in the Trojans' victory. Aeneas lived on as ruler of the new city for only three years, but his son Ascanius ruled Alba Longa for the next 30 years, and some 300 years later the great city of Rome itself would be founded there by his descendants, Romulus and Remus.

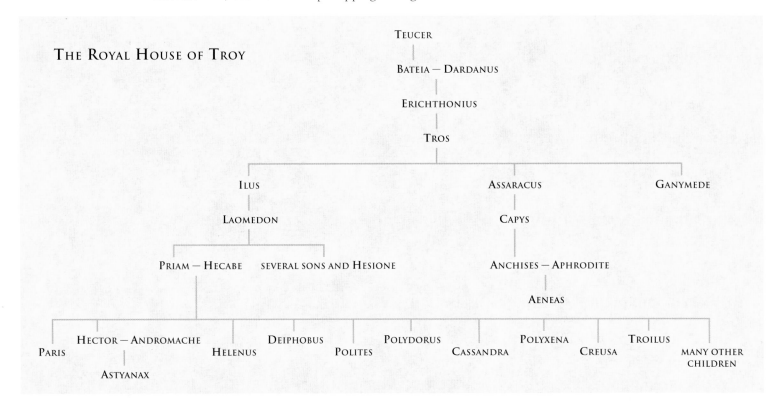

THE ROYAL HOUSE OF TROY

TEUCER

BATEIA — DARDANUS

ERICHTHONIUS

TROS

ILUS   ASSARACUS   GANYMEDE

LAOMEDON   CAPYS

PRIAM — HECABE   SEVERAL SONS AND HESIONE   ANCHISES — APHRODITE

AENEAS

HECTOR — ANDROMACHE   DEIPHOBUS   POLYDORUS   POLYXENA   TROILUS

PARIS   HELENUS   POLITES   CASSANDRA   CREUSA   MANY OTHER CHILDREN

ASTYANAX

MYTHS OF ROME

As a founding myth for a nation and an empire, the story of Aeneas led back not to a warrior god nor to the king of the gods, but to the frivolous, laughter-loving goddess of sexual desire. Such a genealogy was perhaps seen as inadequate by the Romans, who prided themselves on the spread of empire, the rule of law, and good government, none of which was a quality that Venus (Aphrodite) cherished. The second founding myth of Rome offered a different divine origin for the nation, deriving it from Mars (Ares), the god of war, a deity regarded much more favorably by the Romans than the Greeks.

Romulus and Remus

Rhea Silvia was the daughter of King Numitor. When Amulius took the throne from Numitor, he killed the king's son and forced Rhea Silvia to become a Vestal Virgin (priestess of Hestia), so that she would have no husband, sons, or grandsons who might avenge Numitor's overthrow. One day, she was fetching water from the spring in the sacred grove of Mars when the god himself came down from the sky and raped her. Rhea Silvia did her best to conceal her pregnancy, and nine months later, gave birth to twin boys, Romulus and Remus. Amulius did not believe her story about the god, and threw her into the Tiber where the river god Tiberinus saved her life, married her, and transformed her into a goddess.

Amulius ordered the twin babies to be put in a wooden chest and thrown into the river (as in Greek myth, this was to avoid blood-guilt). The Tiber carried them to the Palatine hill where the box opened and they were left stranded under a fig tree. There a she-wolf found them. She had just given birth to cubs of her own, and she was willing to suckle these crying man-cubs as well. The king's swineherd saw this amazing sight, and knew that a god was favoring Rhea Silvia's children. He took the children to his wife, whose own baby had recently been stillborn, and the couple brought up the twin boys as their own sons.

Romulus and Remus grew up with their father's warlike nature, dispensing rough justice to wrong-doers, loving to hunt, and enjoying a good quarrel. One day, when the boys had grown to young men, the herdsmen of Numitor quarreled with the herdsmen of Amulius, while

Above *Romulus and Remus, Legendary Founders of Rome, Suckled by the She-wolf* by Giuseppi Cesari (1568–1640). Romulus and Remus, stranded and left for dead, were not destined to die on the hillside. Instead they were found and cared for by a she-wolf and a wood-pecker. Both of these ani-mals were sacred to the father of the twins, Mars.

Left **The god of the River Tiber with the she-wolf and the twins.** Tiberinus, the god of the River Tiber, was particularly revered in Rome because he rescued its founders. He is often shown holding the Horn of Plenty, to symbolize the fertile power of the water.

Opposite page *Rape of Sabine Women* by Giovanni-Antonio Sodoma (1477–1549). Though they were abducted and forced to marry the Romans, the Sabine women eventually resigned themselves to their new lives. Their intervention not only stopped the killing, but also brought the two tribes together. The Confederation was governed by both King Romulus and the Sabine king, Titus Tatius.

Below *Romulus Marking Out with Furrows the Plans for the Foundation of Rome* by Giuseppe Cesari (1568–1640). When Romulus was declared the official founder of the city, his twin brother was outraged. Relying on augury, they argued over which omen should be recognized. Remus spotted six vultures, whereas Romulus spied twelve. Remus felt he should win regardless of number, because he spied his first.

Romulus was away. Quarrel turned to fight, and Remus was captured and taken to Numitor. Romulus was keen to counterattack and free his brother, but his foster father now revealed the truth of who the twins were. Romulus and he planned not just to rescue Remus, but to regain the kingdom that had been taken from their grandfather, Numitor. At the same time, Numitor was working out the truth of who the twins were, by questioning his captive, Remus. Soon the twins were together once more, ready to mount an attack on King Amulius with Numitor's support. The attack succeeded, Amulius was killed, and Numitor was restored to his kingship.

There are many different versions of the quarrel that destroyed brotherly love between Romulus and Remus. Numitor gave them permission to build a new city, and some say that they quarreled over which hill the city should be built upon. When the omens favored Romulus, he began by digging a trench around the boundaries of the new city, ordering his men to kill anyone who came in without permission. Remus taunted his brother, saying that the trench was far too narrow. "Any enemy will be able to jump over this ditch, just like this," he said, as he jumped across it. Immediately one of the workmen killed him with a spade for entering without permission. Other versions say that Romulus himself killed his brother, saying, "So perish all invaders!" The founding myth of Rome, then, derived its imperial glory not only from the god of war but from brother killing brother. Rome was founded on a crime; but unlike the Greek myths of cursed ruling families, where a curse works its way through generations, this Roman myth ends

with the death of Remus. Romulus became the first king of Rome, and was finally deified as the god Quirinus.

The Rape of the Sabine Women

Romulus was the first king of Rome, but almost all his subjects were men. He badly needed to attract women to the city, and sent messengers to many nearby cities to arrange marriages, but without success, since this new city had a bad reputation for lawlessness. The Romans began to urge war, but Romulus devised a less bloody solution to their problem. He invited the citizens of all neighboring states to attend a festival in Rome, and crowds of people came, mainly from the Sabine state. All the visitors were waiting for the chariot race to begin, when Romulus signaled his men to take hold of every woman in the audience and carry her off. The male visitors were not prepared for a fight, and went home angrily, planning a raid on Rome to fetch their women back and teach the lawless Romans a lesson in hospitality. They hoped that the gods, too, would take revenge, for it was an offense against the gods to violate friendship toward a guest.

Romulus forced the women to marry Roman men, and gave them all Roman citizenship. He believed that they would become reconciled to their marriages if only they stayed in Rome until their first children were born, but the Sabines and the men of the other nearby city-states did not wait that long before raising armies against Rome. Three times Romulus defeated an army and made generous terms with a city-state, but when the Sabines sent their army against Rome and attacked its citadel, the Roman commander's daughter Tarpeia betrayed the city to them. The Sabines had caught her outside the citadel and asked what price she would ask to betray Rome. She looked at the jewelry on the king's arms and said, "I will betray my people for the things that you wear on your arms." That night she opened the gate and asked for her reward. The Sabines gave her what they wore on their arms—shields, not jewels—until

they crushed her to death. Then they threw her body from the top of the citadel's rock, which was known from then on as the Tarpeian Rock. The Sabines took the citadel and then attacked Rome. In the middle of the battle, the Sabine women ran out onto the battlefield, shouting out that they wanted neither their fathers nor their husbands to die. Hearing this, the Sabines made peace with the Romans. The influence of the new city-state was growing.

The Sibylline Books

The Sibylline books consisted of prophecies that one of the Greek sibyls was supposed to have uttered, and that were brought from Greece to Cumae in Italy. The myth of the Sibylline books tells of the Cumaean Sibyl taking the books to Tarquin the Proud, the last king of Rome, and offering them to him for a price. What she offered was nine books of prophecies, and when he refused to pay the price, she burned three of the books. Tarquin still refused to buy the prophecies, and she went away to burn another three of the books. This tactic worked, as he became afraid that he would lose the whole set of prophecies, and he

THE PROBLEM WITH TWINS

The birth of twins was considered so portentous in Greek myth that it was explained supernaturally. Only one of the twins could live as a normal mortal. The other twin must be the child of a god. The myths of Castor and Pollux (Polydeuces), Clytaemnestra and Helen, and Hercules (Heracles) and Iphicles all follow this pattern. There are traces of such a pattern, too, in the story of Romulus and Remus. The twins could not coexist as joint rulers of Rome,

and only Romulus achieved apotheosis, by taking his place as a god with his divine father, while Remus died and was buried as a mortal man.

_____

Above **The Dioscuri (Twins Castor and Pollux).** When Castor was killed, Pollux also wanted to die, but he could not, because he was the son of Zeus. Zeus let him share his immortality with Castor, splitting their time between the upper and lower worlds.

201

agreed to buy the remaining three, even though the asking price was exactly the same for three as for the original nine. In 83 B.C. the Sibylline books were destroyed, and the Romans collected as many similar prophetic utterances as they could from Greece and Asia Minor, with the specific aim of using them for the interpretation of portents. The prophecies were used to interpret such worrying events as earthquakes, plagues, and the arrival of comets. In the early fifth century A.D., this second collection of Sibylline prophecies was also destroyed.

How Horatius Kept the Bridge

When the last king of Rome, Tarquin the Proud, had been overthrown, he gathered an army of Etruscans to force his way back into power. He persuaded King Lars Porsena of Clusium to help him, and their army laid siege to Rome. The city had one particularly

weak point, however, which was a wooden bridge over the Tiber, and if Tarquin's forces captured this bridge, it would certainly mean that Rome could be starved into submission.

The battle began across the Tiber from Rome, and the Etruscans were winning. The Roman line broke, and the soldiers ran back across the bridge with the Etruscans racing after them. Horatius, the commander of the soldiers who were guarding the bridge, knew that in minutes the bridge would fall if his men gave way to panic like the rest of the soldiers. He ordered his soldiers to destroy the bridge, while Horatius himself stood at the far side, ready to defend it single-handedly against all the enemy forces.

The Etruscans were amazed at this man's courage, and the Romans were ashamed by it. Two of Horatius's companions, Spurius and Titus, ran forward to join him, and the three Roman soldiers defeated every

Below *Horatius Cocles Defending the Bridge* by Charles Le Brun (1619–1690). Horatius was greatly rewarded for the way in which he put his own life at risk. As well as land, he also received the honor of having a statue of himself erected in the place of Assembly, the Comitium.

Etruscan who tried to cross the bridge. The other Romans were chopping away the supports of the bridge, and now they called the three men to come back quickly, before it was too late. Spurius and Titus ran back, but Horatius stayed on the enemy side of the Tiber, holding back the Etruscans until the bridge finally collapsed. Horatius prayed to the river god Tiberinus and jumped into the river, wearing the full weight of his armor. The god must have helped him to swim across, and he was welcomed as a hero by the Romans and given as much land as he could plow around in a day.

The Story of Camillus

When Rome was still a small city-state at war with its neighbors, the Etruscans, the Romans besieged the Etruscan city of Veii. Like Troy, it took 10 years to be conquered. In the tenth year, the Roman commander, Camillus, ordered a tunnel to be dug under the city walls, and the Romans overpowered the Etruscans both inside and outside their city. Camillus gave his men permission to rampage through the city but not to injure the temples of the gods. He was particularly concerned not to do any violence to the temple of Juno (Hera), the patron goddess of Veii. He even asked the goddess for permission to take her statue to Rome. The statue nodded and said that she was willing to move, and the Romans took this as a great sign of divine favor.

The next Etruscan city that Camillus besieged was Falerii, and it was here that the schoolmaster betrayed his city to the Romans by taking all his pupils to Camillus's tent and offering them up as hostages. Camillus was too honorable to accept this gift, and ordered the boys to whip their teacher all the way back to Falerii. The Etruscans were so impressed by their enemy's just and honorable code of war that they decided to make peace with him.

The Geese That Saved Rome

Rome now attracted enemies from much farther away. The Gauls of northern Europe invaded Italy and came as far as Rome. They had a huge army and the Romans could not withstand them. It seemed highly likely that Rome would fall. People either fled from the city or assembled on the steep citadel of Rome, the Capitoline hill, fearfully waiting for the invaders to arrive. The Gauls found no resistance as they continued on their rampage, burning and looting and then setting fire to the buildings of Rome. Then they assembled at the foot of the Capitoline hill, looking for an undefended way to climb it and destroy the city entirely. After days of searching, they found a way up the steep rock, and that night, they quietly started to climb up.

On the citadel lived a flock of geese sacred to the goddess Juno. The Romans were all asleep but the geese heard the small sounds of men struggling up the rock and panting for breath. The birds attacked the Gauls, hissing and cackling and beating at the men with their wings. Their noise woke up the Romans, who hurried over to throw the invaders down to their deaths. The geese had saved Rome, and from then on, no goose was sacrificed on the altar of Juno. They had won the right to live out their days as honored guardians of the city.

Left *Horatius Cocles* by Pietro Perugino (c. 1445–1523). The name "Cocles," meaning "one-eyed," came to be identified with Horatius because of his single-mindedness and determination. In historical times, there was a statue of a one-eyed figure that stood at the head of a wooden bridge near Rome.

APOTHEOSIS

Apotheosis is the transformation of a mortal into a god. In Greek myth it occurs at the moment of death for Heracles (Hercules). Some mortal men and women beloved by the Greek gods were transformed into deities; Psyche, for instance, achieved apotheosis after enduring Venus's (Aphrodite's) trials, and Ariadne was transformed into a goddess when she married Bacchus (Dionysus). In Greek and Roman history, there were some rulers who were said to have achieved apotheosis as gods. After the death of Alexander the Great, rulers of his empire were worshipped as gods while alive. Julius Caesar was worshipped after death as the divine Julius, and so, too, were a good many Roman emperors and also some empresses.

Above **Apotheosis of the god Heracles.** The Athenians were the first to worship Heracles as a god, although he was soon honored throughout the Mediterranean world. As his popularity grew, so did the tales of his great feats and exploits.

ENDURING TALES

The Greeks and Romans were not particularly interested either in tales of the beginning of things, or in speculating on the end of the world or life after death. The principal Greek myth about the ending of a world concerns a civilization that preceded the stories of the heroes, nine thousand years before the civilization of classical Greece, and this story can be found only in the writings of the philosopher Plato. The myth of Atlantis was not a widely spread traditional myth, rather a literary artifact, which has enjoyed much wider currency in modern Europe than it ever did in classical Greece or Rome.

Lost Atlantis

According to two of Plato's dialogues, the Critias and Timaeus, Atlantis was an island bigger than Libya and Asia combined. It lay beyond the Pillars of Heracles (Hercules) out in the Atlantic Ocean, closest to Spain. The patron god of the island was Poseidon (Neptune), and he and a mortal woman, Cleito, were the ancestors of its ruling family. Its first ruler was called Atlas, and from his name derived the island's name, Atlantis, and the name of the ocean surrounding it. The island of Atlantis abounded in fertile land, and was full of fruit trees. From underground came the precious metal orichalcum. The main city was a marvel of architecture and sculpture, with wonderfully ornamented palaces and a magnificent temple to Poseidon. Atlantis was well governed, with all of its people knowing their duties to the state and obedient to its laws, which Poseidon had laid down.

For generations, all went well in Atlantis. The Atlanteans obeyed the laws and worshipped Poseidon, and although their island was full of riches, they did not value gold and other treasures over-highly. In the end, though, they became decadent and corrupt, no longer obeying the laws of Poseidon and not content to stay within the boundaries of the realm that Poseidon had allotted them. They built a great empire, sub-duing North Africa from the Pillars of Heracles in the west to Egypt in the east, and all the southern part of Europe except for Greece. When they invaded Greece, the Athenians led a Greek army against them. Little by little, the Atlanteans defeated each city-state until only Athens was left unconquered. Thus it was the Athenians alone who eventually defeated the people of Atlantis and freed all the other regions from their tyranny. Soon after this episode the earth became disturbed with earth-quake and flood. In one day and one night the whole Athenian army was swallowed up in a mighty earthquake, and the city of Atlantis sank into the depths of the sea. According to Plato, the sea was still disturbed by the fall of Atlantis less than 200 years before he wrote these dialogues, with a shoal of mud preventing ships from passing through.

Over the years, many have tried to locate lost Atlantis as an actual physical island, and there are two main competing theories as to its whereabouts. Some think that the myth speaks of a huge eruption that occurred within historical time on the volcanic island of Thera. This massive eruption seems likely to have destroyed the pre-classical Minoan civilization existing on Crete. Others take literally Plato's state-ments about the geographical location of Atlantis, and seek for the island's remains in the Atlantic Ocean, perhaps in the vicinity of

Right **Thera.** According to one story, the island known as Thera developed from a clod of Libyan earth. The god of Lake Tritonis gave it to the Argonaut Euphemus who, following the orders of the god, threw it into the sea. Thera later became part of the Atlantis myth.

THE DEATH OF PAN

Some time in the first century A.D., a ship was sailing past the island of Paxi and a sailor heard a huge voice crying out, "The great god Pan is dead," followed by cries of lamentation. But was this really a voice from the heavens announcing the death of the god? Some scholars of myth believe that the sailor heard the sounds of lamentation from the yearly festival of the god Tammuz ("Dumuzi" in Sumerian myth) who died and was resurrected, as one of his titles was "pan-megas" meaning "all-great." The sailor misunderstood the use of "pan" here as referring to the god Pan. Certainly the worship of Pan, and of the other gods of the Greek pantheon, was not dead by the first century A.D.

Left *Pan* by Adolf Martial Thabard (1831–1905). As well as the god of shepherds and flocks, Pan was also believed to be the god of fertility and male sexuality. Even though Pan was reported to be dead in the first century A.D., shrines, altars, trees, mountains, and even caves that were sacred to Pan were still visited and honored over a century later.

the Azores. Plato's dialogue, the Timaeus, also speaks of a succession of civilizations that are each in turn destroyed by either flood or fire, and this idea also resonates with Mesoamerican myth. The debate continues as to whether Atlantis is an imaginary place in myth or something whose physical remains may one day be recovered by archaeologists.

The End of Greek Myth

In A.D. 312, the Roman Emperor Constantine converted to Christianity, which soon became the state religion. The Emperor Julian's attempt to revive the worship of the Greco-Roman gods as the state religion in A.D. 360 was a failure. The oracles fell into disuse, the temples were abandoned, and the festivals were forgotten. What was never totally forgotten, however, even in the Dark Ages of western history, were the myths of Greece and Rome. When Byzantium fell in the fifteenth century, many of its scholars fled to Italy. The influx of classical literature and learning inspired the art, literature, and science of the Renaissance.

The myths of Greece and Rome have provided subject matter for artists from Leonardo da Vinci to Picasso, and from the Romans on, countries aspiring to literary greatness have measured their achievements against the Greeks' tellings of their myths.

Composers, too, have looked to Greek myth for inspiration, as in the operas dealing with Orpheus and Eurydice, Helen of Troy, and Clytaemnestra's children. Philosophers like Nietzsche have drawn on Greek myth, and psychoanalytic theory has named issues in human development like the Oedipus complex and ailments of the psyche like narcissism after characters in Greek myth. The myths remain potent sources for television series and films, from *Xena* to Disney's *Hercules*. Greek myth still lives, and continues to shape our lives and our understanding of ourselves.

Above **Minoan fleet** (c. 1500 B.C.). After the first Minoan civilization was destroyed, a new Minoan race began, said to be the children of the Argonauts and the women of Lemnos.

Below **Minoan river landscape.** The disappearance of the first Minoan civilization may have inspired the Atlantis myth.

RECOMMENDED READING

The Classical Era

Aeschylus. *The Oresteia: Agamemnon; The Libation Bearers; Eumenides* (translated by R. Fagles). Penguin: London, 1977.

Apollonius. *The Voyage of Argo* (translated by E.V. Rieu). Penguin: London, 1975.

Bremmer, Jan and Nicholas Horsfall. *Roman Myth and Mythography*. University of London: London, 1987.

Bulfinch, Thomas. *The Illustrated Age of Fable*. Harper Collins Publishers: London, 1998.

Carpenter, T. *Art and Myth in Ancient Greece*. Thames & Hudson: London, 1991.

Euripides. *The Bacchae and Other Plays: Ion; The Women of Troy; Helen; The Bacchae* (translated by P. Vellacott). Penguin: London, 1973.

Graf, F. *Greek Mythology*. John Hopkins University Press: Baltimore, 1993.

Graves, Robert. *The Greek Myths*. Penguin: London, 1960.

Hesiod. *The Work and Days/Theogony/The Shield of Herakles* (translated by R. Lattimore). University of Michigan Press: Ann Arbor, 1991.

Homer. *The Iliad* (translated by E.V. Rieu). Penguin: London, 2003.

Homer. *The Odyssey* (translated by E.V. Rieu). Penguin: London, 2003.

Hughes, Ted. *Tales from Ovid*. Faber & Faber: London, 1997.

Kamara, Peter. *Ancient Roman Mythology*. Promotional Reprint Company Ltd.: London, 1996.

Kerenyi, C. *The Heroes of the Greeks*. Thames & Hudson: London, 1997.

Lefkowitz, K. *Women in Greek Mythology*. Duckworth: London, 1986.

Ogilvie, R.M. *The Romans and their Gods*. Chatto & Windus Ltd.: London, 1969.

Ovid. *Metamorphoses* (translated by M. Innes). Penguin: London, 1973.

Scullard, H.H. *Festivals and Ceremonies of the Roman Republic*. Thames & Hudson: London, 1981.

Sophocles. *The Three Theban Plays: Antigone; Oedipus the King; Oedipus at Colonus* (translated by R. Fagles). Penguin: London, 1984.

Virgil. *The Aeneid* (translated by D. West). Penguin: London, 2003.

INDEX

Italic numbers refer to illustrations and maps, while **bold** numbers refer to break-out boxes and family trees.

M

Maenads (frenzied ones) 80, *86*, 87, *88*
magic **147**
Maia **16**, 75
Marathon, bulls at 150–151
mares of Diomedes 122, *123*
Mars (god), *see* Ares (Mars)
Mars (planet) *54*, **54**
Marsyas 76, *76*–77
Medea 139–144, *141*, *144*, *147*, 150
 magic of **147**
Medus 150
Medusa *106*, 106–109, *107*
Megara 117, 128
Megareus **96**
Melanion *146*, 146
Meleager 127, 129, 145–146
Melicertes **96**, 132
Memnon **171**, *171*, 173
Menelaus **162**, 162, *163*, 164–166, *165*,
 168–170, *178*, 178
 Orestes and 181, 183
Menoeceus **96**
Mercury, *see* Hermes
Merope 98, 113
Mesopotamian mythology 68
metamorphosis, *see* transformation
 myths
Metis **16**, 21
Mictlan, *see* Underworld
Midas *81*, 81–82, *82*
Middle East mythology 68
migrations, *see* journey myths (discovery
 and victory)
Milky Way **130**, *130*
Minerva, *see* Athene
Minoan civilisation 152, *205*
Minos, King 93–94, **96**, 152, 154
 bull of 122, *122*
Minotaur 122, *152*, 152, 154–155, *155*
Missing Half (Plato) **48**
Mnemosyne **16**
moon myths *63*, 63
Mopsus *137*, 137
Mount Caucasus 26
Mount Cithaeron 97, 101
Mount Etna *18*, 21
Mount Ida 166–167
Mount Nysa 87
Mount Olympus, Mars **54**
Mount Olympus, Thessaly 14–15, 19,
 23, 51
Mount Parnassus 28, 31, 42–43
mulberries 84
Muses, The **16**, *40*, **40**, 60

musicians 74–80
Myrmidons **191**
Myrrha 54, 56
Myrtilus 161, 162
mythology, lasting reminders of 205

N

naiads 57
Narcissus *69*, 69–71
natural world, *see* animal myths; flower
 and plant myths
Nausicaa **191**
Naxos *156*, 157
Neleus 124, **162**
Nemean lion 117, 119, *119*
Neoptolemus 175, 177
Nephele **96**, 132
Neptune, *see* Poseidon
Nereus 126
Nessus 130
Nestor **162**
New Year, *see* seasons and calendar
Nicippe **162**
night and day, *see* moon myths; sun
 myths
Niobe 38, 159, **162**
Nox (Nyx) **14**, 197
Numitor 199–200
Nycteis **96**
nymphs 57, *136–137*
Nyx (Nox) **14**, 197

O

ocean monsters, Heracles and 127–128
Oceanids **16**
oceans, *see* Poseidon (Neptune)
Oceanus **16**
Ocyrhoe 39
Odysseus (Ulysses) **14**, 14, 165–166,
 168, 169–171, *184*, 184–193, *187*,
 188, *189*, *190–191*, *193*
 as beggar 191–193, *193*
 as trickster 184
 Calypso and *190*
 Cyclops and 185–188
 map of journey *186*
 Palladium and 175
 return of 189–193
 Trojan war 173–175, 177
Oedipus **96**, *97*, 97–104, *98*, *99*, *100*,
 101, *103*
Oenomaus 160–161, *161*

Oenone 167
Oenopion 113–114
offerings, *see* sacrifices and offerings
Oineus 145
Olympian gods, *see* classical mythology
Olympic Games **128**
Omphale *128*, 129
oracles *41*, 41–44, *42*, 46, 94, 97,
 97–99, *see also* sibyls and
 soothsayers
 Deucalion and Pyrrha 29, 31
 Dodona 42
 Heracles and the tripod 128–129, 129
 Jason and 132–133
 Orestes and 180
 Theseus and 147
 Thyestes and 164
 Trojan war 167, 171
Orchamus 71
Orchomenus 117
Orestes **162**, 179–181, *181*, *182*, *183*,
 183
Orion (constellation) 114
Orion (hunter) 113–114, *114*
Orpheus *78*, 78–80, *79*, *80*, 142, *143*
Ouranus (Uranus) **16**, 16–17
oxen, *see* cattle

P

Pactolus River 81–82
Palinurus 196–197
Palladium 175, *175*
Pallas 150, 175
Pallas Athene *93*, 93
Pan **16**, 77, *77*, *79*, *204*
 birth of **79**
 death of **204**
 King Midas and 82
 panic and **77**
 Psyche and 49
 responsibilities of **38**
Pandora **17**, 25, *25*
panpipes *14*, 77, *79*
panthers *90*, 90
Paphlagonia 159–160
Paris (Royal House of Troy) 151, 170,
 178, **198**
 death of Achilles and 173–174
 Eris and 166–167, *167*
 Helen and 168
Pasiphae 152–153, *153*
passion, *see* love and lust myths
Patroclus *171*, 171–172
peacocks *32*, 32

PICTURE CREDITS

The Publisher would like to thank the following picture libraries and other copyright owners for permission to reproduce their images. Every attempt has been made to obtain permission for use of all images from the copyright owners, however, if any errors or omissions have occurred Global Book Publishing would be pleased to hear from copyright owners.

Key: (t) top of page; (b) bottom of page; (l) left side of page; (r) right side of page; (c) center of page.

Alamy: dmrphoto: front and back cover (t).

The Art Archive, London: 64(t), 183(b); Accademia Venice/Dagli Orti (A): 92; Archaeological Museum Delphi/Dagli Orti: 41(t), 44(l), 44(r), 170(t); Archaeological Museum Florence/Dagli Orti: 110(t); Archaeological Museum Mykonos/Dagli Orti: 177(b); Archaeological Museum Naples: 160(t); Archaeological Museum Naples/Dagli Orti (A): 39(b), 45(t), 75(t), 87(t), 91(t), 165(tl), 169(t), 181(b), 185; Archaeological Museum Nauplia Nafplion/Dagli Orti: 173(t); Archaeological Museum Paestum/Dagli Orti: 14(t); Archaeological Museum Palermo/Dagli Orti: 107(t), 186(b); Archaeological Museum Piraeus/Dagli Orti: 38–39(t), 162; Archaeological Museum Sousse Tunisia/Dagli Orti: 90; Archaeological Museum Sparta/Dagli Orti: 165(b); Archaeological Museum Syracuse/Dagli Orti: 113(t), 128(b), 176(b); Archaeological Museum Thasos: 113(b); Archaeological Museum Timgad Algeria/Dagli Orti: 29; Archaeological Museum Tipasa Algeria/Dagli Orti: 160(b); Archaeological Museum Venice/Dagli Orti (A): 53(t), 91(b); Bardo Museum Tunis/Dagli Orti: 188; Bargello Museum Florence/Dagli Orti: 71(b), 104(b); Basilique Saint Denis Paris/Dagli Orti: 164; Biblioteca Apostolica Vaticana: 189(t); Biblioteca Estense Modena/Dagli Orti (A): 54(t), 120(t); Bibliothèque des Arts Décoratifs Paris/Dagli Orti: 76(t), 86(t), 122(t), 128–129(t), 168(t), 203(b); Bibliothèque des Arts Décoratifs Paris/Dagli Orti (A): 8–9; Bibliothèque Inguimbertine Carpentras/Dagli Orti: 94(t); Bibliothèque Municipale Dijon/Dagli Orti: 81(t); Bodleian Library Oxford/The Bodleian Library: 79(t) [Douce 135 folio 35v], Cathedral Museum Ferrara/Dagli Orti (A): 197(t); Château d'Ancy-le-Franc/Dagli Orti: 40; Château de Blois/Dagli Orti: 56; Château de Chambord/Dagli Orti: 190(t), 193(b); Château de Dampierre/Dagli Orti: 192(b); Château de Gue-Pean/Dagli Orti: 167(b);); City Archaeological Coll Milan: 116; Civiche Racc d'Arte Pavia, Italy: 193(t); Civiche Racc d'Arte Pavia, Italy/Dagli Orti: 12; Cyprus Museum Nicosia/Dagli Orti: 28(b); Dagli Orti (A): 27(t), 41(b), 105, 131, 153, 182, 183(t), 187, 205(t); Egyptian Museum Cairo/Dagli Orti: 99; Ephesus Museum Turkey/Dagli Orti (A): 180(t); Fitzwilliam Museum Cambridge/Dagli Orti (A): 59(t); Francesco Venturi: 6–7; Galleria d'Arte Moderna Rome/Dagli Orti (A): 157(t); Galleria Borghese Rome/Dagli Orti (A): 43, 57(b), 64(b), 78, 194(b); Galleria Nazionale Parma/Dagli Orti (A): 173(b); Harper Collins Publishers: 75(b); Heraklion Museum/Dagli Orti: 179(b); Jan Vinchon Numismatist Paris/Dagli Orti: 35(t); La Rocca Sanvitale Fontanellato/Dagli Orti: 61; Moor Park Golf Club/Eileen Tweedy: 30, 32(b); Musée des Arts Décoratifs Paris/Dagli Orti (A): 191; Musée des Beaux Arts Orléans/Dagli Orti (A): 100; Musée des Beaux Arts Rouen/Dagli Orti: 123; Musée de la Civilisation Gallo-Romaine Lyons/Dagli Orti: 87(b); Musée du Louvre Paris: 115, 194–195(t); Musée du Louvre Paris/Dagli Orti: 1, 10–11, 13, 23(b), 25(t), 35(b), 45(b), 47(b), 51(t), 57(t), 60(t), 62(t), 68(t), 80(b), 83(t), 84, 96, 103(b), 108, 110(b), 119(t), 122(b), 130(b), 135(r), 140(t), 145(t), 159(b), 165(r), 170(b), 184(t), 199(b); Musée du Louvre Paris/Dagli Orti (A): 5; Musée Thomas Dobrée Nantes/Dagli Orti: 58; Museo Capitolino Rome/Dagli Orti (A): 199(t), 200(b); Museo di Capodimonte, Naples/Dagli Orti (A): 192(t); Museo di Castelvecchio Verona/Dagli Orti (A): 86(b); Museo Catedràlicio Zamora Spain/Dagli Orti: 163; Museo Civico Alessandria, Italy/Dagli Orti (A): 47(t); Museo Civico Padua/Dagli Orti: 134–135(c); Museo della Civilta Romana Rome/Dagli Orti: 195(b); Museo Correr Venice: 51(b); Museo Nazionale Reggio Calabria/Dagli Orti: 37(b), 172(b), 201(bl), 201(br); Museo Nazionale Taranto/Dagli Orti: 16, 22–23(t), 42(b), 98(t), 154, 175(b); Museo Nazionale Terme Rome/Dagli Orti: 146(t); Museo dell'Opera del Duomo Florence/Dagli Orti: 98(b); Museo del Prado Madrid: 130(t), 140(b); Museo del Prado Madrid/Album/Joseph Martin: 80(t); Museo del Prado Madrid/Dagli Orti (A): 31(b), 109; Museo di Villa Giulia Rome/Dagli Orti: 107(b); Museum of Carthage/Dagli Orti: 65; Muzeul de Constantza Romania/Dagli Orti: 117(t); Muzeul de Sarmezegetusa Romania/Dagli Orti: 2; National Archaeological Museum Athens/Dagli Orti: 17(c), 26(t), 133, 152(b), 181(t), 189(b), 205(b); National Gallery London/Eileen Tweedy: 34, 52, 54(b), 89, 197(b); Palazzo Arco Mantua Italy: 111, 118; Palazzo Barberini Rome/Dagli Orti (A): 168(b), 201(t); Palazzo Pitti Florence/Dagli Orti (A): 19; Palazzo Reale Madrid/Dagli Orti: 36; Palazzo Reale Milan/Dagli Orti: 190(b); Palazzo del Te Mantua/Dagli Orti (A): 20; Palazzo Vecchio Florence: 152(t); Salamanca University/Dagli Orti (A): 24; San Zeno Maggiore Verona, Italy/Dagli Orti (A): 21(t); Siritide Museum Policoro/Dagli Orti: 142(b); Staatliche Glypothek Munich/Dagli Orti (A): 21(b); Villa of the Mysteries Pompeii/Dagli Orti (A): 67; Villa Stuck Museum Munich/Dagli Orti (A): 14(b), 77; Villa Valmarana Vicenza, Italy/Dagli Orti: 179(t).

Classical
MYTHOLOGY

Produced by Global Book Publishing
Level 8, 15 Orion Road, Lane Cove,
NSW 2066, Australia
Ph: (612) 9425 5800   Fax: (612) 9425 5804
Email: rightsmanager@globalpub.com.au

Text and Maps
© Global Book Publishing Pty Ltd 2007